Inequality and Uneven Development in the Post-Crisis World

In the years following the financial crash, two issues have become central to the debate in economics: inequality and the uneven nature of sustainable development. These two issues are at the core of this book which aims to explain three key questions: why inequality has increased so much in the last three decades; why most advanced economies are stagnating or are experiencing moderate economic growth; and why, even where economic growth is occurring, the quality of that growth is questioned.

Inequality and Uneven Development in the Post-Crisis World is divided into three parts. The first part concerns the theoretical aspects of inequality, and ethical issues regarding economics and equality. The second part explores empirical evidence and policy suggestions drawing on the uneven levels of development and unprecedented levels of inequality experienced among advanced economies in the context of global financial capitalism. The third part focuses on sustainable development issues such as full employment, social costs of global trade liberalization, environmental sustainability and ecological issues. Along with inequality these issues are central for capitalism and for economic development.

This volume is of interest to those who study political economy, sustainable development and social inequality.

Sebastiano Fadda is Professor at the Roma Tre University, Rome, Italy, and teaches Advanced Labour Economics at the Department of Economics. He is director of ASTRIL (Interdisciplinary Association for the Study and Research of Labour) and has worked extensively on institutions, economic development and labour economics issues.

Pasquale Tridico is Professor at the Roma Tre University, Rome, Italy, and is a lecturer in Labour Economics and Economic Policy. He is director of a two-year master's degree course (Labour Market, Industrial Relations and Welfare Systems). He is also Jean Monnet Chair of Economic Growth and Welfare Systems and elected General Secretary of the EAEPE. He is the author of *Inequality in Financial Capitalism* (Routledge, 2017).

Routledge Advances in Heterodox Economics

Edited by Mark Setterfield
The New School for Social Research, USA
and
Peter Kriesler
University of New South Wales

Over the past two decades, the intellectual agendas of heterodox economists have taken a decidedly pluralist turn. Leading thinkers have begun to move beyond the established paradigms of Austrian, feminist, Institutional-evolutionary, Marxian, Post Keynesian, radical, social, and Sraffian economics—opening up new lines of analysis, criticism, and dialogue among dissenting schools of thought. This cross-fertilization of ideas is creating a new generation of scholarship in which novel combinations of heterodox ideas are being brought to bear on important contemporary and historical problems.

Routledge Advances in Heterodox Economics aims to promote this new scholarship by publishing innovative books in heterodox economic theory, policy, philosophy, intellectual history, institutional history, and pedagogy. Syntheses or critical engagement of two or more heterodox traditions are especially encouraged.

For a full list of titles in this series, please visit www.routledge.com/series/RAHE

Inequality and Uneven Development in the Post-Crisis World

**Edited by Sebastiano Fadda
and Pasquale Tridico**

Routledge
Taylor & Francis Group
LONDON AND NEW YORK

First published 2018
by Routledge

2 Park Square, Milton Park, Abingdon, Oxfordshire OX14 4RN
52 Vanderbilt Avenue, New York, NY 10017

Routledge is an imprint of the Taylor & Francis Group, an informa business

First issued in paperback 2020

British Library Cataloguing-in-Publication Data
A catalogue record for this book is available from the British Library

Library of Congress Cataloging-in-Publication Data
Names: Fadda, Sebastiano, editor. | Tridico, Pasquale, 1975- editor.
Title: Inequality and uneven development in the post-crisis world /
edited by Sebastiano Fadda and Pasquale Tridico.
Description: Abingdon, Oxon ; New York, NY : Routledge, 2017. |
Includes index.
Identifiers: LCCN 2017002014| ISBN 9781138229563 (hardback) |
ISBN 9781315388823 (ebook)
Subjects: LCSH: Economic development. | Equality—Economic aspects. |
Sustainable development. | Financial crises.
Classification: LCC HD82 .I34125 2017 | DDC 338.9—dc23
LC record available at https://lccn.loc.gov/2017002014

ISBN: 978-1-138-22956-3 (hbk)
ISBN: 978-0-367-59497-8 (pbk)

Typeset in Times New Roman
By Keystroke, Neville Lodge, Tettenhall, Wolverhampton

Contents

PART II
Empirical evidences of inequality

PART III
Sustainable development issues

Figures

Tables

Contributors

Nicholas Black, Alliance Manchester Business School, University of Manchester.

Nicola Caravaggio, Department of Economics, Roma Tre University, Rome.

Gionata Castaldi, Italian Ministry of the Environment, Rome.

Valeria Costantini, Department of Economics, Roma Tre University, Rome.

Alessio D'Amato, Università di Roma Tor Vergata and SEEDS, Rome.

Ismail Ertürk, Alliance Manchester Business School, University of Manchester.

Sebastiano Fadda, Department of Economics, Roma Tre University, Rome.

Georg Feigl, Department of Economics and Statistics, Austrian Federal Chamber of Labour.

Zoltán Gál, HAS Research Centre for Economic and Regional Studies, Hungary and Kaposvar University.

Sven Hergovich, Austrian Federal Ministry of Labour, Social Affairs and Consumer Protection.

Martina Iorio, Department of Economics, Roma Tre University, Rome.

Salvatore Monni, Department of Economics, Roma Tre University, Rome.

Erika Nagy, HAS Research Centre for Economic and Regional Studies, Hungary and University of Szeged.

Julie A. Nelson, Department of Economics, University of Massachusetts Boston.

Elena Paglialunga, Department of Economics, Roma Tre University, Rome.

Riccardo Pariboni, Department of Economics, Roma Tre University, Rome.

Zsuzsanna Pósfai, HAS Research Centre for Economic and Regional Studies, Hungary and University of Szeged.

Werner Raza, ÖFSE – Austrian Foundation for Development Research, Vienna.

Michele Raitano, Department of Economics and Law, University of Rome "La Sapienza".

Miriam Rehm, Department of Economics and Statistics, Austrian Federal Chamber of Labour.

Miklós Szanyi, Institute of World Economy, Hungarian Academy of Science, Budapest.

Pasquale Tridico, Department of Economics, Roma Tre University, Rome.

Mariangela Zoli, Università di Roma Tor Vergata and SEEDS, Rome.

Acknowledgements

This book is an outcome of the contributions presented at the 2015 Summer School of the European Association for Evolutionary Political Economy (EAEPE) by professors and experts in the fields of inequality, sustainable development and ecological economics. The EAEPE Summer School was as usual held in Rome at the Roma Tre University and the local organizers were Sebastiano Fadda and Pasquale Tridico, editors of this book.

Tridico, Jean Monnet Chair of Economic Growth, wishes to acknowledge the contribution of the Jean Monnet Programme – Key Activity 1 (nr: 542598-LLP-1-2013-IT-JMC-CH).

Introduction

Pasquale Tridico and Sebastiano Fadda

In the last years, in particular after the 2007 financial crash, two issues have occupied the economic policy debate in advanced economies. First of all inequality, which became also an issue to analyse as a possible factor causing macro-economic instability and financial crisis, as the financial crash in 2007 showed. Second, sustainable development and in particular ecological issues as the last UN conference in November 2015 in Paris showed. These two issues are at the core of this book which aims to explain why inequality has been increasing so much in the last three decades, and why most advanced economies are stagnating or are experiencing moderate economic growth, and even where economic growth is occurring the quality of that growth is questioned. In fact sustainable development is required that involves in particular long-term economic development, full employment and decent work, equality and environment protection.

However, contrary to most books in this field, inequality and sustainable development will be explored from a broad perspective and with different approaches, not only the *income* inequality dimension and not only *ecological* issues. As far as inequality is concerned, other dimensions such as gender, spatial, generational inequality will be explored. As far as sustainable development is concerned the following issues will be examined: decent work and unemployment, environmental issues, ecosystems, gas emissions and trade costs.

These issues are in fact, in particular among advanced economies, the most pressing items in the policy agenda of governments and international organizations, when they deal with policies concerning economic growth. For this reason the book explores the possibility of reducing inequality and having sustainable development. At the same time inequality and sustainable development are identified as the most important challenges for capitalism nowadays. These challenges could also evolve in open threats to the capitalist regime which is currently governing advanced economies.

From an empirical perspective, the book, in particular in the second and third parts, shows evidence of varieties of inequality and ecological issues, and advances policy suggestions that aim to improve macroeconomic stablity, labour opportunities, welfare states and sustainable development.

The book is divided into three parts. The first part concerns the theoretical aspects of inequality, and ethical issues concerning economics and equality. The second part deals with empirical evidence and policy suggestions drawn from the elaboration of the current uneven development among advanced economies, and inequality within countries in the context of the financial capitalism paradigm governing most advanced economies. The third part focuses on sustainable development issues such as full employment, social costs of global trade liberalization, environmental sustainability and ecological issues. Along with inequality these issues are central for capitalism and for economic development.

In Chapter 1, Pasquale Tridico tries to identify the determinants of the increase in income inequality that rich countries have experienced over the last two decades. The hypothesis is that along with the financialization of economies that has taken place since 1990, inequality increased because labour flexibility intensified, labour market institutions weakened as trade unions lost power, and public social spending started to retrench and did not compensate the vulnerabilities created by the globalization process. Using data from 34 Organisation for Economic Co-operation and Development (OECD) countries from 1990 to 2013, the hypothesis is empirically evaluated.

In Chapter 2, Riccardo Pariboni shows that in the last decades household debt has acted, across the vast majority of OECD countries, as a substitute for stagnant wages in financing private consumption. In this way the demand-generating problems, entailed by a generalized increase in income inequality, have been postponed for a while. Nonetheless, the process proved to be unsustainable, increased enormously the financial fragility of the economy and contributed to the outburst of the Great Recession. In order to assess the macroeconomic implications of these developments, a simple theoretical framework is provided, based on the Supermultiplier model with endogenous credit money.

In Chapter 3, Sebastiano Fadda criticizes the explanations of (and the policies against) unemployment that are still based on traditional views about the working of the economy and particularly of the labour market. According to this view involuntary unemployment is essentially due either to difficulties in 'matching' demand and supply, or to wages higher than the equilibrium level of full employment. The inability of wages to adjust to the equilibrium level is in turn ascribed either to trade unions interfering against the free working of market forces or to dynamics of a New Keynesian kind such as efficiency wages or implicit contracts or 'insider–outsider' models. This framework suggested policies in the European Union failed to reach the supposed aims (employment levels, productivity and growth). Fadda proposes a critical and selected literature survey, which indicates what could be the alternative.

In Chapter 4, Werner Raza argues that the new generation of trade agreements, including the Transatlantic Trade and Investment Partnership (TTIP), aim at deep economic integration. Thus, they are not restrained to reducing conventional barriers to trade like tariffs and quotas, but are essentially focused upon the removal or alignment of non-tariff measures (NTMs) between countries. These are domestic standards, laws and regulations that impede international trade and investment. NTMs extend into core domains of public policy, including health and food safety, environmental regulations and labour laws. Regulation, however, confers both benefits and costs to society. By altering NTMs, far-reaching impacts upon the welfare of society are potentially brought about by trade policy. Yet, in the trade literature NTMs are typically treated as a cost item to business only. Raza purports to show that this standard methodology used to account for NTMs is methodologically insufficient. Building upon the seminal work of institutional economist K.W. Kapp, the author conceptualizes the welfare impacts of new generation trade agreements as social costs of trade. With this he goes beyond the theoretical frame of mainstream trade analysis and is able to systematically scrutinize the distributional impacts of trade-driven regulatory change.

In the last chapter of Part I, Julie A. Nelson argues that our current global economy is characterized by excessive inequality – by vast inequalities in income, wealth, and access to resources and opportunities. It is also characterized by unsustainability, as processes of climate change and environmental degradation, as well as a debasing of the norms and institutions underlying successful commerce, progressively undermine the physical and social foundations of survival and flourishing. Finally, Nelson argues that our economies – and our thinking about economies – are being overwhelmed by financialization, meaning an excessive or exclusive emphasis on financial outcomes, motivations and institutions. This chapter shows that these phenomena have a common root in a deeply held belief that economic life is, by its nature, something separate from the concerns of *care*, for example caring about the poor, the environment or the quality of life. The source of this 'poison in the well' of our thinking about economics is traced in both its historical and gendered dimensions, and its impact on both neoclassical and 'radical' economic thinking is discussed. Rethinking the relationship between economics and care has implications for the economics discipline's ontological, epistemological and behavioural assumptions, and for how we think about ways out' of our current predicament.

Part II opens with a chapter by Michele Raitano who argues that studies on intergenerational inequality investigate the link between offspring's outcomes and the features of family background, assessing whether and to what extent socio-economic inequalities persist in subsequent generations. However, synthetic measures of the correlations between parental characteristics and children's outcomes do not provide information on the processes lying behind such correlations and their different importance across countries. The main aim of this chapter is to shed light on what lies behind the intergenerational transmission of inequalities, following a conceptual framework that identifies several channels of influence on the family background, acting at different stages of the offspring life cycle. The main feature of the framework is that it does not share the common view that it is almost exclusively through education that the intergenerational transmission of inequality may take place. Indeed, it considers that family background can influence, besides education, children's prospects in a more direct way.

Chapter 7 by Nicholas Black and Ismail Ertürk covers the relationship between financialization and inequality by first providing a theoretical understanding of financialized capitalism and then discussing how the behaviour of shareholder value-driven firms and financialized households shapes the dynamics of inequality in present-day capitalism. Through data on financialized economies and households in ten high-income countries the chapter discusses financialization's quantitative properties. And then financialized firm behaviour is discussed by tracing the rise of neo-liberal agency theories that justify shareholder value maximization strategies by managers and consequently legitimizes the growth of the gap between chief executive officer compensation and the average wage which is the main driver of inequality in financialized capitalism.

In Chapter 8, Miklós Szanyi shows that the post-transition economic structure of east-central European countries has been largely shaped by foreign direct investments. Affiliates of multinational companies contributed to the overall modernization and integration of these economies into the global value chains. Their position used to be at the lower end and this resulted in deformations of the national economies, giving fuel to criticism of the FDI-led development model. Two shortcomings stood out in Hungary: strong and even increasing spatial inequalities as well as ownership-related inequalities. Local companies could not keep pace with the quick restructuring process of multinational affiliates. Sometimes they were crowded out of some markets. Thus, the presence of multinational firms and increased competition did not result in advances of local firms' capabilities. The multiplex dual structure could not be dampened very quickly by economic policies. Investment attraction potential of less developed regions has not increased. Nor has local firms' compatibility increased to become suppliers. It seems that the elimination of dual structures needs more fundamental and complex social and economic changes that exceed the scope of capital attraction policies.

In Chapter 9, the key argument of Zsuzsanna Pósfai, Zoltan Gál, Erika Nagy is that processes of financialization have strengthened existing spatial inequalities on various scales through the mechanisms of the housing market on which financial institutions had a decisive role in the 2000s. On a European scale, the period of global capital expansion of the early 2000s meant a rapid liberalization of financial markets and a spiralling increase of private indebtedness on the European semi-periphery. The consequences of the dependency and vulnerability inherent to this system were made explicit by the economic crisis of 2008. Spatial polarization is also enhanced on a subnational scale with a concentration of capital in the core regions of the country, or locally by further marginalizing spaces that do not have access to capital.

In Chapter 10, which starts Part III, Miriam Rehm, Sven Hergovich and Georg Feigl argue that Europe is facing a triple crisis: since the financial crisis growth has been anaemic, high unemployment accompanied by overwork raise issues of quality of life, and both of these are coupled with an urgent need to address ecological concerns arising from climate change. The Stiglitz–Sen–Fitoussi Commission started a new momentum, which has gained a foothold in Europe under the headline of 'Beyond GDP'. However, it is not clear that the lessons from the Beyond GDP debate in the 1970s have been learned. Statistical indicators are an important first step, but decisive political action is needed.

In particular, reducing work time, redistribution and investments in socio-ecological transformation are likely to have positive effects on all three frontiers of the triple crisis.

In Chapter 11, Nicola Caravaggio, Valeria Costantini, Martina Iorio, Salvatore Monni and Elena Paglialunga argue that climate change and sustainability targets are key issues within the global development strategy. Renewable energies are increasingly considered as first best solution to combine development achievements while preserving the ecosystem services. The case of the Brazilian Amazon allows reflecting on potential benefits and controversial issues arising around hydroelectric source. The authors focus on two plants in the Amazon Region: Tucuruí and Belo Monte. To evaluate the two projects a simplified CBA analysis has been carried out. The comparison pointed out both positive and negative aspects of the plants, urging for possible future fairer alternatives in the Amazon.

In Chapter 12, Gionata Castaldi, Alessio D'Amato and Mariangela Zoli argue that domestic energy saving plays a central role in modern society and in designing new energy-related policies. Despite this, the empirical literature on the topic is scarce and usually focused on the industrial sector. In this chapter, the three authors identify, through the implementation of a demand analysis based on the British Household Panel Survey (BHPS), the principal determinants that affect the amount of energy saved by each household and, through the implementation of a household production function, estimate the households' willingness to save. The results help to provide food for thought on the distributional issues connected to domestic energy saving.

Part I

Ethics, pluralism and theoretical approaches

1 The rise of income inequality in rich countries

Pasquale Tridico

Introduction

Over the last two decades at least, income inequality within rich countries has increased. The richest 10 per cent of the population in the Organisation for Economic Co-operation and Development (OECD) countries earn about ten times the income of the poorest 10 per cent; in the late 1980s the richest 10 per cent earned about seven times the income of the poorest 10 per cent (OECD, 2014). At the same time the Gini coefficient increased from about 27 per cent to 33 per cent on average. In a way this contradicts the famous Kuznets curve (1955) according to which inequality increases in the initial phase of the development process, and then decreases as economies become richer. Piketty (2014) already noticed its limitations, and in his recent book he rejects the idea of the bell curve. What he proposes is a horizontal "S" curve – inequality re-increases again when countries reach an advanced stage of development. Following to some extent Piketty's broad conclusions, I focus in this chapter on the years that are probably the ones during which inequality increased the most, namely from 1990 to 2013. During this period the world changed substantially, the structure of rich economies was reshaped, and in most of them the impressive technological progress has led to strong and long waves of transformations. Before that, in the late 1970s, political changes also created the basis for a new paradigm of political economy, first in the United States and in the United Kingdom, and later in most advanced and emerging economies.

This new paradigm, which I call "financial capitalism", is characterised by a strong dependency on the financial sector, by the globalisation and intensification of international trade and capital mobility, and by the "flexibilisation" of the labour market (Epstein, 2005; ILO, 2013). From an economic policy perspective these changes resulted in the partial withdrawal of the state from the economy (i.e. the minimisation of its economic intervention) and the dominance of supply-side policies (i.e. labour flexibility, tax competition for firms and capital, etc.) (Shield, 2012).

In this context, I argue that income inequality increased because labour, which is the most important production factor for income, is seen by the supply-side approach as a cost to be compressed rather than as a fundamental part of aggregate demand to be expanded. In the age of financial capitalism, labour–capital relations are changing, and in most cases labour represents the weaker part. On the one hand, as a result of the conflict between labour and capital, trade unions lost power, and labour market regulations such as labour protection against firing, unemployment benefits, minimum wage and so on weakened. On the other hand, the expansion of labour flexibility, atypical labour contracts and temporary jobs created unstable jobs and therefore unstable consumption (Jha and Golder, 2008).

Moreover, within the aforementioned new paradigm of political economy, the welfare state represents another cost to compress. In order to improve firms' competitiveness and boost economic growth, advocates of the so-called "efficiency thesis" argue social spending needs to be reduced[1] (Allan and Scruggs, 2004; Blackmon, 2006; Castells, 2004). In fact most countries are experiencing a retrenchment of the welfare state or at least a stabilisation of public expenditure. In an age of globalisation and ageing, this corresponds to a per capita reduction in real terms (Adema et al., 2011.

The link between globalisation and inequality has been largely explored in the literature since the Stolper and Samuelson theorem, according to which market integration increases inequality and vulnerability as increased international trade raises the incomes of the owners of abundant factors and reduces the incomes of the owners of scarce factors (Stolper and Samuelson, 1941). Since advanced industrial countries are more capital-intensive economies and abundant in skilled labour, trade is expected to be beneficial for skilled labour and detrimental to unskilled labour, thus increasing income inequality. For labour-intensive economies, which is typically the case of developing countries, trade is expected to increase regional disparities.

Other recent explanations for inequalities were put forward by Van Reenen (2011) who found support for trade-induced technological change associated with inequality. Chusseau and Dumont (2012) show that globalisation, skill-biased technological change and changes in labour market institutions weakening the welfare state explain the increase of inequality in a group of 12 rich countries. Other labour markets arguments explaining inequality have been challenged by Lemieux et al. (2009) and Card et al. (2004) among others. Atkinson et al. (2011) instead point out the changes in taxation that reduced progressivity in particular at the top of the distribution as main drivers of inequality. Similarly Facundo et al. (2013) argue that reductions in the top income tax rate is the most important factor explaining inequality. Finally, researchers have stressed the link between credit availability (as a consequence of increasing inequality) and financial crises (see for instance Perugini et al., 2015) and inequality as the cause for the current financial crisis (Stockhammer, 2013).

My contribution emerges clearly in light of this existing literature since it aims at synthesising most of the causes mentioned above in a single and valid empirical model, stressing in particular the role of financialisation, globalisation and labour market institutions as an explanation of inequality.

To sum up, financialisation, labour flexibility and the weakening of trade unions, plus the retrenchment of the welfare state, are the most important factors in my analysis explaining the explosion of income inequality over the past two decades. The econometric analysis of the chapter uses data from 34 OECD countries from 1990 to 2013, and clearly and robustly suggests all these factors are at play.

The rest of the chapter is organised as follows: in the next section I briefly review the literature regarding the relationship between globalisation and inequality; in the third section I analyse, theoretically and empirically, the relationship between financialisation and labour market legislation and its impact on inequality; in the fourth section I put forward my econometric model; and I conclude with a final section.

Globalisation and inequality

Globalisation is still a generic term, which, in most definitions, is identified as a process of *intensification* of trade, capital mobility, finance and labour flexibility. By contrast, authors such as Hay and Wincott (2012) disagree with such a definition of globalisation and would rather define it as a process not only of *intensification* of those flows but also of *extensive increase*, on a global level, of trade, capital and labour mobility, and technological exchange, among others (Held et al., 1999). Because evidence of this second type of definition of globalisation is missing and since not all countries have taken part in the globalisation process (quite the opposite; globalisation interests a limited, yet increasing, number of countries), they conclude that it would be more appropriate to speak about regionalisation rather than globalisation. For instance, trade, capital and labour mobility increased particularly in the European Union (Europeanisation), among advanced and emerging economies (trans-regionalism) and between North American countries (with regional agreements such as NAFTA), and so on. Hence, the interpretation of globalisation remains quite controversial and an ongoing and evolutionary process.

Nonetheless, while it is true that globalisation affects more advanced and increasingly more emerging economies, typically BRIC countries (Brazil, Russia, India, China and South Africa), it is objectively impossible to deny the intensification of this process and the increase in the number of countries involved in the global economy over the last two decades.

Figure 1.1 is the simplest representation of this kind of globalisation. In particular, a first big wave of globalisation, identified purely according to the *intensive* definition, occurred after 1970, and may have been generated by a new international monetary system, the change in oil prices and the birth of the European Monetary System. However, this first wave of globalisation was unstable and the process of intensification declined during the 1980s. Finally, the process of intensive globalisation, often accompanied by the extensive inclusion of more and more countries, steadily rejuvenated at the end of the 1980s when several institutional, geopolitical and technological changes occurred.

Neoclassical economics strongly supports globalisation, or to be more precise trade openness (defined as imports and exports as a percentage of gross domestic product – GDP) and capital mobility.[2] Lewis (1980) and many economists such as

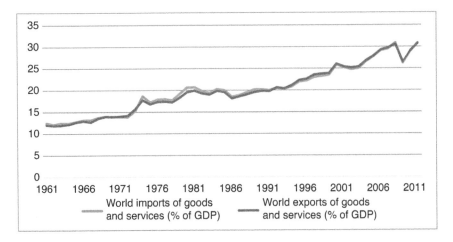

Figure 1.1 Globalisation in terms of trade intensification

Source: World Bank database

Lucas (1993) and Baghwati (2004) believe trade is the engine of economic growth. However, the experience of globalisation so far has shown that the performance of opened economies can vary dramatically (Rodrik, 1999; Rodrik et al., 2004). Openness and integration in the world economy should be accompanied by appropriate institutions, state strategies and particularly by an important welfare state that supports internal cohesion and maintains external competitive advantages. In fact, according to Rodrik (1999), the best-performing countries are the ones that are integrated in the world economy with institutions capable of supporting the impact of globalisation on the domestic market and social cohesion. Countries with poor social institutions, weak conflict management institutions (which means poor welfare states) and strong social cleavages suffer external shocks and do not perform well in the world economy.

Rodrik (2011) and also Stiglitz (2006) offer a sort of guide concerning what should be taken in and what should be left out of the globalisation process. Institutions and policies control, along with a strong government role, is essential in order to compensate for globalisation damages (such as inequality and un-employment) and vulnerabilities (such as employment problems for unskilled workers). In this context, while trade openness could bring advantages and stimulate economic growth, capital mobility would be more problematic for unskilled workers and for employment levels in the country of origin of foreign direct investment (FDI), as I will argue more in detail below.

Nevertheless, for most of the globalisation period, the US has proven the neoclassicals right, showing that to perform well in a globalised economy a country does not necessarily need a strong welfare state. However, the current financial and economic crisis that started in the US in 2007 suggests Rodrik's argument still holds true:

The world market is a source of disruption and upheaval as much as it is an opportunity for profit and economic growth. Without the complementary institutions at home – in the areas of governance, judiciary, civil liberties, social insurance, and education, one gets too much of the former and too little of the latter.

(1999: 96)

For Lucas (1993), international trade stimulates economic growth through a process of structural change and capital accumulation, as in the case of Ireland where, according to Walsh and Whelan (2000), a structural change had already taken place during the 1970s and created conditions that allowed the Irish economy to grow considerably in the 1990s and later in the 2000s. Capital accumulation is determined by "learning by doing" and "learning by schooling" in a process of knowledge and innovation spill-overs. A country that protects its goods made with intensive skilled work from international competition by raising tariffs on them will see a domestic increase in the price of those goods. Skilled workers' wages will increase and research and development (R&D) will become more expensive. Consequently, investments in R&D will decrease, and growth will be negatively affected. On the contrary, removing tariffs on those goods will cause a reduction in their price, a reduction in the cost of R&D, and thus an increase in investments in R&D, with positive effects on growth (Lucas, 1993).

This argument, however, does not take into consideration the inequality and uneven development caused by trade liberalisation and intensification via wage differentials. This issue was already raised by Stolper and Samuelson as we saw previously. Similarly, increased capital flows are expected to raise income inequality in advanced industrial economies because capital outflows from capital-rich countries to least developed countries (LDCs) reduce domestic investment and lower the productive capability and demands for labour in these economies (Ha, 2008; Tsebelis, 2002). Since a reduction in total capital in the production process increases the marginal productivity of capital and reduces the marginal effect of labour, capital outflows increase the income of capital relative to labour, thus exacerbating income inequality. In particular, because FDI outflows from advanced industrial economies tend to be concentrated in industries with low-skilled labour in the home country (Lee, 1996), rapidly rising FDI outflows often reduce the demand for low-skilled labour and increase income gaps in industrial-ised countries. In fact, several studies find that FDI outflows is associated with expanded income inequality in industrialised countries (Leamer, 1996; McKeown, 1999; Wood, 1994).

Empirically, it is interesting to observe the expansion of FDI, which experi-enced a strong increase in the 1990s due to the liberalisation of capital markets, followed by a collapse at the beginning of the 2000s due to the global uncertainty caused by the international events of September 11, 2001 (as shown in Figure 1.2). A further and bigger increase in FDI flows can be observed immediately after and up to the financial crash of 2007, reaching a peak in 2006–07. The current crisis, marked by financial instability and depression, caused a further squeeze

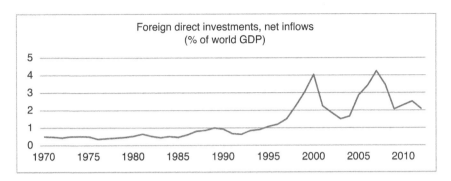

Figure 1.2 FDI in the world economy

Source: World Bank database

in FDI, although it remains at a substantially higher level than at the beginning of the 1990s.

Another argument that needs to be taken into consideration is the impact of economic integration in terms of trade openness and FDI on public finance. This is relevant because obviously public policies affect redistribution and therefore inequality. First of all, it can be stated that financial openness is negatively associated with government size, as Liberati (2007) concluded in his empirical paper. Beyond the size of governments, however, it is very difficult to find conclusive answers concerning the relations between economic integration and public finance. As Gastaldi and Liberati (2011: 343) in their literature review paper conclude: "according to the available empirical literature, the most likely answer is *we do not know*". Studies and researches present contrasting results and a definite conclusion in this filed is impossible to release.

Globalisation, however, poses several challenges to national economies and governments. One of the most important is its effect on inequality, both within and between countries, and its impact on welfare state sustainability. The debate about these challenges has been very lively, and it has produced two main interpretations. The first one states that globalisation reduces the size of welfare states because the latter constitutes a cost for firms. Higher levels of welfare spending necessitate higher levels of income tax, payroll taxes and/or corporate tax which all reduce profit prospective and increase firms' costs. Firms would therefore be pushed to go abroad unless government retrenched social spending and reduced taxes. Thus, in order to maintain high levels of investment and employment in the country, the welfare state needs to be reduced under the process of globalisation. This famous interpretation is known as the "efficiency thesis". This thesis was developed within the neoclassical and neoliberal paradigm, and it argues that globalisation has forced (or should force) states to retrench social welfare in order to achieve a market-friendly environment, improve its competitiveness and attract increasingly mobile international capital (Allan and Scruggs, 2004; Blackmon, 2006; Castells, 2004).

The efficiency thesis is contrasted with the "compensation thesis", which argues that because globalisation increases inequality, welfare states need to increase. In other words, globalisation pressures governments to expand welfare expenditures in order to compensate the domestic "losers" of the globalisation process (Brady et al., 2005; Rodrik, 1998; Swank, 2002).

It is true that with the rise of outsourcing practices and FDI outflows, globalisation has improved the position of capital with respect to labour. Firms' decision to move capital and production across countries has distributional effects: the position of low-skilled workers in industrial countries is worsened by a combination of (1) globalisation and (2) new technology. The first increases the bargaining power of capital against labour, with the consequence of easing capital owners' procurement of tax reductions and welfare retrenchment (Chusseau and Daumont, 2012). States are willing to embark on tax competition among themselves in order to keep investments and production at home. The second has a direct and negative impact on unskilled labour and income distribution without welfare support and social institutions (Tisdell and Svizzero, 2003).

In this context, wage shares in the richest countries have declined dramatically, as Figure 1.3 suggests, with negative consequences on aggregate demand and on income distribution.

The new macroeconomic consensus of the last two or three decades is strictly linked to, if not completely correspondent with, the Washington Consensus doctrine, which called for the implementation of some institutional forms that

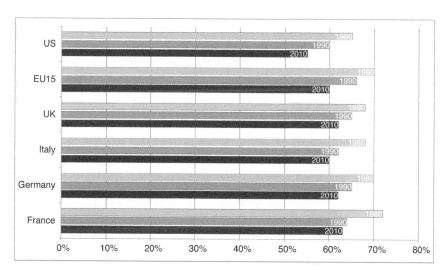

Figure 1.3 Wage share as a percentage of GDP in selected OECD countries

Note: the unadjusted wage share is calculated as total labour compensation of employees divided by value added

Source: Author's own elaboration on the ILO (2013)

better suit the globalisation process such as the financialisation of the economy and the introduction of labour flexibility in the economy (see Tridico, 2012).[3] Acemoglu (2011) argues that the policies implemented over the last two decades in particular were more closely aligned with the preferences of a minority of high-income voters. Instead of redistributive policies favouring low- and middle-income constituents, politicians implemented financial deregulation policies favouring a small group of influential high-income earners (many of whom worked in, or directly benefited from, the financial sector).

To sum up, inequality has increased in most advanced and emerging economies over the last two decades – an era of growing interconnectedness of the world economy – as many studies have already shown (Atkinson, 1999; Galbraith, 2012; Milanovic, 2011; Piketty, 2014), and a simple look at Gini coefficients across countries exposes this trend.

In the next section, I examine the main factors underpinning this development and then, in the following section, I will put forward a model that tries to explain the determinants of inequality.

Financialisation, labour market institutions and inequality

Financialisation is defined in several ways by scholars from the political sciences, sociology and economics. Most of these definitions, however, converge towards the identification of the financialisation process in a political economy phenomenon where there is a growing dominance of capital financial systems over bank-based financial systems (Krippner, 2005), or more broadly the increasing role of financial motives, financial markets, financial actors and financial institutions in the operation of domestic and international economies (Epstein, 2005: 3–4). This process culminated, according to the Bank for International Settlements, in a daily volume of foreign exchange transactions of about 2 trillion dollars in 2006, just before the financial crash of the summer 2007. This is more or less equivalent to the GDP of France. In contrast, in 1989, this volume was about 500 billion dollars per day (BIS, 2013).

Financialisation (a process that involves a set of institutions and financial tools) and labour flexibility (a set of labour market policies that increase the ease for businesses to fire and hire workers, and to cut wages) are two general categories of institutional arrangements that have gone hand in hand in particular during the last two decades, although not everywhere. They have been introduced across the world by countries, in varying degrees, in order to take advantage of the globalisation process which most policy makers and governments believe will boost their national economy. Labour flexibility has increased almost everywhere in Europe and in advanced economies over the last 20 years. However, some countries, such as Austria, Belgium, France and Germany, have retained more rigid labour markets. Other economies, such as Denmark, Sweden, Finland and the Netherlands, introduced higher levels of flexibility along with higher levels of security (OECD, 2013). Countries such as the US, the UK and Ireland increased (or maintained) their already very flexible labour markets. Finally, Mediterranean

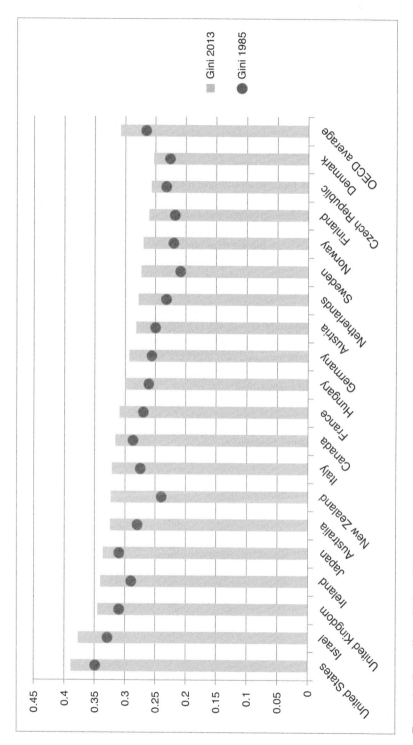

Figure 1.4 Inequality – Gini coefficient

Source: OECD

countries such as Italy, Spain and Greece and most of the former communist economies in Europe combined very hybrid situations (of liberal and corporative elements) with an increased level of labour flexibility.

The political and economic roots of the financialisation process, which brought about a new financial-led growth regime, can be found in the 1970s (Jessop, 2002). After the fall of the Soviet Union, Alan Greenspan, who rose to oversee the US Federal Reserve at the end of the Reagan administration, believed that the world economy could expand greatly through the globalisation of the financial sector (Greenspan, 2007; Semmler and Young, 2010). Many other economies followed the American example of a financial-led regime of accumulation, which used other institutional forms such as flexible labour and the nexus of compressed wages in order to increase firms' competitiveness (Tridico, 2012). Shareholders sought higher dividends because they invested their own capital in firms, taking on a higher level of risk. Since the economic growth of advanced economies under financial capitalism has not been higher than under previous phases (the so-called Fordist period), as Figure 1.5 shows,[4] it follows that wages should be compressed in order for shareholders to obtain higher dividends. However, wages have not followed the increases in productivity and profits continued to soar (as has been the case in most of advanced countries and in particular in US).

Similarly, Lin and Tomaskovic-Devey (2011) argue that the increasing reliance by firms on earnings realised through financial channels generated surplus from production, strengthening owners' and elite workers' negotiating power relative to other workers. This resulted in the exclusion of most workers from revenue and therefore in the increase of inequality.

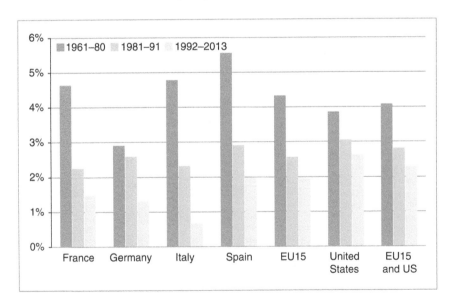

Figure 1.5 Average GDP growth in the EU15 and the US, 1961–2013

Source: World Bank database

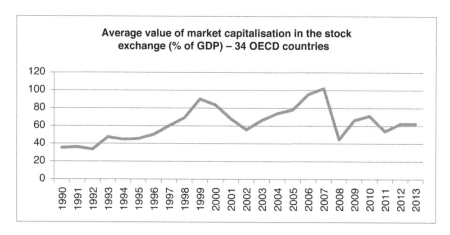

Figure 1.6 Financialisation

Source: World Bank database

In light of these developments, labour flexibility and wage contraction were functional in obtaining this result (higher dividends for shareholders), at least in the short run. As far as financialisation is concerned, Figure 1.6 shows the expansion of financialisation among OECD economies over the past two decades. The variable here is the World Bank's "Market capitalization of listed [domestic] companies" as a percentage of GDP.[5] One can observe an important increase in the 1990s, driven probably by the "dot.com" bubble; the fall after September 11, 2001; another consistent increase with a bubble that reached its peak in 2006 driven by the housing sector; and finally the crash of 2007–8 and the following stabilisation after 2012 to a level that is almost double than the average value of 1990 (more than 60 per cent of GDP versus less than 40 per cent).

More specifically, the highest level of financialisation is found in Anglo-Saxon economies (particularly the US, the UK, Australia and Canada, which have enormous values of financialisation – between 100 and 150 per cent of GDP), while the lowest levels of financialisation are in continental Europe, with the notable exception of Switzerland. The US promoted neo-liberalism as a main ideological paradigm for globalisation and financialisation through global, multi and bilateral measures under pressure from all the major international financial institutions, multinational corporations and Wall Street institutions (Epstein, 2005).[6]

Within financial capitalism, the bargaining position of capital relative to labour in higher-income countries increased importantly. As Feenstra (1998: 46) observes, the impact of globalisation on changing the bargaining position of labour and capital has far-reaching consequences. The decline in union power, particularly within trade-oriented industries, may well account for a portion of the increased wage inequality in the US and in other countries (Borjas and Ramey, 1995; Gordon, 2012).

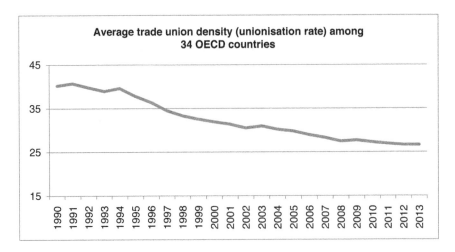

Figure 1.7 The decline of trade union density

Source: Author's own elaboration on OECD data

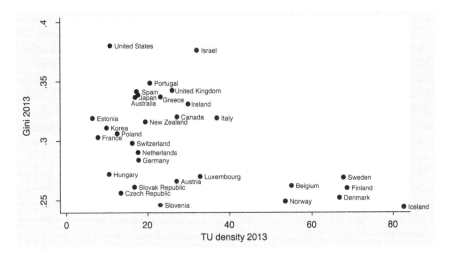

Figure 1.8 Trade unions and inequality

Source: Author's own elaboration on OECD data

In the US there is a very clear relation between decline in trade union membership and inequality in the twentieth century. Gordon (2012) argues that between the New Deal, which granted workers basic collective bargaining rights among other important things, and the end of 1960s "labor unions both sustained prosperity, and ensured that it was shared". Since the 1970s and in particular during the Reagan administration, "unions came under attack—in the workplace, in the courts, and in

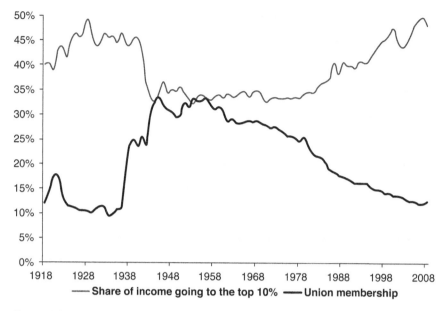

Figure 1.9 Unionisation and share of income to the top 10 per cent

Source: Reproduced from Gordon (2012)

public policy. As a result, union membership has fallen and income inequality has worsened—reaching levels not seen since the 1920s" Gordon (2012).

The decline in unionisation rates has contributed to the weakening of labour market institutions such as labour protection against firing and hiring, the level and duration of unemployment benefits with the introduction of constraints concerning eligibility and the reduction in most of the cases of their length and amount, the minimum wage and so on. In the Appendix a list of nine labour market indicators (the seven in Table 1A.1, plus employment protection legislation (EPL) and trade union density in Table 1A.2) is presented. Out of them, a factor analysis was carried out in order to establish the most important elements explaining variation among the variables. This resulted in a principal component that, when scattered in a plot against the inequality index (Gini in 2013), produces Figure 1.10. This figure displays a clear correlation between the two: the higher the score of the principal component (more protection in the labour market) the lower the Gini level, and vice versa.[7]

The OECD's EPL indicator is probably the most important labour market indicator. It measures the general level of worker protection in the labour market and consequently the level of labour flexibility (it varies between 0 for very low protection and 6 for very high protection). In essence, it shows the level of protection offered by national legislation with respect to regular employment, temporary employment and collective dismissal – in other words, regulation that

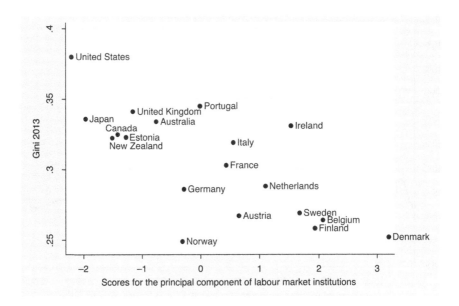

Figure 1.10 Inequality and labour market indicators

Source: Author's own elaboration on OECD data

allows employers to fire and hire workers at will (OECD, 2004). Figure 1.11 shows the evolution of the average level of EPL among OECD countries from 1990 to 2013. Its decline clearly underlines an increase in labour flexibility.

A flexible labour market with compressed wages needs to be supplemented by available financialisation, credit and developed financial tools to sustain

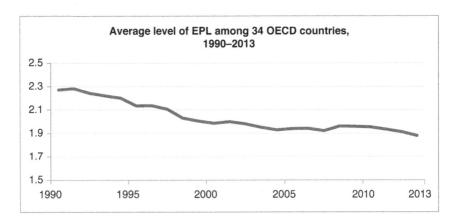

Figure 1.11 Labour market flexibility

Source: Author's own elaboration on OECD data

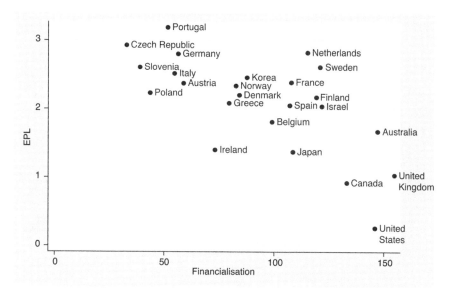

Figure 1.12 Correlation scatter between financialisation and labour flexibility (EPL) in 2013

Source: Author's own elaboration on the OECD and World Bank database

consumption, which otherwise would be compressed by low and unstable wages (Brancaccio and Fontana, 2011). Therefore, a large number of financial tools were invented to finance consumption, postpone payments, extend credit and create extra consumption (Tridico, 2012). That being said, it is difficult to establish a causal relation: we cannot be certain whether financialisation required labour flexibility or if increased labour flexibility brought about hyper-financialisation. A simple, but important, correlation (Figure 1.12) between these two complementary institutional forms of neoliberalism seems more likely.

Labour flexibility allows for the reduction of firms' labour costs and thus wage savings at the expense of wage earners, that is consumers. In such a situation, inequality increases and aggregate demand is restricted because consumption decreases.

It is very interesting to notice an inverse relationship between inequality and the EPL index (labour flexibility): the lower the EPL (higher flexibility), the higher the inequality. Continental and Scandinavian European countries have a higher EPL (lower flexibility) and lower inequality relative to Anglo-Saxon and Mediterranean countries, which generally show the opposite values of higher inequality and lower EPL (higher flexibility).

As a result, one can see in Figures 1.12 and 1.14 that high financialisation is typically associated with high labour flexibility and high Gini coefficients. More interesting is the parallel trends of these variables: when financialisation increases,

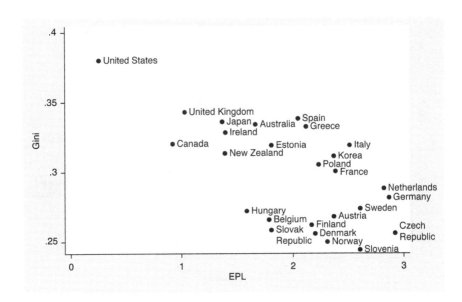

Figure 1.13 Correlation scatter between inequality and EPL in 2013

Source: Author's own elaboration on the OECD

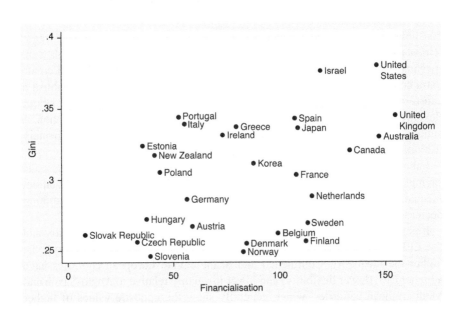

Figure 1.14 Correlation scatter between financialisation and inequality in 2013

Source: Author's own elaboration on OECD and World Bank database

both flexibility and inequality increases, as the correlation scatters seem to suggest. In other words, as has been argued elsewhere (Tridico, 2012), the rise of inequality generated an increased demand for credit, which translated into a credit expansion provided for by accommodating monetary policies and financial deregulation. One should take particular notice of the particular path of Scandinavian countries (especially Sweden and Finland) which display a relatively high degree of financialisation, yet are able to contain inequality (which nevertheless is increasing) with their strong welfare states (along with other labour market institutions).

Finally, this series of correlations and scatters suggest that what contributes to the increase or decrease of inequality seems to be the choice of the socio-economic model that each country built during the decades after the Second World War. More specifically, what is most relevant is the set of policies that each country is currently able to implement in order to cope with the challenges of globalisation both in terms of income distribution and competitiveness (Rodrik, 1999). These include in particular social protection against unemployment and low wages, welfare programmes against poverty, health and education policies, social policy for housing and so forth. As Figure 1.15 shows, there seems to be a clear relationship between inequality and welfare expenditures in the sense that countries that spend more on welfare generally have a lower level of inequality.[8]

After the Second World War and particularly since 1960, countries, especially those in Europe, invested increasing shares of their GDP on developing welfare

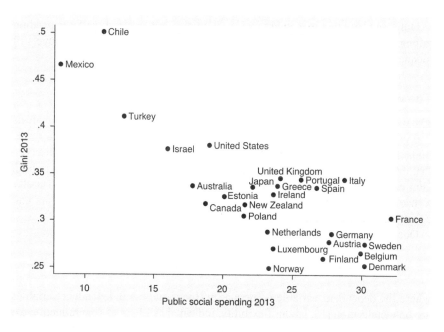

Figure 1.15 Inequality (Gini) and public social expenditure (percentage of GDP)

Source: Author's own elaboration on the OECD data

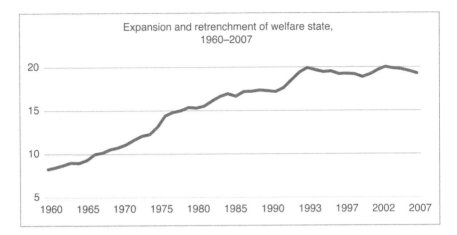

Figure 1.16 The welfare states since 1960 (public social expenditure, percentage of GDP)

Source: Author's own elaboration on OECD data

states. This trend continued until the beginning of the 1990s. After that, and particularly after the peak reached in 1993, governments started to retrench welfare states, and welfare expenditure was lower at the eve of the financial crisis in 2007 than in 1993 (OECD, 2012).

Only countries that managed to keep relatively high levels of welfare spending (along with the other variables discussed) have managed to keep low levels of inequality, as the model in the next section shows.

The model

The model that I put forward in this section takes into consideration the analysis and the correlations discussed previously. The objective is to identify the determinants of inequality over the last two decades in rich countries. I have observed that inequality has increased in the past two decades or more, according to both Gini coefficient and the Palma ratio and other indicators. In my model I prefer to use the Gini coefficient since it has a wider coverage in terms of years and countries than other ratios.

Our model is represented by the following equation:

$$Ineq = \alpha + \beta_1 F - \beta_2 EPL - \beta_3 TU - \beta_4 S + \varepsilon$$

where the dependent variable is inequality (Ineq) and the independent variables are financialisation (F), labour flexibility, indicated as LF, or as (the reduction of) EPL (employment protection legislation), trade union density (TU) and public social spending (S). I use panel data for 34 OECD countries from 1990 to 2013, for a total of 816 observations.

Interestingly enough the correlation matrix in the Appendix (Table 1A.3) does not show the existence of auto-correlation problems among the independent variables, and it may be difficult to argue in favour of a reverse causality between the dependent and the independent variables of our model, that is the reduction of welfare state, the weakening of trade unions and the increase of labour flexibility, although endogeneity may always exist to some degree.

The regression results are very interesting and confirm our hypothesis. I use a GLS model with a random effect to establish the relation, verified through the Hausman test against the fixed effect. The GLS model (I) produces very robust results, according to which inequality increases when (1) financialisation increases (i.e. the level of market capitalisation as defined previously), when (2) labour

Table 1.1 Regression results for inequality (Gini, 1990–2013)

	Random-effects GLS regression		Fixed-effect regression
	Number of obs = 816 Number of groups = 34 Panel = 1990–2013		
	Model I	**Model II** (with control var)	**Model III**
Var	*Coeff (St. er. in brackets)*	*Coeff (St. er. in brackets)*	
Financialisation (F)	.0000502	.0000459	.0000451
P>|z|	(.000019)	(.0000214)	(.000021)
	0.008**	0.032**	0.032**
EPL (LF)	−.0040886	−.0051814	−.0061798
P>|z|	(.0021277)	(.0024638)	(.0025251)
	0.050**	0.035**	0.015**
TU density (TU)	−.0005735	−.0005768	−.0004044
P>|z|	(.0001389)	(.0001975)	(.0002232)
	0.000*	0.003*	0.070***
Social spending (S)	−.000829	−.0010213	−.0007598
P>|z|	(.0002327)	(.0003015)	(.000301)
	0.000*	0.001*	0.012**
Unemployment		.0000153	−.0000472
P>|z|		(.0002661)	(.0002632)
		0.954	0.858
FDI		.0000543	.0000384
P>|z|		(.0000604)	(.000059)
		0.369	0.515
Import		−.0001758	2.92e-06
P>|z|		(.0001385)	(.0001501)
		0.204	0.984
Economic growth		.0001935	.0001312
P>|z|		(.0002315)	(.0002276)
		0.403	0.565

(continued)

Table 1.1 Regression results for inequality (Gini, 1990–2013) *(continued)*

Var	Random-effects GLS regression		Fixed-effect regression
	Number of obs = 816 Number of groups = 34 Panel = 1990–2013		
	Model I	**Model II** *(with control var)*	**Model III**
Var	*Coeff (St. er. in brackets)*	*Coeff (St. er. in brackets)*	
Tertiary education level P>|z|		−.0001815 (.0003467) 0.600	.0001228 (.000372) 0.741
Time dummies (years 1990–2013)	YES	YES	YES
Constant P>|z|	.3530048 (.0124588) 0.000*	−.2291932 (.4890413) 0.639	.2456811 (.5126353) 0.632
	R-sq = 0.2437	R-sq = 0.3167	R-sq = 0.1447
	Wald chi²(4) = 32.55	Wald chi²(10) = 40.36	Prob > F = 0.0009
	Prob > chi² = 0.0000	Prob > chi² = 0.0000	

Hausman Test (RE vs FE):
  b (RE) = consistent under Ho and Ha; obtained from xtreg
  B (FE) = inconsistent under Ha, efficient under Ho; obtained from xtreg
  Test: Ho: difference in coefficients not systematic
  chi²(10) = (b − B)'[(V_b − V_B)^(−1)](b − B) = 101.88 Prob > chi² = 0.0000

Notes: * indicates significance level at 1%

Source: Author's own elaboration

flexibility increases (i.e. EPL decreases), when (3) trade unions are weaker (i.e. TU density declines) and when (4) the level of public social spending decreases. All coefficients are statistically significant at least at the 5 per cent level.

Thus, we can consider the following output (RE GLS model):

$$Gini = .35 + .00005 * F_{ij} - .004 * EPL_{ij} - .0006 * TU_{ij} - .0008 * S_{ij}, \text{ with } i = \text{country},$$
and j = year

Model III shows the results of the fixed effect regression, which are not consistent against the random effect and therefore are not advised by the Hausman test performed. In Model II I include some relevant control variables such as the unemployment rate, import (as a percentage of GDP), FDI inflow (as a percentage of GDP), economic growth and tertiary education level, plus the years (time). All these variables are used for the same timespan covered by the panel, namely

1990–2013. As the regression table suggests, adding these variables to the initial model does affect the results (they are all statistically insignificant), since the co-efficients for our variables of interest (F, EPL, TU and S) stay approximately the same. This means that higher unemployment rates do not affect inequality levels, so long as the welfare state of that country is able to compensate the unemployed. Moreover, the other two control variables suggest that an open economy is not condemned to increased inequality if this economy has a stronger welfare state, powerful trade unions, a more rigid labour market and social institutions which mitigate the negative effects of globalisation. This seems to be the case, for instance, with the very competitive Scandinavian and continental European economies which are also countries where inequality is low.

Conclusion

This chapter argues that the increase in inequality, which has been very marked over the last two decades, is due to a radical change to the main features of the socio-economic model of advanced economies. This change involves a shift towards financialisation, a pressure on labour through increased labour flexibility, the decline of trade unions' power and the retrenchment of public social spending. My sample was composed of data for 34 OECD countries during the period between 1990 and 2013. The econometric analysis produced very interesting results and the regression confirmed my hypothesis that inequality increases when the level of labour flexibility and the level of financialisation of the economy increases, and when trade union density and public social spending declines. The introduction of control variables such as the unemployment rate, FDI, imports, economic growth or tertiary education level does not alter the results.

These results pose further challenging questions to governments and policy makers. First of all, whether inequality negatively affects economic performance; and secondly whether inequality negatively affects government revenues and fiscal performance. Important answers have already been found by Winkelmann and Winkelmann (2010) who find a robust inverse relation between the size and the income of middle class (and economic performance) and inequality, and by Larch (2012) who found evidence that a more unequal distribution of income can harm fiscal performance of a country. More recently, evidence from the International Monetary Fund (IMF) (see Ostry et al., 2014) and the OECD (see Cingano, 2014) have also found that high levels of inequality were associated with lower economic growth, suggesting that there is no "big trade-off" between equality and efficiency. Hence, economic and fiscal policies in the post-2007 financial crisis should take into consideration their distributional implications.

The financialisation of advanced economies, as I have discussed in this chapter, has occurred since the end of the 1970s in the US and the UK and since the end of the 1980s in Western Europe and in other advanced economies. It increased rapidly in the 1990s and in the 2000s, with negative effects on inequality. Compensations in the financial sector soared enormously in the last two decades, beyond any reasonable link with labour productivity. The globalisation of the economy which occurred during the same period, as I argued, increased the power of capital in relation to labour, and trade unions lost power, contributing to the deterioration of labour market institutions. During the process of financialisation and globalisation of economies, which identifies the shift towards what I called financial capitalism, labour markets were affected by radical changes too, involving above all an increase in labour flexibility. As I argued, a flexible labour market with compressed and low wages needs to be supplemented by credit consumption and developed financial tools to sustain consumption. Hence, a strong correlation between financialisation and labour flexibility was identified in my empirical analysis, suggesting complementarities between these two phenomena. Labour market institutions such as protections against firing and hiring weakened, and contracts for temporary jobs increased. This process is captured in my argument by the trend of the EPL indicator which has decreased on average in my sample. In this context, labour was continuously under pressure, contributing to the worsening of income distribution and therefore to the increase in inequality. Finally, income distribution was worsened by the retrenchment of the welfare state (illustrated in my argument by the stagnation in public social spending) in advanced economies, mostly with the justification that firms would be more competitive and economies could attract more capital – the so-called "efficiency thesis".

This argument does not conflict with Piketty (2014), Atkinson et al. (2011) and Facundo et al. (2013), who maintain that inequality has risen since the 1970s mostly because taxation reduced progressivity in particular at the top of the distribution. Quite the opposite: the shift towards a model where trade unions are less important, social spending declines, financialisation becomes dominant and labour flexibility regulates industrial relations as main drivers of inequality is very consistent with the lack of progressivity in taxation argument. All these policies and institutions are coherently part of the financial capitalism model in which inequality increased.

Obviously, there is a strong variation in the independent variables among the countries analysed and strong variation also exists with regards to inequality. Usually continental European countries, which have lower inequality levels, have lower levels of financialisation and labour flexibility, and higher levels of trade unions density and social spending. Conversely, Anglo-Saxon countries, which have higher inequality levels, have higher levels of financialisation and labour flexibility, and lower levels of trade union density and social spending. Mediterranean countries, new European Union member states (from Central and Eastern Europe) and emerging economies, which have increasing levels of inequality, are also increasing their levels of financialisation and of labour flexibility, while they are lowering their levels of trade union density and social spending. These worrying changes constitute strong signals to policy makers who wish to reduce income inequality.

Appendix

Table 1A.1 Labour market indicators

	Active policy 2012 (% of GDP)	Passive policy 2012 (% of GDP)	Coverage (in % of workers) of trade unions 2009–11	Level of coordinated bargaining wage	Length of unemployment subsidies (months) 2011	Substitut. rate for unempl. subsidies (% 2009 11)	Minimum wage, hourly (US$ PPP)	Scores of the principal component analysis
Australia	0.29	0.51	99.00	6.00	9	0.55	10.5	-.75
Austria	0.75	1.29	60.00	0.00	48	0.22		.65
Belgium	0.81	2.08	96.00	0.33	48	0.59	10.1	2.07
Canada	0.24	0.59	31.50	0.00	11	0.59	7.8	-1.41
Chile	0.1	0.23	48.00	0.00	18	0.71	2.9	2.07
Denmark	2.1	1.7	82.00	0.00	24	0.55		3.19
Estonia	0.29	0.44	80.00	4.00	24	0.49	2.8	-1.15
Finland	1.03	1.45	90.00	1.67	23	0.54		1.93
France	0.9	1.45	95.00	3.33	24	0.69	10.7	.43
Germany	0.69	0.98	63.00	0.00	12	0.60		-.28
Ireland	0.91	0.57	44.00	0.00	12	0.36	9.0	1.53
Italy	0.45	0.34	80.00	0.67	8	0.63		-.19
Netherlands	0.98	0.37	82.00	3.67	38	0.68	9.5	1.09
New Zealand	0.29	0.35	17.00	0.00	48	0.23	8.7	-1.49
Norway	0.54	0.3	72.00	0.00	24	0.67		-.31
Portugal	0.49	0.44	62.00	0.00	24	0.78	4.0	-.010
Sweden	1.33	0.59	92.00	0.00	35	0.60		1.67
UK	0.41		34.80	0.00	6	0.17	8.0	-1.15
US	0.12		13.10	0.00	23	0.57	7.3	-2.20

Note: data concerning most of these labour market indicators, on the basis of which the factor analysis was run and the score of principal component in the last column was extracted, are not available for all 34 OECD countries, but only for 19 as this table suggests

Source: author's own elaboration on OECD data

Table 1A.2 Descriptive statistics for the regression of Table 1.1

	Financialis. 2013 (% GDP)	Financialis. avg. (% GDP)	EPL 2013	EPL avg.	TU density 2013	TU density avg.	Social spending 2013 (% GDP)	Social spending avg. (% GDP)	Inequality (Gini 2013)	Inequality (Gini avg.)
Australia	85	92	1.27	1.11	17	26	19	15.2	0.32	0.32
Austria	27	21	1.84	1.94	27	36	28.3	25.5	0.28	0.27
Belgium	62	57	2.09	2.46	55	54	30.9	26.3	0.26	0.27
Canada	111	95	0.59	0.59	27	30	17.2	16.9	0.32	0.31
Chile	117	97	2.81	2.81	15	15	10	10.8	0.50	0.51
Czech Republic	19	23	2.18	2.01	13	25	20.5	18.0	0.26	0.25
Denmark	72	54	1.79	1.95	67	72	30.2	26.9	0.25	0.23
Estonia	11	23	2.40	2.09	6	14	16.1	15.9	0.32	0.34
Finland	63	85	1.86	1.88	69	74	30.6	25.6	0.26	0.25
France	70	64	3.00	2.99	8	8	32	27.9	0.31	0.29
Germany	44	40	2.00	2.34	18	25	25.6	24.5	0.29	0.27
Greece	18	41	2.18	3.29	21	27	24.3	18.7	0.34	0.34
Hung	17	19	1.42	1.42	11	21	22.1	22.1	0.29	0.29
Iceland	21	62	1.18	1.18	83	88	17.1	15.7	0.25	0.26
Ireland	52	54	1.01	0.90	30	39	21.9	18.6	0.30	0.31
Israel	57	61	1.46	1.46	32	55	15	15.9	0.38	0.36
Italy	24	31	2.26	2.97	37	36	28.7	23.1	0.32	0.32
Japan	62	74	1.12	1.40	18	21	23	14.4	0.34	0.33
Korea Republic	105	60	2.25	2.55	10	12	10.2	5.7	0.31	0.31
Luxembourg	123	149	3.00	3.00	33	41	23.4	20.9	0.28	0.27
Mexico	45	31	2.05	3.05	14	16	7.9	4.5	0.48	0.49
Netherlands	84	92	1.88	2.00	18	22	24.6	23.8	0.28	0.29
New Zealand	48	42	1.20	1.06	19	25	20.8	19.1	0.32	0.33
Norway	51	43	2.67	2.67	54	55	22	20.8	0.25	0.26
Poland	36	20	1.99	1.69	13	20	20.7	20.0	0.30	0.33

Portugal	31	32	2.50	3.57	21	23	25.8	17.0	0.34	0.37
Slovakia	5	6	1.80	1.81	17	29	18.7	18.3	0.26	0.26
Slovenia	14	18	2.21	2.22	23	42	23.8	14.5	0.25	0.25
Spain	74	65	2.31	2.91	17	17	27.3	21.2	0.34	0.33
Sweden	107	92	1.71	2.17	68	77	28.2	28.8	0.27	0.24
Switzerland	171	187	1.36	1.36	16	20	19.9	16.5	0.29	0.30
Turkey	39	25	3.59	3.62	5	11	12.5	6.8	0.41	0.44
UK	124	128	0.70	0.71	25	30	22.5	19.4	0.34	0.34
US	119	115	0.25	0.25	11	13	18.6	15.1	0.39	0.37
OECD	62	62	1.88	1.11	17	21	21.7	15.2	0.32	0.32

Note: the average (avg.) is for the whole period (1990–2013)

Source: author's own elaboration on OECD data

Table 1A.3 Correlation matrix

	Gini	EPL	TU_dens.	SocSpend	Financ.	FDI_IN	Import	Growth	Unemploy.	Tert_edu_level
Gini	1.0000									
EPL	0.2721	1.0000								
TU_dens.	-0.4535	-0.0640	1.0000							
SocSpend	-0.6734	-0.0973	0.4489	1.0000						
Financ.	-0.1215	-0.3800	-0.0052	0.0938	1.0000					
FDI IN	-0.0301	-0.0449	0.0266	0.0737	-0.0258	1.0000				
Import	-0.3201	0.0846	0.0344	0.2808	-0.0122	0.1158	1.0000			
Growth	0.0726	-0.0198	-0.0649	-0.2520	0.0976	0.0386	-0.0424	1.0000		
Unemploy.	0.0265	0.1894	-0.0247	0.1909	-0.2615	-0.0130	0.0408	-0.1132	1.0000	
Tert_edu_level	-0.2507	-0.5556	0.1603	0.1372	0.4599	0.0109	-0.0719	-0.0978	-0.1940	1.0000

Acknowledgements

I wish to thank Paolo Liberati for his useful comments. I wish to thank also the participants of the First World Congress of Comparative Economics, held in Rome at the Roma Tre University (25–27 June 2015), where the paper on which this chapter is based was first presented. The usual disclaimer applies.

Notes

1 I will come back to this later.
2 Interestingly enough, the IMF has recently backtracked with regards to capital market liberalisation, arguing that opening capital markets in developing economies could increase economic instability if an appropriate regulatory environment was not put in place (IMF, 2014).
3 It has to be said that in the last years, in particular after the 2007 financial crash, the Washington Consensus along with other mainstream policies has evolved, and the main advocates of those policies have started to acknowledge failures and mistakes (IMF, 2014).
4 Figure 1.5 shows that GDP growth during Fordism (which is usually identified by the period before 1980) is higher than growth during both the transition period (which is usually identified by the period during the 1980s, in particular the decade 1981–1991) and post-Fordism (or the period of globalisation and finacialisation) which is identified by the last period from 1992 until today. For more details on the periodisation of Fordism and post-Fordism, see Jessop (2002).
5 Financialisation is captured by the variable "market capitalisation" (also known as market value) which is the share price multiplied by the number of shares outstanding. Listed domestic companies are the domestically incorporated companies listed on the country's stock exchanges at the end of the year. Listed companies do not include investment companies, mutual funds or other collective investment vehicles.
6 Interestingly enough, financialisation also took place in Scandinavian economies. This is consistent with the results of Engelen et al. (2010) and van der Zwan (2014), who show that financialisation takes place everywhere, including in countries with strong welfare states. However, here the high level of social expenditure is able to contain inequality (which is nevertheless increasing in Scandinavian countries too). The highest percentage of financialisation in terms of GDP is Switzerland, while, in terms of absolute value, the US is the most financialised market, followed by the UK.
7 A similar result is obtained by Butcher et al. (2012) and by Autor et al. (2015) who found that minimum wages have little effect on employment but do have impacts on wage inequality, in particular in the UK and in US during the 1990s and 2000s.
8 I have also included here three emerging countries: Chile, Turkey and Mexico, new OECD countries, which, although they are outliers with respect to the values of the other OECD countries, fit well with the discourse and constitute a group in themselves (with very low levels of social spending and very high inequality).

References

Acemoglu, D. (2011), "Thoughts on inequality and the financial crisis" (presentation held at the American Economic Association). Paper available from http://economics.mit.edu/files/6348 (last accessed 07/11/2013).

Adema, W., Fron, P. and Ladaique, M. (2011), "Is the European Welfare State Really More Expensive? Indicators on Social Spending, 1980–2012 and a Manual to the OECD Social Expenditure Database (SOCX)", *OECD Social, Employment and Migration Working Papers*, No. 124, OECD Publishing.

Allan, J. P. and Scruggs, L. (2004), "Political Partisanship and Welfare State Reform in Advanced Industrial Societies", *American Journal of Political Science*, 48(3): 496–512.

Atkinson, A. B. (1999), "Is Rising Inequality Inevitable? A Critique of the Transatlantique Consensus", WIDER Annual Lectures No. 3, Helsinki.

Atkinson, A. B., Piketty, T. and Saez, E. (2011), "Top incomes in the long run of history", *Journal of Economic Literature*, 49(1): 3–71.

Autor, D., Manning, A. and Smith, C. (2015), "The Contribution of the Minimum Wage to U.S. Wage Inequality over Three Decades: A Reassessment", mimeo, http://economics.mit.edu/files/3279.

Bhagwati, J. (2004), *In Defense of Globalization*, Oxford: Oxford University Press.

BIS (2013), Triennial Central Bank Survey, Bank for International Settlements, Monetary and Economic Department, Basel.

Blackmon, P. (2006), "The State: Back in the Center of the Globalization Debate", *International Studies Review*, 8(1): 116–119.

Borjas, G. J. and Ramey, V. A. (1995), "Foreign Competition, Market Power, and Wage Inequality", *The Quarterly Journal of Economics*, 110(4): 1075–1110.

Brady, D., Beckfield, J. and Seeleib-Kaiser, M. (2005), "Economic Globalization and the Welfare State in Affluent Democracies, 1975–1998", *American Sociological Review*, 70: 921–48.

Brancaccio, E. and Fontana, G. (2011), "The Global Economic Crisis" (Introduction), in E. Brancaccio and G. Fontana (eds) *The Global Economic Crisis: New Perspective on the Critique of Economic Theory and Policy*, Abingdon: Routledge.

Butcher, T., Dickens, R. and Manning, A. (2012), "Minimum Wages and Wage Inequality: Some Theory and an Application to the UK", CEP discussion paper no. 1177.

Card, D., Lemieux, T. and Craig Riddell, W. (2004), "Unions and Wage Inequality", *Journal of Labor Research*, 25(4): 519–62.

Castells, M. (2004), "Global Informational Capitalism", in D. Held and A. G. McGrew (eds) *The Global Transformations Reader: An Introduction to the Globalization Debate*, Malden, MA: Blackwell.

Chusseau, N. and Dumont, M. (2012), "Growing Income Inequalities in Advanced Countries", ECINEQ WP 2012 – 260, Paris.

Cingano, F. (2014), "Trends in Income Inequality and its Impact on Economic Growth", OECD *Working Papers*, No. 163, OECD Publishing.

Engelen, E., Konings, M. and Fernandez, R. (2010), "Geographies of Financialisation in Disarray: The Dutch Case in Comparative Perspective", *Economic Geography*, 86(1): 53–73.

Epstein, G. (2005), *Financialisation and the World Economy*, Cheltenham: Edward Elgar.

Facundo, A., Atkinson, A. B., Piketty, T. and Saez, E. (2013), "The Top 1 Percent in International and Historical Perspective", *Journal of Economic Perspectives*, 27(3): 320.

Feenstra, R. C. (1998), "Integration of Trade and Disintegration of Production in the Global Economy", *Journal of Economic Perspectives*, 12(4): 31–50.

Fitoussi, J.-P. and Saraceno, F. (2010), "Inequality and Macroeconomic Performance, Documents de Travail OFCE 2010–13, Observatoire Francais des Conjonctures Economiques.

Galbraith, J. K. (2012), *Inequality and Instability*, Oxford: Oxford University Press.

Gastaldi, F. and Liberati, P. (2011), "Economic Integration and Government Size: A Review of the Empirical Literature", *Financial Theory and Practice*, 35(3): 328–384.

Gordon, C. (2012), "Union Decline and Rising Inequality in Two Charts", Economic Policy Institute, www.epi.org/blog/union-decline-rising-inequality-charts/.

Greenspan, A. (2007), *The Age of Turbulence: Adventures in a New World*, London: Allen Lane.

Ha, E. (2008), "Globalization, Veto Players, and Welfare Spending", *Comparative Political Studies*, 48(6): 783–813.

Hay, C. and Wincott, D. (2012), *The Political Economy of European Welfare Capitalism*, Basingstoke: Palgrave Macmillan.

Held, D., McGrew, A., Goldblatt, D. and Perraton, J. (1999), *Global Transformations: Politics, Economics and Culture*, Cambridge: Polity.

ILO (2013), Global Wage Report 2012/13 Wages and Equitable Growth, Geneva: International Labour Office.

IMF (2014), *The IMF's Approach to Capital Account Liberalization*, Washington, DC.

Jessop, B. (2002), *The Future of the Capitalist State*, Cambridge: Polity.

Jha, P. and Golder, S. (2008), *Labour Market Regulation and Economic Performance: A Critical Review of Arguments and Some Plausible Lessons for India*, Geneva: International Labour Office.

Krippner, G. R. (2005), "The Financialisation of the American Economy", *Socio-Economic Review*, 3(2): 173–208.

Kuznets, S. (1955), "Economic Growth and Income Inequality", *American Economic Review*, 45 (March): 1–28.

Larch, M. (2012), Fiscal Performance and Income Inequality: Are Unequal Societies More Deficit-Prone? 65(1): 53–80.

Leamer, E. (1996), "Wage Inequality from International Competition and Technological Changes: Theory and Country Experience", *The American Economic Review*, 86(2): 309–314.

Lee, E. (1996), "Globalization and Employment: Is Anxiety Justified?", *International Labour Review*, 135(5): 485–497.

Lemieux, T., MacLeod, W. B. and Parent, D. (2009), "Performance Pay and Wage Inequality", *Quarterly Journal of Economics*, 124(1): 1–49.

Lewis, A. (1980), "The Slowing Down of the Engine of Growth: Nobel Lecture", *American Economic Review*, 70(4): 555–564.

Liberati, P. (2007), "Trade Openness, Capital Openness and Government Size", *Journal of Public Policy*, 27(2): 215–247.

Lin, K.-H. and Tomaskovic-Devey, D. (2011), "Financialization and US Income Inequality, 1970–2008", mimeo. http://papers.ssrn.com/sol3/papers.cfm?abstract_id=1954129.

Lucas, R. (1993), "Making a Miracle". *Econometrica*, 61(2): 251–257.

McKeown, T. J. (1999), "The Global Economy, Post-Fordism, and Trade Policy in Advanced Capitalist States", in H. Kitschelt, P. Lange, G. Marks and J. Stephens (eds) *Continuity and Change in Contemporary Capitalism*, Cambridge: Cambridge University Press.

Milanovic, B. (2011), "Global Inequality and the Global Inequality Extraction Ratio: The Story of the Past Two Centuries", *Explorations in Economic History*, 48: 494–506.

OECD (2004), "Employment Outlook" (Chapter 2), *Employment Protection Regulation and Labour Market Performance*, Paris: OECD Publishing.

OECD (2012), Social Expenditure database. www.oecd.org/els/social/expenditure.

OECD (2013), "Protecting Jobs, Enhancing Flexibility: A New Look at the Employment Protection Legislation", in *OECD Employment Outlook*, Paris: OECD Publishing.

OECD (2014), "Focus on Inequality and Growth", Paris: OECD Publishing.

OECD (various years), Employment outlook (online database). www.oecd.org/els/oecd-employment-outlook-19991266.htm

Ostry, J. D., Berg, A. and Tsangarides, C. G. (2014), "Redistribution, Inequality, and Growth", IMF staff discussion paper, Washington, DC.

Perugini, C., Hölscher, J. and Collie, S. (2015), "Inequality, Credit and Financial Crises", *Cambridge Journal of Economics*, 39(1), doi:10.1093/cje/beu075.

Piketty, T. (2014), *Capital in the Twenty-First Century*, Cambridge, MA: Belknap Press.

Rodrik, D. (1998), "Why Do More Open Economies Have Bigger Governments?", *Journal of Political Economy*, 106: 997–1032.

Rodrik, D. (1999), *Making Openness Work*, Baltimore, MD: Johns Hopkins University Press.

Rodrik, D. (2011), *The Globalization Paradox: Democracy and the Father of the World Economy*, New York: W.W. Norton & Company.

Rodrik, D., Subramanian, A. and Trebbi, F. (2004), "Institutions Rule: the Primacy of Institutions over Geography and Integration in Economic Development", *Journal of Economic Growth*, 9(2): 131–165.

Semmler, W. and Young, B. (2010), "Lost in Temptation of Risk: Financial Market Liberalization, Financial Market Meltdown and Regulatory Reforms", *Comparative European Politics*, 8(3): 327–353.

Shield, S. (2012), *The International Political Economy of Transition: Neoliberal Hegemony and Eastern Central's Europe Transformation*, Abingdon: Routledge.

Stiglitz, Joseph E. (2006), *Making Globalization Work*, New York: W.W. Norton & Company.

Stockhammer, E. (2013), "Why Have Wage Shares Fallen? A Panel Analysis of the Determinants of the Functional Income Distribution". Condition of Work and Employment no. 35, International Labour Organization, Geneva.

Stolper, W. F. and Samuelson, Paul A. (1941), "Protection and Real Wages", *Review of Economic Studies*, 9(1): 58–73.

Swank, D. (2002), *Global Capital, Political Institutions, and Policy Change in Developed Welfare States*, New York: Cambridge University Press.

Tisdell, C. and S. Svizzero (2003), "Globalization, Social Welfare, and Labour Market Inequality", Working Paper no. 20, University of Queensland.

Tridico, P. (2012), "Financial Crisis and Global Imbalances: Its Labour Market Origins and the Aftermath", *Cambridge Journal of Economics*, 36(1): 17–42.

Tsebelis, G. (2002), *Veto Players: How Political Institutions Work*. Princeton, NJ: Princeton University Press.

van der Zwan, N. (2014), "Making sense of financialisation", *Socioeconomic Review*, 12(1): 99–129.

Van Reenen, J. (2011), "Wage Inequality, Technology and Trade: 21st Century Evidence", *Labour Economics*, 18(6): 730–41.

Walsh, P. and Whelan, C. (2000), "The Importance of Structural Change in Industry for Growth", *Journal of the Statistical and Social Inquiry Society of Ireland*, 29: 1–32.

Winkelmann, L. and Winkelmann, R. (2010), "Does Inequality Harm the Middle Class?", *Kyklos*, 63(2): 301–316.

Wood, A. (1994), *North–South Trade, Employment and Inequality*, Oxford: Clarendon Press.

2 Income inequality, household debt and growth

Riccardo Pariboni

Introduction

The last decades have witnessed dramatic institutional and socio-economic transformations, which have been labelled by some scholars as the "neoliberal cycle".[1] Their most evident aspect has probably been a pronounced increase in inequality in the distribution of income and a prolonged and generalized stagnation of real incomes for workers and wage earners in the lowest deciles of population, across a vast majority of Organisation for Economic Co-operation and Development (OECD) countries (see Christen and Morgan, 2005; Fitoussi and Saraceno, 2010; Atkinson et al., 2011; Kumhof et al., 2015; Hein, 2015; and Kapeller and Schütz, 2015 for a detailed account of these trends in different countries).

Nonetheless, the relative fall in households' purchasing power has not been accompanied, up to the onset of the Great Recession, by any decrease in their spending that, on the contrary, kept growing steadily,[2] allowing mainstream commentators to depict the period started in the 1980s as the Great Moderation Era. These phenomena prompted a growing interest in the macroeconomic effects and implications of household debt which, according to many authors of different persuasions (see, for example, Cynamon and Fazzari, 2008, 2010, 2015, 2016; Barba and Pivetti, 2009; Palley, 2009; Rajan, 2010; Dejuán, 2013; Stockhammer, 2015) has been, in the last decades, one of the main engines of growth and has acted as a substitute for wages in financing private consumption. I consider this suggestion extremely plausible and I will try to provide a simple, stylized interpretative framework to include debt-driven autonomous consumption among the determinants of aggregate demand and growth, an inclusion that might also be useful to assess the sustainability of such a growth process and eventually contribute to explain the recent crisis.

The chapter proceeds as follows. The first section provides a short and essential sketch of some relevant economic facts that involved, during the last 30 years, almost all the Western countries, especially with respect to the trends in income distribution and debt accumulation. In the second section an analysis of the causes behind the process of household indebtedness is outlined, along the lines put forward by Thorstein Veblen. The third section introduces and clarifies the Sraffian Supermultiplier approach to growth, with its focus on the role of the autonomous components of demand. The fourth section analyses the macro-economic implications of debt-financed consumption through an extended Supermultiplier model with endogenous credit money. Some interesting findings on the stability of the debt/debtors' income and on the adjustment of the rate of accumulation to the rate of credit-financed consumption are presented here. The last section summarizes the aforementioned results and concludes.

A brief historical perspective on income distribution and household debt during the neoliberal era

It is almost impossible to constrain a multidimensional and complex political and socio-economic process like neoliberalism into a single and straightforward definition. For the same reason, the 30-plus years in which this has proved to be the perhaps most influential and pervasive ideology are not explainable as the simple application of a fixed bunch of given political and economic prescriptions, even if we limit our attention to the Western world. Nonetheless, from the theoretical point of view and following Palma (2009) in his attempt to reconcile the Marxian and the Foucaldian interpretations on this issue, we can look at it as a "technology of power" that has been able to generate a spontaneous consensus, necessary for the acceptance of any institutional arrangement in a democratic system, towards the adoption of such measures as the deregulation of the financial and of the labour markets, the dismantle of the welfare state, the downsizing of the state and of its tasks, the reduction of the progressive nature of taxation, the strategic relevance accorded to the military industrial sector and all the other options that configure the counter-offensive of capital that followed the decades of the Keynesian consensus. We can look at the policy's priority change that occurred between the end of the 1970s and the beginning of the 1980s in the United States and in the United Kingdom, with the shift from full employment to the fighting of inflation (Barba and Pivetti, 2012) as the starting point of the process, whose main features will be sketched below.

Some stylized facts

Income inequality

The path-breaking works of Piketty and Saez[3] on extended time series of pre-tax incomes describe very clearly the alternate cycles in personal income distribution the US passed through,[4] showing a strong redistribution from the lowest deciles to the top. In particular, after the Great Depression the share of income accruing to the top decile fell sharply and remained basically stable for more or less the 30 years of the post-World War II Golden Age. In contrast, since the last years of the 1970s, a constant upward swing has taken place, up to the restoration of the pre-1929 share at the end of the first decade of the twenty-first century. This has been accompanied by a general reduction of the wage share all over the Western world, as has been argued and proved in detail in several recent contributions.[5]

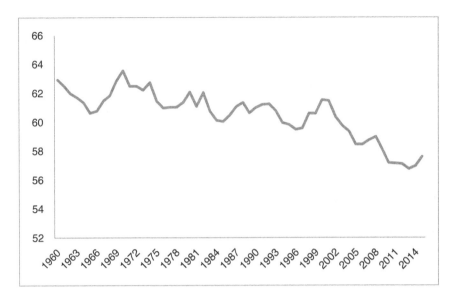

Figure 2.1 Adjusted wage share in the US

Source: Ameco online database

The debt explosion and the housing bubble

As pointed out in Setterfield (2010) and Onaran et al. (2011), the joint consideration of two different tendencies in the US – on the one side the clear increase in income inequality, on the other side the trend of the consumption/gross domestic product (GDP) ratio – seems to pose a puzzle for Keynesian theory. Indeed, in the last 30 years we have observed for the American economy a consumption boom, as it is shown in Figure 2.2, which seems to be counter-intuitive with respect to the standard assumption[6] that the propensity to consume out of wages is higher than the propensity to consume out of profits.

The answer to this apparent puzzle lies in the fact that, in the light of the mentioned aspects about income distribution and of the additional evidence that neither exports nor investment have performed in such a way to be identifiable as the drivers of the quite good macroeconomic performance of US in the last three decades (Setterfield, 2010), the US and more generally the Western capitalist economies have been able to activate such "margins of compensation" (Palley, 2002) that allowed them to more than compensate the aggregate demand-generating problems related with the worsening of income distribution.

The most important of these margins, namely "a high rate of demand growth financed by unprecedented household borrowing" (Cynamon et al., 2013, p. 2), is easily recognizable looking at the steady increase – experienced in the US in the last 60 years – of total credit to households as a percentage of GDP, up to the sudden stop and downturn begun in the aftermath of the first symptoms of the Great Recession.[7]

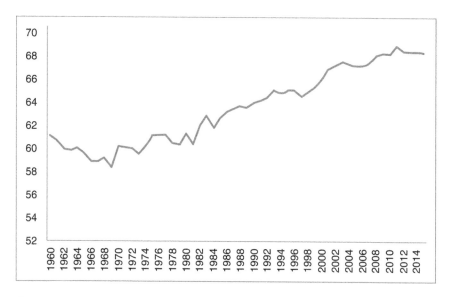

Figure 2.2 Consumption/GDP in the US, 1960–2014

Source: World DataBank, World Development Indicators

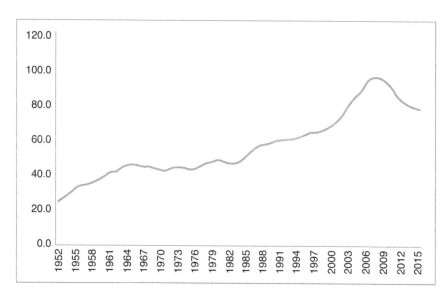

Figure 2.3 Total credit to households and non-profit institutions serving households in the US, 1952–2015 (percentage of GDP)

Source: Financial Accounts of the United States, Fred Economic Data

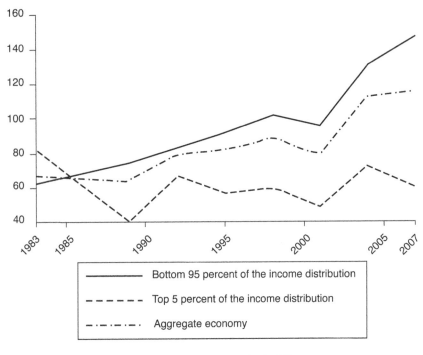

Figure 2.4 Debt to income ratios by income group in the US

Source: Kumhof et al. (2015)

Moreover, the fact that the subjects recurring to debt to finance their consumption were in most of the cases the same that were experiencing the worsening in their income share is confirmed by Figure 2.4 and by the finding of Christen and Morgan (2005, p. 148) of a "strong positive effect of income inequality on household debt relative to disposable income". In a more neoclassical vein, Iacoviello (2008) supports this view, finding in his empirical work on the US in the 1963–2003 period that income inequality has been the main determinant of the debt explosion. Curiously enough, in the theoretical model behind the test, borrowers repay their debt with probability one and there is no possibility of default, rendering for this reason the model unfit to assess the macroeconomic consequences of the process ongoing in those years.

The stock prices boom represented another important stimulus for households to consume over their concrete possibilities, on the basis of the expectation of further appreciations of the value of their assets. The other leading actor of the story, and especially for the US, has been the housing market bubble. As argued by Kotz (2008) through the analysis of the ratio between housing price index and the homeowners' equivalent rent, with this second term being a standard indicator of the value of owning a house, the US passed through, starting from the beginning of the twenty-first century, a period of housing price increase mainly explained by speculative purchases based on the (up to a certain point) reasonable expectation of further increases in these prices.

Thanks to peculiar institutional features of the US credit market,[8] for some years it has been possible for homeowners to extract equity, through renegotiations of the terms of existing mortgages, from the increasing value of their houses, used as a sort of ATM, and to use these amounts to finance not only durable consumptions but current expenses too. As pointed out by Christen and Morgan (2005), being home equity withdrawals[9] and mortgage refinancing classified as mortgage debt, this latter has been used as a de facto substitute for consumer credit and credit cards. This result is confirmed also by Barba and Pivetti (2009), who show the sharp increase in the mortgage equity withdrawal/disposable income ratio. The authors also identify the 1986 Tax Reform Act – which eliminated the deductibility from income tax of several interest payments, but maintained it on mortgages interests – and more generally the credit promotion policies developed by the US government from the 1980s as major generating causes of this phenomenon.

To conclude, what finance has been able to operate is a disconnection of "final demand from distribution through massive process of substitution of loans for wages and wealth effects" (Barba and Pivetti, 2012, p. 127). Unfortunately, this process could not go on indefinitely. The chain of events[10] (see Vercelli, 2011) begun with the first symptoms of a housing crisis in the US (2006) and the spike in the prices of oil, raw materials and food (2007–2008), which was followed by the Federal Reserve decision to raise the discount rate in order to restrain inflation, was just the detonator that demonstrated how problematic was the process that had been going on since three decades. Adjustable rate mortgages became hardly repayable by many households, especially those whose creditworthiness standards were classified as sub-prime. The collapse of real estate prices[11] that followed meant that home equity withdrawals were no longer available to replace wages as a source of purchasing power. As is easily understandable, all the process was strongly self-reinforcing, causing the sudden fall in the value of all the derivatives containing mortgages and leading banks and financial institutions to write down or write off from their balance sheets securities for the value of billions of dollars and to drastically cut down the flow of credit conceded to households and firms, with the further tragic consequences on aggregate demand.[12] The rest of the story is very well known and is nowadays known as the Great Recession.

Consumerism, income distribution and debt-financed conspicuous consumption

In reference to the standard formulations about aggregate consumption proper of Keynesian theory, according to which consumption is generally passive with respect to the level of income, it is possible to move forward and try to include the very well-known insights on conspicuous consumption derived from the classic work of Veblen ([1899] 1975), which over a century ago underlined the individuals' concerns about the social visibility of consumption. According to this approach, households' preferences are socially mediated, evolve endogenously with respect to the environment and present a strong propensity for status considerations. Consumption has no longer the simple task of satisfying individuals' material necessities; it also becomes an indicator of the social position and the adherence to both a certain social structure and a common ground of values and habits. Moreover, in a context of extremely fragmentary information and heavy uncertainty, households will tend to be driven in their behaviour by social norms, which are mainly determined by the habits and the behaviour of the reference groups, in general constituted by wealthier and successful households.

Compared to the time of Veblen's book, society has significantly changed; nonetheless the relevance of Veblen's original intuition is nowadays perhaps further amplified. While the reference group traditionally relevant for the creation of the aspiration levels was identified in the neighbourhood (that is a concept of physical proximity), today the external influences of consumption patterns have enormously widened through mass media. The post-World War II period witnessed, at least in the US,[13] the first relevant traces of opulent consumption mediated by the new media, as pointed out by, for example, Galbraith ([1958] 1968). The years of the neoliberal era have been characterized by a radical speeding-up in this process: advertising and television in general have contributed to the creation of a fascinating and continuously evolving ideal standard of life, based on compulsive consumerism and continuous generation of new needs that the individuals perceive to be imperatively satisfied if they want to be integrated and accepted in their social structure of reference.[14] No surprise that the average consumer has been caught in a consumers' arms race[15] (Frank, 1997) and no surprise that the evolution of consumption aspirations has taken place quite independently of the evolution of the per capita income of the vast majority of population. Paradoxically two different and opposite tendencies overlapped in the last 30 years: the continuous increase in aspired consumption standards has been paired with the steady deterioration of income distribution and with the related stagnation in the purchasing power for the lowest deciles of population, which are also the more reactive to the "keeping up with the Joneses" effect.[16]

It is exactly at this point of the story that household debt comes into play, called upon to fill the gap between the desired, target level of consumption and the level that is possible to finance out of wages and earned incomes.

The last decades have also shown a twin aspect of this phenomenon: the attitude of households towards indebtedness has significantly changed, in response to the necessity of sustaining levels of consumption that the mere flow of income proceeding from the working activity cannot simply afford. In a self-reinforcing process, the desire to keep up with the richer reference points in the extended neighbourhood has made debt more socially acceptable, allowing the catching up households to overcome their actual income possibilities and contributing to the previously mentioned consumers' arms race. This has obviously required that the financial system provided access to consumer credit to a wider range of working class families.

A decisive contribution to the spread of the social acceptance of debt has also taken place through continuous financial innovations,[17] also with the proliferation of less and less transparent financial instruments. This financial evolution "democratized" the access to credit, opened the doors of credit to segments of population traditionally excluded and allowed the consumption boom that begun in the 1970s (see Cynamon and Fazzari, 2013).

It is worth noticing that, over the last 30 years, households have not got into debt just to afford frivolous consumption and to emulate lifestyles beyond their economic means. Indeed, the period under consideration has also been characterized by the spread of political prescriptions such as a minimal state, welfare retrenchments and privatizations, with the result that an increasing number of households has been forced to pay for services, strictly necessary for everyday life, that until then had traditionally been provided by the state and financed out of general taxation. In this respect, at least two paradigmatic cases can be mentioned, especially regarding the US, for their crucial contribution to the accumulation of an enormous stock of household debt: student loans taken out in order to pay increasing university fees (Guttmann and Plihon, 2010; Wray, 2011b) and financial liabilities to medical providers[18] (Doty et al., 2008; Himmelstein et al., 2009; Jacoby and Holman, 2010). In the remainder of the chapter a simple model will be sketched, with the purpose of building a stylized interpretative framework able to deal with the historical developments described above.

The Supermultiplier

In this section I will introduce a baseline version of the Sraffian Supermultiplier model, proposed by Serrano (1995) and further discussed and applied in Cesaratto et al. (2003) and in Freitas and Serrano (2015). In this approach income distribution is treated, according to the classical tradition, as exogenously determined by social and historical factors concerning the bargaining power of the opposite classes, by customs and social norms about the fairness of remunerations and other social habits. Accordingly, the model does not presume any automatic relation between the rate of accumulation and distribution or, in Garegnani's words (Garegnani, 1992, p. 64), "a long-period rise in investment needs not alter distribution in order to generate the corresponding savings", due to the fact that the rise in the output level caused by the increase in effective demand generates endogenously the necessary amount of savings. In the short period the adjustment of savings to investment will take place through a degree of capacity utilization above the normal one. On the other hand, in the long run the process of accumulation is called to adapt capacity to demand, with the objective of producing at the desired level of capital utilization. Furthermore, associated with the given technology and real wage, a Sraffian system of normal, competitive relative prices is assumed to hold.

The basic structure of the model is given by the following equations:

$$Y_t = C_t + I_t + G_t + (X_t - mY_t) \tag{1}$$

$$C_t = c(1 - \tau)Y_t + C_t^a \tag{2}$$

$$Z = G + X + C^a \tag{3}$$

$$I_t = h_t Y_t \tag{4}$$

$$Y_t = \frac{Z_t}{s + m - h_t} \tag{5}$$

Y_t, the current level of output, is equal to aggregate demand, which is the sum of consumption, investment, public expenditure (G) and net exports (X – mY), where *m* is the marginal propensity to import (equation 1). Consumption (equation 2) can be split into an induced component, financed out of wages and profits, and an autonomous component, financed out of endogenous credit money (C_t^a). As usual in the literature, *c* is the aggregate marginal propensity to consume and τ is the tax rate. Equation 3 defines autonomous demand (Z) as the sum of public expenditure, exports and autonomous consumption, "all those expenditures that are neither financed by the contractual (wage and salary) income generated by production decisions, nor are capable of affecting the productive capacity of the capitalist sector of the economy" (Serrano, 1995, p. 71). Investment is completely induced, based on the assumption that entrepreneurs invest to endow themselves with the capacity necessary to produce the amount they are demanded at normal prices. In its simplest version, defining *h* as the marginal propensity to invest of capitalist firms, this is represented by equation 4. With s = 1-c(1-τ) equal to the aggregate marginal propensity to save, we can express the long period, demand-determined output as the autonomous components Z multiplied by the so-called Supermultiplier (equation 5).[19]

While the level of output described by equation 5 does not necessarily imply a normal utilization of the productive capacity, at the same time a continuous tendency towards the latter is in operation, as can be seen from the following set of equations.

$$\dot{h} = h_t \gamma (u_t - 1) \tag{6}$$

$$g_t = g_t^z + \frac{\dot{h}}{s + m - h_t} \tag{7}$$

$$g_t^K = h_t \frac{u_t}{v} - \delta \tag{8}$$

$$\dot{u} = u(g - g^K) \tag{9}$$

According to equation 6, firms continuously attempt to adjust their capital stock, investing more when the degree of capacity utilization is higher than its normal level[20] and less otherwise, with γ being a positive reaction coefficient.

From equations 5 and 6, it is possible to derive g, the output rate of growth (equation 7), while the rate of accumulation g^K is given by equation 8. Equation 9 simply describes the law of movement of the degree of capacity utilization. Imposing $\dot{h} = \dot{u} = 0$ in the system given by equations 6 and 9, we obtain the equilibrium position[21] of the model, characterized by

$$Y_t^n = \frac{z_t}{s + m - v(\delta + g_t^z)} \tag{10}$$

$$g_t = g_t^K = g_t^Z$$

$$u_t = 1 \tag{11}$$

$$h* = v(g^Z + \delta)$$

If a given rate of growth of autonomous demand is sufficiently persistent, output and productive capacity of the economy tend to the position represented by the so-called "fully adjusted" Supermultiplier (equation 10). Along the equilibrium path, all the relevant variables evolve according to the rate of growth of the autonomous components, capacity is normally utilized and entrepreneurs adjust their propensity to invest in order to maintain this desired degree of utilization (equation 11).

Household debt and the Supermultiplier

It is possible to use a modified version of the model introduced in the previous section, with endogenous credit money supplied by the banking system, to analyse the growth effects of household debt accumulation.

In particular, I use modified consumption functions, similar to those presented in the neo-Kaleckian literature on the topic:[22]

$$C_t^W = c_W[(1 - \Pi)Y_t - (r + \phi)D_t] + B_t \tag{12}$$

$$C_t^\pi = c_\pi[\Pi Y_t + rD_t] \tag{13}$$

Π is the profit share, r is the interest rate, considered given for the sake of simplicity; D_t is equal to the stock of debt at time t and ϕ to the percentage of principal's repayment. Equation 12 shows that workers/debtors consume a fraction of their disposable income – given by their share in income minus the service of the accumulated debt – plus B,[23] the amount borrowed in the period. At the same time, according to equation 13, capitalists/creditors consume a lower[24] fraction of their income. Capitalists, as owners of the banks, receive the interest payments on debt from workers. It is assumed that only workers borrow in order to finance part of their consumption.[25] This is just a simplification, given that also capitalists in OECD countries have been borrowing in the last decades. Nonetheless, the phenomenon has been more pronounced in the workers' case and the ratio of debt over disposable income has increased comparatively much more in lower income groups (see Stockhammer, 2015, pp. 947–948).

Coherently with an endogenous credit money approach, as presented for example in Palley (1997) and Lavoie (2003), I assume that the credit flow is endogenously determined by the demand for loans and it is provided by the banking system, without being constrained by the amount of deposits held by the same banks. In other words, loans create deposits and the banking system accommodates any request of funds by households, if it perceives it as profitable and if predetermined parameters of creditworthiness are respected. This implies also that "banks can lend without affecting the consumption of their owners" (Palley, 1994, p. 374, footnote 2). This allows us to treat B as autonomous consumption, "that part of aggregate consumption financed by credit and, therefore, unrelated to the current level of output resulting from firms' production decisions" (Freitas and Serrano, 2015, p. 261).

Neglecting for the moment the existence of autonomous components of demand other than autonomous, debt-financed, consumption we have that

$$Y_t = c_W[(1 - \Pi)Y_t - (r + \phi)D_t] + B_t + c_\pi[\Pi Y_t + rD_t] + h_t Y_t \tag{14}$$

$$Y_t = \frac{B_t - (c_W - c_\pi)rD_t - c_W \phi D_t}{1 - c_W(1 - \Pi) - c_\pi \Pi - h_t} \tag{15}$$

Collecting the autonomous consumption terms as $C_t^a = B_t - (c_w - c_\pi)rD_t - c_w \phi D_t$,[26] we have that, in equilibrium, $g^Y = g^{C^a}$. This shows that, as argued in the previous section, given a sufficient amount of time, demand and output will tend to evolve at the rate of growth of the autonomous components of demand, in this case autonomous consumption.

The reliance on the credit conceded by the banking system leads to a growth process that can go on indefinitely only if banks are willing to keep conceding loans indefinitely. The problem is that banks' behaviour is not driven by demand support concerns. Instead, we can reasonably assume that they continue to lend up to the point they perceive it as too risky and no more profitable. In this respect, it can be interesting to trace the path of the debt/debtors' income ratio, as a measure of the financial solidity of the economy. This ratio is a fundamental indicator of workers' solvency and therefore it is one of the most important parameters on whose basis the banking system will decide whether to keep supplying credit or not. Stated otherwise, if banks observe that the borrowers' solvency ratio approaches or even exceeds a predetermined ceiling, they can reasonably be assumed to stop granting credit (and/or to increase the rate of interest and the repayment coefficient demanded on the stock of debt), provoking in this way a fall in aggregate demand and possibly triggering a recession, induced by a negative growth rate for autonomous consumption and the related process of deleveraging.

It can be proved that the rate of growth of autonomous consumption, g^{C^a}, and the rate of growth of debt, g^D, tend to coincide. As a first step, I divide by D both sides of $C_t^a = B_t - (c_w - c_\pi)rD_t - c_w\phi D_t$. Given that $\frac{dD}{dt} = B - \phi D$, from which $B/D = g^D + \phi$ follows, I get $C^a/D = g^D - (c_w - c_\pi)r + (1 - c_w)\phi$. Taking the logarithm of this equation and deriving it with respect to time, we have that $\dot{g}^D = (g^{C^a} - g^D)[g^D - (c_w - c_\pi)r + (1 - c_w)\phi]$. Assuming that $g^D > (c_w - c_\pi)r - (1 - c_w)\phi$,[27] this tells us that the rate of debt accumulation changes as long as it is different from g^{C^a} and converges to the latter (if $g^{C^a} > g^D$, then $\dot{g}^D > 0$), so that in equilibrium $g^{C^a} = g^D$, both equal to g^Y, as argued above.

Having assumed that in the simple economy represented by equation (15) only workers borrow to finance their consumption, it is possible to conclude that the ratio $d_t = D_t / (1–\Pi)Y_t$ is stable as long as the wage share is constant, given that in equilibrium the numerator and the denominator grow at the same rate. Any increase in the profit share, on the contrary, does not affect the *rate of growth* of output but decreases the disposable income of debtors[28] and worsens the d ratio. This result is coherent with the arguments presented in Barba and Pivetti (2009), where the authors provide an interpretation along these lines of the processes which led to the Great Recession: debt-financed consumption directly affects the course of aggregate income and consequently also of indebted workers' income. Nonetheless, if indebtedness comes with a marked increase in income inequality, the richest fraction of population tends to appropriate most of the income's increase generated by the expansion of consumption financed out of credit.

The inclusion into the model of the other autonomous components of demand, which I call Q, adds a new relevant dimension to the analysis of the stability of the debt/income ratio. With $Z_t = C_t^a + Q_t$, we have that

$$g_t^Z = g_t^{C^a} \frac{C_t^a}{Z_t} + g_t^Q \frac{Z_t - C_t^a}{Z_t} \tag{16}$$

where the rate of growth of Z is a weighted average of the rates of growth of its components, with the weights represented by the components' share in Z.

With this in mind, it is easy to see that if debt-financed consumption grows more rapidly than the other terms of Z we have that $g^D > g^Z = g^Y$ and, even with a constant wage share, the ratio of debt over debtors' income continuously increases. This is due to the fact that, in this scenario, the accumulation of debt is faster than the growth of the whole autonomous part of demand, which determines the rate of growth of output.

It is possible to conclude that the sustainability of the private debt position of an economy depends, among other things, on the rate of growth of public expenditures and exports. Indeed, these two autonomous demand components contribute to the determination of the output growth rate together with credit-financed consumption. As it has been argued, the growth differential between C^a, whose evolution tends to shape the pattern of the stock of personal debt, and the other parts of autonomous demand is a major factor in explaining the path of the households' debt to income ratio.

Conclusions

A prolonged worsening in income distribution is likely to have negative effects on the level of consumption, unless a counteracting positive level of autonomous consumption is at work (or, so long as it is possible, a continuous reduction in workers' propensity to save). In a genuine demand-led growth model, where investment is dependent on the expected rate of growth of demand and not on distributive variables, this has negative effects also on the level of aggregate long-period output, given the autonomous components of demand. Moreover, if the process of income polarization is continuous over time, it also affects the rate of growth of output, and not only its level. To offset this effect, a continuous increase in the rate of growth of autonomous demand is required. As we have seen, serious problems could arise if this is brought about through a sustained rise in debt-financed household consumption, which leads the economy to an increasing financial fragility that could not be sustainable indefinitely. As many authors have argued, this is what happened at the onset of the Great Recession, as a consequence of the lengthy trends in income distribution and household debt accumulation that characterized the neoliberal era.

In this chapter, I have tried to investigate the macroeconomic consequences of a growth process driven and fuelled by household debt. For this purpose, I have relied on an extended version of the Supermultiplier model, integrated with an explicit consideration of household debt financed through endogenous credit money. One of the main results of this contribution regards the stability (or instability) of the outstanding debt/debtors' income ratio, which has been proven to be affected, among other things, by the growth differential between autonomous consumption (and debt) and the other autonomous components of demand. This implies that the sustainability of the private debt position of an economy depends also on the external performance of the country and on an active role of the public sector in warranting the necessary stability to aggregate demand.

Notes

1 See Harvey (2007) and Vercelli (2015).
2 See Onaran et al. (2011) and Cynamon and Fazzari (2015, 2016).
3 See, for example, Piketty and Saez (2003, 2006) and Atkinson et al. (2011).
4 The majority of the empirical data reviewed here refers to the United States, given their paradigmatic, general relevance for the development of capitalist economies and the enormous amount of data and studies available. Of course, there are many institutional peculiarities, in some cases quite relevant, which are not just extendable to the European countries. Nevertheless, the qualitative conclusions should not be affected by such discrepancies.
5 See, for example, Atkinson et al. (2011); Kumhof et al. (2015); Hein (2015); and Kapeller and Schütz (2015).
6 See Kaldor (1955–56) for a detailed discussion.
7 The same general trend for the household debt/GDP ratio is confirmed by the findings in Christen and Morgan (2005), Papadimitriou et al. (2005), Tridico (2012) and Cynamon and Fazzari (2016).

8 See Barba and Pivetti (2009, in particular pp. 114–116) for a discussion of the role of home equity loans and HELOC (Home Equity Lines of Credit) in financing household consumption in the US.

9 This term refers to the mentioned activity through which a household can "increase its borrowing based on an increase in the market value of their house" (The CORE Project, 2015, p. 38).

10 For an alternative, strictly neoclassic, narrative of the events, see, for example, Justiniano et al. (2013), where the fall in the house prices is seen as a consequence of changes in the household preferences concerning housing.

11 See, for example, Justiniano et al. (2013, p. 4) for a picture of the trend in house prices in the 1970–2013 period.

12 The phenomena shortly described are part of a broader historical and institutional process, fundamental to understand properly the outcomes we are actually observing: namely what has been identified in the Minskyan literature as the transition of the global financial system toward a "money manager capitalism", defined in terms of an "economic system characterized by highly leveraged funds seeking maximum total returns in an environment that systematically underprices risk" (Wray 2011a, p. 7) and that has elsewhere been called and defined as "financialisation", meaning with this term the "increasing role of financial motives, financial markets, financial actors and financial institutions in the operation of the domestic and international economies" to use Epstein's (2005, p. 3) words. These factors co-generated and amplified all the events described. See also Orhangazi (2008) and Onaran et al. (2011).

13 An interesting insight is provided in Wisman (2013), where the author maintains that "because Americans believe they are individually responsible for their own social standing, they feel strongly compelled to demonstrate status and hence class identity through consumption" (p. 931).

14 See Cynamon and Fazzari (2010) for a discussion of the influence of mass media in the process of expansion of the social reference groups.

15 In a situation in which the consumer strives to reach the consumption levels of the richer households, a sort of "expenditure cascade" is observable, where the desire of emulation leads households to consume more, with the result that this increased spending level generates endogenously new needs that tend to become the new driving norm, endowed with its own increased desired level of consumption, self-reinforcing the process in a potentially endless race.

16 See also Kim et al. (2014) and Kapeller and Schütz (2014).

17 In this regard, it is interesting to notice how this "supply side" factor is seen in some mainstream analysis as the main, or perhaps only, cause of the credit cycle observed especially in the last ten years. For instance, according to Mian and Sufi (2009), the post-2002 loosening and the following tightening, begun in 2007, of credit standards explain the spike and the subsequent fall, after the first symptoms of the Great Recession, in the household debt/GDP ratio. Another supply side explanation (e.g. Shiller, 2007 or Mian and Sufi, 2011) stresses the boom in house prices as the principal cause of the cycle, which allowed the appreciation of the collateral backing the households" debt and the consequent increase in the possibility to borrow. On the other hand, from a Keynesian perspective, Barba and Pivetti (2009) identify the 1986 US Tax Reform Act and more generally the credit promotion policies developed by the US government as major co-generating causes of the household debt explosion.

18 According to Himmelstein et al. (2009, p. 3), medical bill problems contributed to 57.1 per cent of all bankruptcies in 2007.

19 To have an economically meaningful result, the condition $s + m - h > 0$ must hold.

20 I define the actual degree of capacity utilization as the ratio of actual over normal output, with the latter being in general lower than full capacity output (see Steindl, 1952 and Kurz, 1986). It follows that the normal degree of capacity utilization is equal to one ($u_n = 1$).

21 See Freitas and Serrano (2015), Lavoie (2014) and Allain (2015) for an explicit analysis of the dynamic stability of the equilibrium.
22 See, for example, Dutt (2006), Palley (2010) and Hein (2012). See also Pariboni (2016) for a detailed critique of the treatment of debt-led growth proposed in the neo-Kaleckian literature.
23 An explicit and formal discussion of the determinants of the workers" demand for loans is outside the scope of this chapter. However, also on the basis of the previous sections, it can be reasonably assumed to be affected by a complex set of circumstances like: the cut in public social expenditures (the indirect wage) and the related rise in the prices of fundamental services like health and education; consumption externalities generated by wealth effects among the top quintiles; and the shrinkage of the wage share. These factors forced households to get into debt, "in an attempt to protect the welfare of their families and to maintain, if not improve, their relative social status" (Wisman, 2013, p. 930).
24 As with most of the literature (see, for example, Kaldor, 1955–56), it is assumed that capitalists have a lower marginal propensity to consume than workers.
25 Moreover, it is assumed that workers can borrow and save at the same time, following with this respect Kim et al. (2014), since savings and debt are not a perfect substitute for them. A further assumption is that, in case workers deposit their savings in a bank account, the interest they earn on this is negligible with respect to the interest they have to pay on the amounts borrowed, reinforcing the imperfect nature of competition in the real world credit markets.
26 The term $(c_w - c_\pi)rD_t + c_w \phi D_t$ can be seen as negative autonomous consumption.
27 The condition imposed derives from the assumption that autonomous consumption is greater than 0: from $B - (c_w - c_\pi)rD - c_w \phi D > 0$, dividing by D and recalling that B/D $= g^D + \phi$, we obtain $g^D > (c_w - c_\pi)r - (1 - c_w)\phi$.
28 A decrease in the wage share could also, in principle, have a positive effect on the *level* of household debt, contributing to worsening of the *d* ratio.

References

Allain, O. (2015), "Tackling the instability of growth: a Kaleckian–Harrodian model with an autonomous expenditure component", *Cambridge Journal of Economics*, 39(5), 1351–1371.

Ameco online database.

Atkinson, A.B., Piketty, T. and Saez, E. (2011), "Top incomes in the long run of history", *Journal of Economic Literature*, 49(1), 3–71.

Barba, A. and M. Pivetti (2009), "Rising household debt: Its causes and macroeconomic implications – a long period analysis", *Cambridge Journal of Economics*, 33(1), 113–137.

Barba, A. and M. Pivetti (2012), "Distribution and accumulation in post-1980 advanced capitalism", *Review of Keynesian Economics*, Inaugural Issue, 126–142.

Cesaratto, S., Serrano, F. and A. Stirati (2003), "Technical change, effective demand and employment", *Review of Political Economy*, 15(1), 33–52.

Christen, M. and M. Morgan (2005), "Keeping up with the Joneses: Analyzing the effect of income inequality on consumer borrowing", *Quantitative Marketing and Economics*, 3(2), 145–173.

CORE Project, The (2015), *The Economy*, February 2015, Beta version, available online at http://read.core-econ.org/material.

Cynamon, B.Z. and S.M. Fazzari (2008), "Household debt in the Consumer Age: Source of growth-risk of collapse", *Capitalism and Society*, 3(2), 1–32.

Cynamon, B.Z. and S.M. Fazzari (2010), "The end of the Consumer Age", in B.Z. Cynamon, S.M. Fazzari and M. Setterfield (eds), *After the Great Recession: Keynesian Perspectives on Prospects for Recovery and Growth*, Cambridge: Cambridge University Press.

Cynamon, B.Z. and S.M. Fazzari (2013), "Inequality and household finance during the Consumer Age", Levy Economics Institute of Bard College working paper no. 752.

Cynamon, B.Z. and S.M. Fazzari (2015), "Rising inequality and stagnation in the US economy", *European Journal of Economics and Economic Policies: Intervention*, 12(2), 170–182.

Cynamon, B.Z. and S.M. Fazzari (2016), "Inequality, the Great Recession and slow recovery", *Cambridge Journal of Economics*, 40(2), 373–399.

Cynamon, B.Z., Fazzari, S.M. and M. Setterfield (2013), "How the Great Moderation became a (contained) depression and what to do about it", Trinity College Department of Economics working paper 13–03.

Dejuán, Ó. (2013), "The debt trap", in Ó. Dejuán, E. Febrero and J. Uxó (eds), *Post-Keynesian Views of the Crisis and its Remedies*, London: Routledge.

Doty, M.M., Collins, S.R., Rustgi, S.D. and J.L. Kriss (2008), "Seeing red: the growing burden of medical bills and debt faced by US families", *Commonwealth Fund publications*, 42, 1–11.

Dutt, A.K. (2006), "Maturity, stagnation and consumer debt: a Steindlian approach", *Metroeconomica*, 57(3), 339–364.

Epstein, G.A. (2005), *Financialization and the World Economy*, Cheltenham: Elgar.

Fitoussi, J.P. and F. Saraceno (2010), "Inequality and macroeconomic performance", OFCE no. 13.

Frank, R.H. (1997), "The frame of reference as a public good", *Economic Journal*, 107(445), 1832–1847.

Freitas, F. and F. Serrano (2015), "Growth rate and level effects, the stability of the adjustment of capacity to demand and the Sraffian supermultiplier", *Review of Political Economy*, 27(3), 258–281.

Galbraith, J.K. [1958] (1968), *The Affluent Society*, Harmondsworth: Penguin Books.

Garegnani, P. (1992), "Some notes for an analysis of accumulation", in J. Halevi, D. Laibman and E. Nell (eds) *Beyond the Steady State: A Revival of Growth Theory*, London: Macmillan.

Guttmann, R. and D. Plihon (2010), "Consumer debt and financial fragility", *International Review of Applied Economics*, 24(3), 269–283.

Harvey, D. (2007), *A Brief History of Neoliberalism*, Oxford: Oxford University Press.

Hein, E. (2012), "Finance-dominated capitalism, re-distribution, household debt and financial fragility in a Kaleckian distribution and growth model", *PSL Quarterly Review*, 65(260), 11–51.

Hein, E. (2015), "Finance-dominated capitalism and redistribution of income: A Kaleckian perspective", *Cambridge Journal of Economics*, 39(3), 907–934.

Himmelstein, D.U., Thorne, D., Warren, E. and S. Woolhandler (2009), "Medical bankruptcy in the United States, 2007: Results of a national study", *The American Journal of Medicine*, 20(10), 1–6.

Iacoviello, M. (2008), "Household debt and income inequality, 1963–2003", *Journal of Money, Credit and Banking*, 40(5), 929–965.

Jacoby, M.B. and M. Holman (2010), "Managing medical bills on the brink of bankruptcy", *Yale Journal of Health Policy, Law and Ethics*, 10(2), 240–298.

Justiniano, A., Primiceri, G.E. and A. Tambalotti (2013), "Household leveraging and deleveraging", NBER working paper no. 18941.

Kaldor, N. (1955–56), "Alternative theories of distribution", *The Review of Economic Studies*, 23(2), 83–100.

Kapeller, J. and B. Schütz (2014), "Debt, boom, bust: A theory of Minsky–Veblen Cycles", *Journal of Post-Keynesian Economics*, 36(4), 781–813.

Kapeller, J. and B. Schütz (2015), "Conspicuous consumption, inequality and debt: The nature of consumption-driven profit-led regimes", *Metroeconomica*, 66(1), 51–70.

Kim, Y., Setterfield, M. and Y. Mei (2014), "A theory of aggregate consumption", *European Journal of Economics and Economic Policies: Intervention*, 11(1), 31–49.

Kotz, D.M. (2008), "Contradictions of economic growth in the Neoliberal Era: Accumulation and crisis in the contemporary US economy", *Review of Radical Political Economics*, 40(2), 174–188.

Kumhof, M., Rancière, R. and P. Winant (2015), "Inequality, leverage and crises", *American Economic Review*, 105(3), 1217–1245.

Kurz, H. (1986), "Normal positions and capital utilisation", *Political Economy*, 2(1), 37–54.

Lavoie, M. (2003), "A primer on endogenous credit-money", in L.P. Rochon and S. Rossi (eds) *Modern Theories of Money: The Nature and Role of Money in Capitalist Economies*, Cheltenham: Elgar.

Lavoie, M. (2014), *Post-Keynesian Economics: New Foundations*, Cheltenham: Elgar.

Mian, A. and A. Sufi (2009), "The consequences of mortgage credit expansion: Evidence from the US mortgage default crisis", *The Quarterly Journal of Economics*, 124(4), 1449–1496.

Mian, A. and A. Sufi (2011), "House prices, home equity-based borrowing and the US household leverage crisis", *American Economic Review*, 101(5), 2132–2156.

Onaran, Ö., Stockhammer, E. and L. Grafl (2011), "Financialisation, income distribution and aggregate demand in the USA", *Cambridge Journal of Economics*, 35(4), 637–661.

Orhangazi, Ö. (2008), "Financialisation and capital accumulation in the non-financial corporate sector: A theoretical and empirical investigation on the US economy: 1973–2003", *Cambridge Journal of Economics*, 32(6), 863–886.

Palley, T.I. (1994), "Debt, aggregate demand, and the business cycle: An analysis in the spirit of Kaldor and Minsky", *Journal of Post Keynesian Economics*, 16(3), 371–390.

Palley, T.I. (1997), "Endogenous money and the business cycle", *Journal of Economics*, 65(2), 133–149.

Palley, T.I. (2002), "Economic contradictions coming home to roost? Does the US economy face a long-term aggregate demand generation problem?", *Journal of Post Keynesian Economics*, 25(1), 9–32.

Palley, T.I. (2009), "The limits of financial instability hypothesis as an explanation of the crisis", IMK working paper 11–2009.

Palley, T.I. (2010), "Inside debt and economic growth: A neo-Kaleckian analysis", in M. Setterfield (ed.) *Handbook of Alternatives Theories of Economic Growth*, Cheltenham: Elgar.

Palma, J.G. (2009), "The revenge of the market on the rentiers: Why neo-liberal reports of the end of history turned out to be premature", *Cambridge Journal of Economics*, 33(4), 829–869.

Papadimitriou, D.B., Shaikh, A.M., Dos Santos, C.H. and G. Zezza (2005), "How fragile is the US economy?", Levy Economics Institute of Bard College Strategic Analysis.

Pariboni, R. (2016), "Household consumer debt, endogenous money and growth: A supermultiplier-based analysis", *PSL Quarterly Review*, 69 (278), 211–233.

Piketty, T. and E. Saez (2003), "Income inequality in the United States, 1913–1998", *The Quarterly Journal of Economics*, 118(1), 1–39.

Piketty, T. and E. Saez (2006), "The evolution of top incomes: A historical and international perspective", *American Economic Review*, 96(2), 200–205.

Rajan, R. (2010), *Fault Lines: How Hidden Fractures Still Threaten the World Economy*, Princeton, NJ: Princeton University Press.

Saez, E. (2015), "Striking it richer: The evolution of top incomes in the Unites States (updated with 2014 preliminary estimates)", mimeo.

Serrano, F. (1995), "Long period effective demand and the Sraffian Supermultiplier", *Contributions to Political Economy*, 14, 67–90.

Setterfield, M. (2010), 'Real wages, aggregate demand and the macroeconomic travails of the US economy: diagnosis and prognosis', Trinity College Department of Economics Working Paper 10–05.

Shiller, R.J. (2007), "Understanding recent trends in house prices and homeownership", NBER Working paper no. 13553.

Steindl, J. (1952), *Maturity and Stagnation in American Capitalism*, Oxford: Blackwell.

Stockhammer, E. (2015), "Rising inequality as a cause of the present crisis", *Cambridge Journal of Economics*, 39(3), 935–958.

Tridico, P. (2012), "Financial crisis and global imbalances: Its labour market origins and the aftermath", *Cambridge Journal of Economics*, 36(1), 17–42.

Veblen, T. [1899] (1975), *The Theory of the Leisure Class*, New York: Kelley A.M.

Vercelli, A. (2011), "Economy and economics: The twin crises", in E. Brancaccio and G. Fontana (eds) *The Global Economic Crisis: New Perspectives on the Critique of Economic Theory and Policy*, London: Routledge.

Vercelli, A. (2015), "The Neoliberal trajectory, the Great Recession and sustainable development", in P. Arestis and M. Sawyer (eds) *Finance and the Macroeconomics of Environmental Policies*, Basingstoke: Palgrave, pp. 37–73.

Wisman, J.D. (2013), "Wage stagnation, rising inequality and the financial crisis of 2008", *Cambridge Journal of Economics*, 37(4), 921–945.

Wray, R. (2011a), "Minsky crisis", Levy Economics Institute of Bard College working paper no. 659.

Wray, R. (2011b), "What reform? What recovery? Why those who never saw 'it' coming cannot be trusted with reform", 2011 Mecpoc Lecture, Franklin College.

3 Unsustainable unemployment and sustainable growth

A long-run perspective

Sebastiano Fadda

Introduction

The explanations of (and the policies against) unemployment are still based on traditional views about the working of the economy and particularly of the labour market. According to this view involuntary unemployment is essentially due either to difficulties in "matching" demand and supply, or to wages higher than the equilibrium level of full employment. The inability of wages to adjust to the equilibrium level is in turn ascribed either to trade unions interfering against the free working of market forces or to dynamics of a new-Keynesian kind such as efficiency wages or implicit contracts or "insiders–outsiders" models.

This view is nothing but an extension to macroeconomics of the microeconomic principle of equilibrium of the individual firm in a perfect competition world. Ignoring the role of aggregate demand, the demand for labour can simply be assumed as a decreasing function of wage levels due to decreasing marginal productivity of factors. But if aggregate demand is considered, the alleged growth of employment as a consequence of falling wages requires to assume the existence of either the so called "Keynes effect" or the "Pigou effect". The first relies on the increase of investment demand due to the fall of interest rate which follows the increase in real money supply when prices fall as a consequence of declining wages; the second relies on the increase in consumer demand due to the increase in the real value of financial assets, assuming consumption demand to be a function of wealth as well of income.

As is well known, several objections can be raised against the actual working of these effects. Just to mention a few, consider the elasticity of investment to interest rates, or the role of the real rate of interest, or the strategic behaviour of consumers in times of falling prices.

The possible co-existence of equilibrium wage level with disequilibrium in the labour market and equilibrium between aggregate demand and supply has been proved by Clower (1965) in opposition to the Walrasian general equilibrium model. The distinction between "notional" and "effective" aggregate demand allowed Malinvaud (1977) to then clarify the distinction between "classical" and "Keynesian" unemployment, pointing out two different obstacles to the achievement of full employment: on the one hand the relation between wages and marginal productivity of labour and on the other hand the insufficient effective aggregate demand.

In this frame the economic policies suggested by the European Union and generally implemented by member states with heavier unemployment problems have taken a rather funny shape. On one side a cut in wages has been advocated and attained, while on the other side the awareness of its negative effect on aggregate demand has been handled with the idea that foreign demand would have compensated the fall in domestic demand. But unfortunately the supposed fall in prices due to reduced wages was not able to compensate the productivity gap to the extent necessary to gain competitiveness in the world, and particularly the European, market.

Consciousness, although late acquired, of the failure of such approach in dealing with the problem of unemployment has recently pushed our policy makers to reduce the emphasis on the supply side of the labour market (which has been the main limit of the Lisbon Strategy and the following updates) and to address the issue of aggregate demand. But with regard to its components of consumer and investment demand the approach has not been appropriate, since it has fundamentally underestimated the role of disposable income distribution as far as the first is concerned and overestimated the role of the interest rate with regard to the second.

Obviously, supply-side labour policies are necessary in order to reduce frictional and structural unemployment: the Beveridge curve needs to be shifted to the left and the rise of the natural rate of unemployment has to be avoided. But the real issue nowadays is: since the achievement of equilibrium between labour demand and supply is obstructed by the two constraints (one relative to wage-marginal productivity ratio and one relative to insufficient effective demand) is it possible to increase aggregate demand up to the point of totally removing the second constraint? In other words, can demand management policies make aggregate demand and output grow to such extent as to be able to absorb all the labour supply (allowing for structural and frictional unemployment)? If not, the target of full employment should be abandoned and commitment should be turned to deal with the problem of those who cannot be involved in productive activity not because of "matching" problems, but because they exceed the labour input requirements of the economic system. In the following sections we shall explore this question, first by reconsidering the definition of full employment and of "labour demand", then by questioning the compatibility between technical progress and the target of full employment, and finally by considering policies to conciliate increasing technical progress with ensuring full employment.

The notion of full employment and of demand for labour

In order to proceed it is necessary to emphasize first some aspects of these two notions. Clearly a situation of full employment is not one in which everybody has got a paid job. People not in working age, people who are not willing to work, people whose qualifications do not match the qualifications required to fulfil the vacancies and people who are late in the process of finding out and fulfilling the vacancies are all people without a job who do not contradict a situation of full employment. When no other people than these are jobless there is full employment, which is to say that labour demand and labour supply are numerically equivalent. But this apparently straightforward definition suffers ambiguities both on operative and conceptual grounds. On operative ground, considering the supply side it's difficult to account for people who are willing to work but do not engage in positive actions of job search and for people who would be willing to work only under particular conditions. On the demand side, while it's easy to measure that segment of demand that has been matched by supply (that is, people in employment) it is awkward to take accurate account of that segment that has not been matched by supply (unfilled vacancies). On the theoretical level, the above definition of full employment is tied to the notion of "clearing of the market" and it corresponds "to the point of intersection between the supply curve and the demand curve" (Robinson 1937, p. 171). But if the assumption is made that both the demand and the supply functions are sensitive to endogenous variables besides the real wage, the notion of full employment based on the clearing of the aggregate labour market becomes ambiguous. It would be better to adopt another conceptual definition, such as the one given, again, by Joan Robinson (ibid., p. 15) that "no one employer can increase his staff without reducing the staff of some other employer", or "one entrepreneur can increase the amount of labour he employs only by reducing the amount employed by someone else". Still clearer is the notion of full employment adopted by Keynes, which, in addition, is also connected with the notion of aggregate demand. According to Keynes the condition of full employment is the one in which the size of employment is inelastic with respect to rising effective demand; that is when, for a given technology, output cannot growth because of lack of labour force.

> a zero elasticity of supply for output means that an increase of demand in terms of money will lead to no change in output; that is to say, prices will rise in the same proportion as the money demand rises. Inflation will have no effect on output or employment, but only on prices . . . Indeed, the condition in which the elasticity of the supply of output as a whole is zero is, I now think, the most convenient criterion for defining full employment.
>
> (Keynes 1973, p. 106)

In other words, output can grow only if technology and productivity increase and, it has to be noticed, conversely if technology and productivity increase, full employment can be maintained only if output grows. This can be considered the basis for the subsequent warning by Keynes about "technological unemployment".

Coming to the conceptual definition of "demand for labour" it has to be refined in one fundamental aspect. Whatever the variable on which it is considered dependent, it cannot be meant in terms of "workers", but in terms of "quantity of work", possibly hours of work. The technology of the economy, in fact, defines the input coefficients of labour in terms of quantity of work and not of workers.

Converting the quantity of work into quantity of workers requires a passage of institutional nature (as such subject to discretionary changes): precisely, the hours of work per employee. In fact the total output of an economy is given, again *for a given technology*, by productivity per hour multiplied by the number of hours worked per employee multiplied by the number of workers actually employed. As a consequence, for a given productivity per hour, total output may change even when the number of employees does not change provided the hours worked per employee do change, or, vice versa, when the hours worked per employee do not change if the level of employment changes. Similarly, total output may remain constant if both variables change but in opposite and compensating directions. These qualifications are of great importance when dealing with the real question: whether it is possible to achieve the target of full employment through appropriate aggregate demand management in case of technical progress and increasing productivity.

Technical progress and technological unemployment

When introducing the role of technical progress with regard to the goal of full employment it must be borne in mind that although it can be neutral, or labour saving or capital saving, either in the Hicks or in the Harrod sense, it is always labour saving in absolute terms because it always reduces the labour input coefficients of production. Therefore it always implies a rise of labour productivity. This concept is very tricky, as it is nearly indistinguishable from the productivity of any other factor of production (Fadda 2013), and the growth accountancy does not give satisfying answers to the problem. Still, for our purpose we can use the crude concept of labour productivity as the ratio between total output and total labour input. Therefore we identify technical progress with its effect of increasing labour productivity.

In order to explore the relationship between the goal of full employment and the presence of technical progress the first step has to be devoted to the question of the impact of rising productivity on the level of employment. This problem can be (and it has been) considered under an empirical perspective and under a theoretical approach. The empirical perspective generally leads to the conclusion that historically no positive relationship has emerged between productivity growth and unemployment. The classical standard reference is to the fact that since the worries of Luddism started to pervade the world of workers, the predictions of massive unemployment due to technological change have always proven false. More detailed empirical investigations reach more refined conclusions, sometimes revealing that although in the short run there may be a positive relationship it disappears or turns negative in the long run. Two empirical studies, though, are particularly worth mentioning. The first (Benigno 2010), based mainly on US data, finds out a positive relationship between productivity growth and employment in the long run, but a negative one between a rise in the variance of productivity growth and employment. The explanations could be grounded on the slow process of adjustment of wages to productivity growth (Ball and Mankiw

2002; Pissarides 2009), which would let production costs decline, profits increase, and consequently the demand for labour rise because of more investment and economic growth. On the other hand, in case of a downwards shift of the pace of productivity growth the increase in wages according to expectations would make profits shrink, causing a reduction in the demand for labour in order to protect profits.

The second bunch of empirical considerations that I think worth mentioning comes from J. Mason (2015). The data that he reports show that "Ten-year periods with high growth of productivity invariably also have low unemployment rates; periods of high average unemployment are invariably also periods of slow productivity growth". This is as far as the US is concerned, plus Japan and some other countries, while many other countries show inverse relationships. Relative to these data it can be observed in the first place that the causal direction of the relationship is not established. It may well be that technical progress and productivity growth are able to speed up the growth of the economy so that the demand for labour rises, but it may also be the other way round: when unemployment falls and labour becomes scarce employers are stimulated to speed up the process of innovation, also increasing the level of output due to high aggregate demand. In addition, changes in output and employment could be strongly influenced by monetary and fiscal policy, something which obviously would discredit any straight relationship between productivity and employment. A second observation concerns the different shapes that the above correlation shows in different countries. This really poses a problem: there must be other aspects (which are to be detected) able to affect this relationship. It may be differences in the kind of innovation, it may be differences in labour market institutions and regulations, it may be differences in the world trade position, it may be differences in content and timing of economic policy. When dealing with the problems of maintaining the target of full employment in the long run in the presence of technical progress these aspects will prove of fundamental importance.

A final but essential consideration about the empirics of the evolution of this relationship is that the historical trend cannot be assumed to continue as such in the future. There is no reason to believe that the new inventions of the future will have the same effect on the labour market as in the past. There is no reason to say that the growth of output will have in the future the same pace of the past. Perhaps in the past all kinds of polluting activities did not have significant effects on climate change, but they do in the present, and probably will do to a larger extent in the future. Similarly, the fact that all the past predictions have proven wrong says nothing about how the variables involved are going to behave in the future. It is not correct to infer from the past the evolution of the future. So, being unable to rely on past experience, particularly in times of deep and fast changes, we are forced to look for light in the theory.

Economic theory on this topic is mainly derived from neoclassical approaches. Among the classical economists, Ricardo (1817) in his well-known Chapter 31 on machinery saw a conflict between mechanization and employment, while Marx saw in the growth of the "organic composition of capital" on the one hand a way of forcing wages to subsistence level but on the other hand a root from which an underconsumption crisis of the system would develop (Marx 1993).

Neoclassical models generally deny a negative effect of productivity increase on employment in the long run although they admit it could temporarily appear in the short run. "Many structural shocks that initially create a positive trade-off between productivity and unemployment set in motion a dynamic path of adjustment involving capital accumulation or decumulation that in principle can eliminate the trade off" (Gordon 1995, p. 4). In Solow's model of growth, full employment is unaffected by technical progress, since an increase in investment will accompany the shift of the production function as well as the increase in the capital/labour ratio. Even according to Layard's approach the equilibrium unemployment rate is not affected by changes in technology: "Unemployment in the long run is independent of capital accumulation and technical progress" (Layard et al. 1991, p. 107). Rowthorn, on the other hand has objected that these conclusions are valid only on the assumption of a unit elasticity production function (Rowthorn 1999). The theoretical literature on this theme is vast, but definitely not conclusive, and it looks right to agree with Blanchard, Solow and Wilson when they state that

> theoretical arguments are unlikely to settle the issue, precisely because it turns so decisively on the reaction of aggregate output to (favorable or unfavorable) productivity shock. The problem is located at the intersection of the demand side and the supply side, the least developed and most controversial area of economic theory.
>
> (Blanchard et al. 2007, p. 5)

The complexity of the issue and the various interconnections and possible lines of causation among the involved variables can be summarized as follows.

Consider first the relationship between growth and productivity. A first line of causation goes from productivity to growth and implies a positive effect of the first on the latter. This effect is attributed to reduction of unit costs, which will allow the aggregate supply curve to shift down. If the aggregate demand curve remains unchanged the result will be an increase in aggregate output. But the aggregate demand curve may shift left or right according to what will happen to investment and consumer demand. If the aggregate demand curve shifts right, output will increase still more. Nevertheless, the direction of causality between productivity and growth can be reversed. Growth may be the cause of increasing productivity by virtue of the pro-cyclical conduct implied by Okun's law or by technical progress embodied in the new investments required to enlarge productive capacity or also by the pressure towards labour-saving innovations coming from tighter labour market conditions.

Turning to consider the relationship between productivity and employment, a two-way causation can also be detected. On the one hand productivity growth is bound to affect the level of employment either positively if the consequent growth is strong enough or negatively if growth is not enough to compensate for labour substitution. In addition, structural effects may take place regarding polarization, wages and long-term unemployment owning to skill-biased technical change. On the other hand a reverse positive causation may go from employment growth to productivity as a consequence of increasing labour scarcity and wages, while increasing unemployment and declining wages would lead to a slowdown of productivity. The positive impact of employment on productivity would also mitigate the price rise, lessening in this way the constraints of the Phillips curve.

A similar view about these relationships, which will also help to answer the question of whether full employment in the long run is compatible with continuous technical progress, can be found in Pasinetti's approach (Pasinetti 1993). Technical progress will reduce labour coefficients of production at different paces in different sectors. Some sectors will be stronger affected than others. Taking account of these different reductions, plus the different output dynamics of each sector, plus the weight of each sector in the aggregate output, plus the creation of new productive sectors, it is possible to establish the net balance in aggregate terms between the destruction and the creation of new jobs that follow the introduction of technical progress. As Pasinetti says, in different historical periods it could well be that this balance is positive, and that only problems of adjustment of the labour force, mobility, education and training would arise. In that case appropriate active labour policies would be sufficient to put things right. But it may also be that this balance is negative, and it will be so when the rate of output growth in aggregate terms is not sufficient to compensate for the destruction of jobs operated by technological innovation. In this case no active labour policies would be able to find employment for the loss of jobs that cannot be replaced. This is the problem that Keynes forecasted when he said:

> We are being afflicted with a new disease of which some readers may not yet have heard the name, but of which they will hear a great deal in the years to come – namely, technological unemployment. This means unemployment due to our discovery of means of economising the use of labour outrunning the pace at which we can find new uses for labour.
>
> (Keynes 1930)

Should we give up the goal of full employment?

The problem is how to cope with the possible situation foreseen by Keynes, or, in other words, how to avoid full employment being held back by technical progress. It is clear that what is true at the industry level is also true for the economy as a whole: aggregate labour demand is bound to increase with productivity growth if aggregate output is sufficiently elastic, while it will decline if aggregate output is not adequately elastic. Therefore the final and also long-run impact on employment depends on the elasticity of both consumer and investment demand. Both price and income elasticities have to be considered. Obviously, since the labour coefficient reduction affects also additional output, its rate of growth has to be higher than the rate of reduction of labour inputs per unit of production in order to compensate for the job destruction caused by technical progress. A particular interpretation of the production function makes the problem still worse. Considering, as Summer does (Summer 2013), a production function of the kind $Y = F(\beta K, L + \lambda(1-\beta)K)$, where one unit of capital is equivalent to λ units of labour, it is possible to make a distinction between two uses of the stock of capital: one part for the customary use and the other part to substitute for labour. As more capital will be reallocated to substitute for labour, output will increase but, being larger the stock of effective labour and smaller the stock of conventional capital, the wage level will decline. In view of this last effect it is not sure that output will grow, and then: "rapid productivity growth associated with inelastic demand leads to fewer and fewer people being engaged in the activity" (Summers 2013, p. 4). It is important at this point to notice that this could give a further and more general explanation of the different impact of increasing productivity on employment in different countries as mentioned above: it is not the absolute intensity of technical progress that matters, but the ratio between this and the rate of economic growth. Obviously behind the different growth rates there are different factors in different countries.

Within this frame the question becomes: in times of increasingly rapid technical progress will consumer and investment demand be able to grow at a higher speed so as to achieve the goal of full employment? And if not, are there any measures that could be adopted to make full employment achievable or should we abandon the goal of full employment altogether?

The question can be split into two parts. The first part is: are we in times of such "dangerously" rapid technical change as to hinder the possibility of full employment? And the second is: what can be done if we are really there or nearly there?

The literature on the nature and consequences of the present rapid increase of technical change is burgeoning and it sounds like we are witnessing something completely different from the past. It is not like substituting looms for workers or trains for horses. It is far beyond the information and communications technology (ICT) revolution, as it looks like progressively transferring to robotics most of the tasks up to now performed by human workers. Jeremy Rifkin (1995) began many years ago to foresee mass unemployment as the fundamental problem of the twenty-first century. Martin Ford (2009) expects the workers expelled by technological innovation from productive activity not to be able to find employment in other sectors in the next few decades. The race against machines (Brynjolfsson and McAfee 2011) is such as to bring Frey and Osborne (2013) to predict that 47 per cent of jobs currently existing in the US will vanish in the next two decades, while Jeremy Bowles (2014) foresees a net loss of 50 per cent of today's jobs in Europe in the next decades. On several occasions Ulrich Beck (2009) has drawn attention to the prospect that in the next decade employment of only 50 per cent of the working-age population would be enough to produce all the goods and services demanded in advanced countries. More recently, some projections of the possible impact of the so-called fourth industrial revolution ("Industry 4.0") on the labour market show a substantial net loss of jobs (Chui 2015; Ford 2015; WEF 2016). The cyber revolution, with the use of big data, advances analytics, internet of things, advanced robotics, learning machines and 3D printing, will undoubtedly have dramatic implications for the change of skill requirements of the workforce, but will also destroy more jobs than it will be able to create. According to a recent British report (Glover 2016), employment in manufacturing is projected to decline in Britain at a rate of 0.9 per cent per annum between 2015 and 2022; while in Germany no significant impact on the level of employment is expected (Walwei 2015), due also to the powerful attraction that the improved efficiency and profitability of the whole German industrial system will exert on location decisions. At a global level, the report published by the World Economic Forum in January 2016 (WEF 2016), taking into account 15 of the world's largest economies, estimates a loss of 7.1 million jobs over the next five years due to the fourth industrial revolution. In front of this, 2.1 million new jobs are estimated to be created in other sectors, leaving a net loss of 2 million jobs.

It seems therefore that we are close to the point at which the speed of job destruction caused by such rapid and deep technological progress will hardly be offset by job creation due to additional consumer and investment demand. The production of all the goods and services needed to match aggregate demand would require the employment of only a fraction of the available labour; or, reciprocally, if all the available labour were employed this would lead to overproduction, which in turn would revert the economy to crises and unemployment. It seems that we have reached at an aggregate level that paradoxical situation depicted by Bertrand Russell with reference to a single industry.

> Suppose that, at a given moment, a certain number of people are engaged in the manufacture of pins. They make as many pins as the world needs, working (say) eight hours a day. Someone makes an invention by which the same number of men can make twice as many pins: pins are already so cheap that hardly any more will be bought at a lower price. In a sensible world, everybody concerned in the manufacturing of pins would take to working four hours instead of eight, and everything else would go on as before. But in the actual world this would be thought demoralizing. The men still work eight hours, there are too many pins, some employers go bankrupt, and half the men previously concerned in making pins are thrown out of work. There is, in the end, just as much leisure as on the other plan, but half the men are totally idle while half are still overworked. In this way, it is insured that the unavoidable leisure shall cause misery all round instead of being a universal source of happiness. Can anything more insane be imagined?
>
> (Russell 1935, p. 16)

Obviously Russell didn't imagine that either rising wages in the pin sector or falling prices of pins could have increased the demand for other goods in such a way as to employ all the workers dismissed in the pin industry. This is what is accounted for in multisectoral models, where cross-elasticities of demand play a fundamental role in ascertaining the impact of technical progress on employment. But if the reduction of labour input coefficients is extended to all the economy, if the substitution of human work with machines or robots pervades all sectors, then the preservation of same levels of aggregate employment is conditional on adequate increase of aggregate production. The problem, therefore, is whether it is possible for aggregate demand to grow to such a required level. The problem may also be exacerbated by the fact that the initial fall in unemployment will work towards a reduction in consumer demand. Unless the pace of aggregate output growth is higher than that of aggregate productivity increase (measured as a weighted average of all sectors) it will be impossible to avoid a fall in employment as a consequence of technological change, and therefore it will impossible to maintain the goal of full employment.

Since it is out of question the possibility and also the opportunity of slowing down the path of innovation (it wouldn't make sense to delay the reduction of the human effort required per unit of production), it is on the other side of the ratio, that is the speed of output growth, that possible actions are to be considered if the goal of full employment is to be maintained.

Of course, monetary and fiscal policies must come to play in this regard, as well as real public policies such as industrial policies, agricultural policies, research policies, and so on. But since consumer demand is the key variable, both in itself and in its role relative to the investment function, it is also towards its growth that action should be directed. To this end, a most effective and structural measure would be to attain a less unequal income distribution. As Keynes said, "measures for the redistribution of incomes in a way likely to raise the propensity to consume may prove positively favourable to the growth of capital" (Keynes 1967, p. 373).

Although empirical evidence and theoretical debates are less than conclusive about the impact of unequal distribution on the rate of growth, the prevailing hypothesis is that a negative relationship exists between the two (Fadda 2015). The available measures towards a reduction of income inequality range from those directed to affect the market distribution (before tax and transfers) to those directed to change the disposable income distribution. Although the first ones should be preferred, also the second ones could be effective if well designed. Careful design is required to avoid distortive effects that could turn to be worse than the inequality they are meant to correct (Fadda 2015). Transfers, both in money and in kind, could be particularly effective in rising aggregate demand beyond the level reached with the original market distribution.

Social expenditure could be a second and powerful tool to control the ratio between productivity increase and output growth. The provision of public goods and social services financed out of taxation of top incomes or through public debt would help to support aggregate demand.

A third way of providing a stimulus to labour demand when jobs are lost because of technological change is that of stimulating (actually with specific policies aimed at exploiting the possibilities open by same technological progress) the production of new goods and new services to which a growing paying demand could be addressed. This additional demand could come from either the wage increase due to productivity growth or from the price fall, and would reflect the evolution of needs and tastes as the standard of living rises.

All these measures are right, but they might not be enough to solve the problem. In case of excessively wide gap between labour demand and supply and in case of accelerating and deep technical change, relying only on these measure could lead to an obsessive search for a continuous increase of the rate of growth. GDP growth would be pursued, in this case, not for the sake of generating social welfare and responding to social needs, but only for the sake of creating new jobs, in an endless spiral escalation. Furthermore, in the long run such a rate of growth could easily prove to be unsustainable under several points of view. Because neither natural resources nor human needs are unlimited, this process would tend to crash in the long run against a destructive consumeristic exasperation or/and against an insuperable crises of overproduction. The measures mentioned above are useful and also necessary as part of countercyclical and stabilization policy, but their ability to reach and maintain full employment in a world of continuous deep and accelerating technical progress of the kind we are starting to witness is doubtful, not to say illusory. Actually the economy may be trapped between an *unsustainable rate of growth and an unsustainable rate of unemployment*. The need to escape this trap requires that other options be considered.

The reduction of working time

An alternative way to conciliate increasing technical progress, full employment and "sustainable" growth comes from the distinction made above between the reduction of labour input coefficients and the reduction of "workers" coefficients. Taking account of this, the problem could be reduced to an elementary arithmetical sequence. If the total amount of working hours required for an output that equals aggregate demand falls and this total amount is divided by the number of workers, the result is the number of work hours per worker which is needed to keep constant the level of employment. If the starting point is one of full employment, the achievement of the result of this calculation would neutralize the job destruction effect of technical progress; and the advantage of productivity increases would be entirely translated on the variable of working time per worker.

Undoubtedly, the historical evolution shows a path of working hours' reduction, although this has been caused more by workers' demands for better quality of life than by deliberate labour policy choices. From the original working time with no limits of regulatory or contractual kind of the first industrial revolution, a first step forwards was the English Factory Act of 1833, which imposed a limit of eight hours a day for workers aged between 9 and 13 and of 12 hours for workers aged between 14 and 18. Later, in 1850, a limit of 10 working hours a day was imposed for everyone. In France the revolutionary government imposed in 1848 a general limit of 10 hours a day in Paris and 11 in the provinces. In Italy, in 1860 the daily working hours were about 15, while in 1923 a length of 8 hours per day and 48 per week was established by law. Collective agreements in the 1970s reduced it to 40 hours in five days. More recently, tentative measures for further reductions have been discussed in France and Germany.

Table 3.1 Average annual hours actually worked per worker in some OECD countries, 2015

Country	No. of hours
Germany	1,371
Netherlands	1,419
Norway	1,424
Denmark	1,457
France	1,482
Luxembourg	1,507
Belgium	1,541
Switzerland	1,590
Sweden	1,612
Austria	1,625
Finland	1,646
Australia	1,665
United Kingdom	1,674
Spain	1,691
Japan	1,719
Italy	1,725
United States	1,790
Portugal	1,868
Poland	1,963
Russian Federation	1,978
Greece	2,042
Korea	2,113
Mexico	2,246

Source: OECD Statistics

A description of the comparative situation at the present time is given in Table 3.1.

It is worth noticing that countries that have an average working time per worker comparatively higher than others (such as Greece and Italy) are known to have also a lower productivity per worker, and vice versa.

The above simple arithmetical sequence could be refined in the following way. Suppose an economy is at full employment and an accelerated and deep technical progress takes place. Then, full employment could be maintained by adjusting the productivity per worker through a reduction of working hours in proportion to the rate of growth of productivity per hour *minus* the rate of growth of aggregate demand. Of course this kind of rule implies that productivity per hour is intended in the "crude" sense mentioned above, and that the average changes be weighted for the different sectors or industries of the economy.

Even so, the implementation of this rule, its conversion into measures of economic policy, is far from simple. Three main problems arise. The first is concerned with the organization of production processes, the second with the behaviour of wages, the third with differences in sectoral productivity changes.

With regard to the first, let's imagine that technological innovations yield in the firm an increase of the ratio between output and labour input; that is an increase of labour productivity in the above sense. It would be awkward for the firm to reduce proportionally the working time of employees such as to leave the number of employed unchanged. This would be technically difficult for more than one reason.

In the first place, the technology of each production process does not offer an elasticity of substitution between factors such as to permit movements along a "continuum", in a kind of "fine tuning", to match increases in productivity with corresponding splitting of the specific task of one worker into different complementary workers. There are discontinuities (of different extent according to specific tasks and stages of the production process) that, if disregarded by hasty redistributions of the working time, would create a disruption in the process that would neutralize all the gain of productivity increases.

In the second place, the reduction in total unit costs due to technological change would reflect different changes in variable and fixed costs. Possibly, changes in fixed costs (such as cleaning, maintenance, administration, recruitment and so on) would be unaffected by changes in the process of production; therefore the reduction in total unit costs would be less than proportional to the increase in labour productivity so that a general cut in the working time proportional to the average increase in labour productivity would increase total unit costs making it impossible for the firm to maintain the same level of competitiveness in the market. In fact the conversion of productivity increases into shorter working time should be carefully designed in a thorough restructuring of production operations and of firm organization. The option between fewer working hours per day or fewer working days per week is also available. In any case an absolute proportionality between productivity growth and working time reduction could hardly be managed.

The second problem is relative to wage levels. Ignoring the first problem and assuming that in a manufacturing process the increase in productivity per worker was accompanied by a strictly proportional reduction in the hours worked per worker, the labour cost per unit of production would be constant if the worker's wage was kept constant. In this case the wage level would not benefit from the increase in productivity. If, on the contrary, workers wanted to transfer to wages some of the productivity benefit, the proportion between productivity growth and working time reduction should change accordingly. In other words, workers are faced with a trade-off between change in wages and change in working time, and this would consequently affect the level of employment. With regard to this an important point has to be made. In the case of a working time reduction being generally imposed as a measure of economic policy, workers can still individually keep the choice about this trade-off and decide either to engage in other short-time paid jobs or make themselves available for overtime work (unless these choices were effectively discouraged or prohibited). In this case any positive impact of shorter working time on employment would vanish. The probabilities of making these choices are of course linked to the individual preference functions; a greater utility attributed to income rather than to free or leisure time would clearly encourage them – something that is not unlikely to happen, given the growing tendency of these times to engage in a kind of social competition in terms of consumption and status symbols exhibition.

The third problem would arise if the same general reduction of working time were extended to all the economy while different sectors have different rates of productivity increase. Obviously this would cause either an exit from the market of the firms in the sectors with lower (or nil) productivity growth, or a change (which could be very substantial) in relative prices. If the society thinks such consequences inappropriate, the government could act through taxes, transfers and subsidies to restore the previous equilibrium. An intervention of this kind happened in Sweden in the mid-1990s with the fundamental cooperation of trade unions' collective bargaining (Erixon 2008).

We can conclude that great care has to be taken in designing this kind of policy, but that with a careful combination of growth policy and working time management it is possible to maintain the goal of full employment even in times of heavy job destructive technical progress.

Now a similar but quite different question has to be asked: can a shortening of the working time be used as a measure to curb the rate of unemployment even when the economy is far below full employment and unemployment is not caused by technical progress? What can be done when there is not enough technical progress to be converted into reduction of working time to fill the wide gap between demand and supply of labour? In this case the persistence of unemployment (apart from frictional and structural unemployment for which effective active labour policies are appropriate) would be caused either by wages above the equilibrium level or by insufficient aggregate demand. When the latter is the case the question is whether (as long as aggregate demand stimuli are time taking or ineffective) it could be of some help to act to convert the total labour input of the economy into a larger number of job places through a reduction of the working time. It has to be said that this possibility is prejudicially opposed by those who think that the labour force unable to find jobs in the production of goods and services for the market should be employed in jobs to satisfy social needs (such as the so-called "third sector" activities, no-profit, and so on). In their view this would have a double advantage: it would lessen the drive towards consumerism (because "absolute" needs and not "relative" needs would be involved) and it would raise real wages because private expenditure for basic social needs would decline (Valli 1996). It would be better to consider the implementation of this perspective as complementary rather than an alternative to the above perspective of "redistribution" of jobs. In fact it is exposed to the risk of state paternalism and, in any case, its public financing would require a sufficient level of market production.

Another radical opposition to the perspective of shortening the working time in order to increase employment comes from the argument that the supposed increase would be swept away by entrepreneurs' readiness to pay higher wages for more productive workers working longer: since shorter working time and lower unemployment would "worsen the quality of a worker's effort; then a maximizing firm has an incentive to substitute a higher wage for fewer workers. A decrease in standard working hours thus may not result in a lower unemployment rate" (Chun 2002, p. 367). This argument, though, is based on the unproven assumption of Shapiro efficiency wage flavour, that "an increase in unemployment rate motivates the worker to furnish much more effort" (ibid.), and vice-versa.

The main problem of trying to create more jobs by reducing working time beyond the increase in productivity rests in the relationship with wages. In fact, should the shortening of working time remain within the limits of the increase in productivity, as long as the necessary organization adjustments are made, no rise in labour cost per unit of production would occur. But if this measure exceeds the increase in productivity, the only alternative is between wage cuts and rising production costs. The first choice could be dealt with in the frame of the trade-off between income and leisure time, while the second could be tackled with cutback of non-labour costs and with infra-industry and international harmonization to avoid loss in competitiveness. Both could be eased with state intervention. Since what matters to workers is disposable income and to entrepreneurs gross labour costs, a reduction of tax and social security contribution would help protect both net wages and labour costs for unit of production. The most effective use of work-time reduction for the sake of employment with state subsidies has been made in Germany during the last recession: short-time work was the "German answer" to the economic crisis. The number of short-time workers strongly increased in the recession and peaked at more than 1.5 million. Without the extensive use of short-time work, unemployment would have risen by approximately twice as much as it actually did (Brenke et al. 2011), although state intervention seems to have led to abuses after the end of the crisis.

If a general reduction of working hours imposed by law encounters several problems of the kind just described, an easier path is to create space for flexible and gradual reductions based on personal choices or collective agreements. On this line it would be possible to agree voluntary marginal reductions of working time joined with wage reductions, such as longer periods of unpaid vacations, or longer unpaid temporary leaves for various purposes, or even the possibility of sabbaticals. Another option could be to free the part-time work from its features of forced, precarious, peripheral and unskilled job and to extend it to voluntary opportunities also for central well-structured tasks requiring high responsibilities and high skills.

Still more, retirement regulations could allow for flexible retiring ages, with gradual reduction of working time linked to progressive inclusion of young workers in the firm. But in this way the concept of working time per worker that we have been referring to becomes closer to that of working time per person. The ratio between total hours worked and total population is bound to decline if the number of pensioners and their life expectancy rise and the entry into the labour force of youngsters is delayed. This process doesn't lead to a decline of working hours per worker; on the contrary it could lead to an increase and would act against the work-sharing perspective. Finally, agreements and regulations that make overtime work less costly than standard work should be avoided.

All these operative lines must be carefully designed and organically conceived as part of a coherent strategy. In order to make such strategy of shortening working time viable and not disruptive of the economy, three pre-conditions are required: first, an efficient labour market based on the principle of "flexicurity"; second, an improved work organization within the firm following the lines of the "lean production"; third, a good degree of international coordination among national regulatory systems and among workers and entrepreneurs' representatives.

Conclusion

A short conclusion can be drawn as follows.

In order to lessen unemployment of a "classical" nature, measures concerning wage moderation and active labour market policies are needed; but these are not sufficient in order to achieve full employment.

When unemployment of a "Keynesian" nature (as Malinvaud calls it) pervades the economy, the implementation of policies aimed at expanding effective demand is also needed. But even these might not be sufficient when "technological unemployment" arises.

When the path and the depth of technical change are such as to make it impossible for the rate of sustainable growth to keep up with the rate of increase in productivity in order to ensure full employment, then a shortening of the working time per worker becomes also necessary.

This measure, though, has to be carefully designed in order to avoid distortions and negative effects on the economy when applied to specific productive sectors. Careful calibration and overall reorganization of operational tasks of the productive process of the firms are also needed. In addition, it should also be framed in a context of international coordination and harmonization.

In the meantime, a set of gradual reforms to help an initial redistribution of the work for which effective demand exists could be adopted, such as a reorgan-ization of "part-time" work, a lengthening of vacations and temporary leaves, a better regulation of overtime work and a flexibility in retirement age. All this should allow a better distribution of the benefits of technical progress, instead of technology improvements being used to slacken the labour market by maintaining constant the working time and making more workers compete for fewer jobs and declining wages.

On these lines one should carefully think about the following Keynes plea. Considering the deep practical knowledge of the economy possessed by Keynes no one could think of him as just a visionary utopian.

> I would predict that the standard of life in progressive countries one hundred years hence will be between four and eight times as high as it is to-day. . . .
> For many ages to come the old Adam will be so strong in us that everybody will need to do some work if he is to be contented. We shall do more things for ourselves than is usual with the rich to-day, only too glad to have small duties and tasks and routines. But beyond this, we shall endeavour to spread

the bread thin on the butter – *to make what work there is still to be done to be as widely shared as possible.* Three-hour shifts or a fifteen-hour week may put off the problem for a great while. For three hours a day is quite enough to satisfy the old Adam in most of us! . . . But beware! *The time for all this is not yet.* For at least another hundred years we must pretend to ourselves and to every one that fair is foul and foul is fair; for foul is useful and fair is not.

(Keynes 1930, pp. 370–373, emphasis added)

References

Ball, L. and G. Mankiw (2002), 'The Nairu in Theory and Practice', *Journal of Economic Perspectives*, 16(4): 115–136.

Beck, U. (2009), *World at Risk*, Polity Press.

Benigno, P., Ricci, L. and Surico, P. (2010), 'Unemployment and Productivity in the Long Run: The Role of Macroeconomic Volatility', IMF Working Paper, no. 259.

Blanchard, O., Solow, R. and Wilson, B.A. (2007), 'Productivity and Unemployment', MIT Economics, Blanchard Papers.

Bowles, J. (2014), 'The Computerisation of European Jobs', Bruegel, Blog Post, 24 July. www.bruegel.org/2014/07/the-computerisation-of-european-jobs/

Brenke, K., Rinne, U. and Zimmermann, K.F. (2011), 'Short-Time Work: The German Answer to the Great Recession', IZA Discussion Paper no. 5780.

Brynjolfsson, E. and A. McAfee (2011), *Race Against the Machine*, Digital Frontier Press.

Chui, M., Manyika, J. and Miremadi, M. (2015), 'Four fundamentals of workplace automation', *McKinsey Quarterly*, November. www.mckinsey.com/business-functions/digital-mckinsey/our-insights/four-fundamentals-of-workplace-automation

Chun-chieh Huang, Juin-jen Chang, Ching-chong Lai and Chung-cheng Lin (2002), 'Worker Productivity, Working Time Reduction, and the Short-Run and Long-Run Employment Effects', *Scottish Journal of Political Economy*, 4: 357–368.

Clower, R.W. (1965), 'The Keynesian Counter-Revolution: A Theoretical Appraisal', in F. Hahn and F. Brechling (eds) *The Theory of Interest Rates*, Macmillan.

Erixon, L. (2008), "*The Rehn–Meidner Model in Sweden: Its Rise, Challenges and Survival*", working paper, Stockholm University. http://people.su.se/~erixo/R-M2008b-1.pdf

Fadda, S. (2013), *Produttività, Contrattazione e Patto Sociale*, in Quaderni di Rassegna Sindacale, no. 2.

Fadda, S. (2015), 'Income inequality: What Causes It and How to Curb It', in S. Fadda and P. Tridico (eds), *Varieties of Inequality*, Routledge.

Ford, M. (2009), *The Lights in the Tunnel*, Acculant Publishing.

Ford, M. (2015), *Rise of the Robots*, Basic Books.

Frey, C. and Osborne, M. (2013), *The Future of Employment*, Oxford Martin School WP.

Glover, P. (2016), *The Future of Productivity in Manufacturing. Strategic Labour Market Intelligence Report*, UK Commission for Employment and Skills.

Gordon, R. (1995), 'Is there a Trade Off Between Unemployment and Productivity Growth?', NBER Working Paper no. 5081.

Keynes, J.M. (1930), 'Economic Possibilities for Our Grandchildren', *in Essays in Persuasion*, W.W. Norton & Co, 1963.

Keynes, J.M. (1967), *The General Theory of Employment, Interest and Money*, Macmillan.

Keynes, J.M. (1973), *Collected Writings of John Maynard Keynes*, vol. 14, Macmillan, St Martin Press for the Royal Economic Society.

Layard, R., Nickell, P.R.G. and R. Jackman (1991), *Unemployment: Macroeconomic Performance and the Labour Market*, Oxford University Press.

Malinvaud, E. (1977), *The Theory of Unemployment Reconsidered*, Basil Blackwell.

Marx, K. (1993), *Capital*, Volume III, Penguin Classics.

Mason, J.W. (2015), 'Unemployment and Productivity Growth', The Slack Wire, 8 January.

Pasinetti, L. (1993), *Dinamica Economica Strutturale*, Il Mulino.

Pissarides, C.A. (2009), 'The Unemployment Volatility Puzzle: Is Wage Stickiness the Answer?', *Econometrica*, 77: 1339–1369

Ricardo, D. (1817), *On the Principles of Political Economy and Taxation*, Dover Publications Inc.

Rifkin, J. (1995), *The End of Work*, Tarcher/Putnam.

Robinson, J. (1937), *Essays in the Theory of Employment*, Macmillan.

Rotman, D. (2013), 'How Technology is Destroying Jobs', *MIT Technology Review*, 12 June.

Rowthorn, R. (1999), 'Unemployment, Wage Bargaining and Capital Labor Substitution', *Cambridge Journal of Economics*, 23(4): 413–425.

Russell, B. (1935), *In Praise of Idleness and Other Essays*, Allen & Unwin.

Summers, L. (2013), 'Economic Possibilities for our Children', NBER Reporter, no. 4.

Valli, V. (ed.) (1996) *Proposte eretiche per l'occupazione*, Rosenberg & Sellier.

Walwei, U. (2016), 'Digitalization and Structural Labour Market Problems: The Case of Germany', ILO Research Paper 2016/17.

WEF (2016), *The Future of Jobs*, World Economic Forum, Geneva.

4 Shifting the social costs of trade

Non-tariff measures as the new focus of trade policy

Werner Raza

Introduction

During the last years, major industrialized countries have embarked on negotiating a new generation of free trade agreements (FTAs). These new trade agreements aim at what Robert Lawrence has termed "deep integration", that is "integration that moves beyond the removal of border barriers" (Lawrence 1996: 8). These new FTAs which include inter alia CETA (Canada–EU Trade Agreement), TPP (Trans-Pacific Partnership Agreement) or TTIP (Transatlantic Trade and Investment Partnership Agreement) stand out in terms of economic importance and scope. They are indeed very comprehensive and include a plethora of topics and issues, including services and investment liberalization, public procurement and cooperation in all matters of trade-related regulations with a view to dismantle so-called unnecessary regulation or harmonize diverging regulations between the trading parties.

Since trade and investment between much of the industrialized world is already very open, trade liberalization in the conventional meaning of the term is only a minor issue in these negotiations. Average tariff rates between the European Union and the United States, for instance, already stand at less than 3 per cent for manufactured goods (BMWT/ifo 2013: 39). Hence, removing remaining tariffs will have only limited effects. Most of the economic effects are expected to come from the alignment, i.e. the (i) harmonization, (ii) mutual recognition or (iii) eventual elimination of diverging national regulations. Therefore the focus of negotiations in the new generation trade agreements lies on *non-tariff measures* (NTMs). These are procedures, laws and regulations other than tariffs or quotas that impede trade and investment, respectively, between two or more countries.

Efforts towards deep integration started already with the Uruguay Round of the GATT (1986–1994), e.g. in the fields of intellectual property rights, services and government procurement. More recent efforts during the World Trade Organization Doha Round, particularly in the areas of investment liberalization, competition law or domestic regulation in services, were, however, stifled by developing and emerging country opposition (Nölke and Claar 2012). Thus, efforts towards deep integration trade agreements were redirected to the bilateral and regional level, with the US and EU proactively pursuing this regulatory agenda in their bilateral trade policies since the mid-2000s. The regulatory agenda of the EU in these bilateral agreements has gradually become more comprehensive, with TTIP and CETA arguably constituting the most advanced examples of deep integration trade agreements.

Mainstream economic theory suggests that the alignment of NTMs will entail cost savings that will transfer into higher income and growth. Not surprisingly, then, economic analysis has made considerable efforts to include NTMs in its assessment exercises of the effects of FTAs. On a conceptual level, conventional trade economics treats NTMs either as a cost to business or as rents accruing to companies, the removal or alignment of which raises economic welfare. However, NTMs that come for instance in the form of sanitary and phyto-sanitary measures, or health and safety standards, arguably confer a benefit to society. As Beghin et al. (2012: 360) write: "The message remains that when market imperfections are present, the interface between NTMs, trade and welfare is more complex than the simple dominant mercantilist message." Thus a proper treatment of NTMs in trade impact assessments would call for an analysis of both costs and benefits of NTMs for society. In other words, in addition to the cost savings for businesses, the consequences of a NTM removal or alignment for the social benefits that this NTM has so far conferred upon society have to be investigated as well.

This issue is relevant across a wide range of technical standards and regulations, but particularly pertinent in the case of highly sensitive public policy areas like food safety standards, health standards or environmental regulations. Given the broad scope of the new generation trade agreements, it should thus come as no surprise that civil society organizations and social movements have become increasingly concerned about the implications of the new FTAs on social welfare.

In the second section of this chapter, I will first scrutinize the analytical treatment of NTMs as trade costs by mainstream trade economics. Some technical improvements by incorporating cost–benefit analysis notwithstanding (third section), I purport to show that the treatment of NTMs in trade impact assessments is still insufficient and indeed misleading on methodological grounds. From this I will move on to ask what methodological options for the assessment of social benefits of regulation exist that go beyond the prevailing approach (fourth section). A final section concludes. My discussion uses some of the most influential studies on the economic effects of TTIP as reference points.

The treatment of NTMs as trade costs in conventional trade analysis

Trade economists have been aware of the importance of NTMs for a long time. But as long as trade liberalization was largely confined to tariff reduction, the analytical treatment of NTMs was of no particular concern. This changed within the last two decades or so, when it became increasingly evident that the focus of trade negotiations shifted towards including a growing number of technical standards and regulations, administrative procedures, or services sector liberalizations, the latter being intimately linked to regulatory issues. During the last 20 years a broad literature has emerged that aims at providing various techniques to quantify the economic importance of NTMs. Regardless of the particular metric applied, NTMs are conceptualized as a cost to trade, i.e. as an element that is a restriction to trade. Thus, the principal challenge lies in quantifying the magnitude of this restrictiveness. Once this is achieved NTMs can be added to other components of trade costs. Depending on specific assumptions on the "actionability" of these trade costs, i.e. the degree to which one believes they can be reduced or aligned by a trade agreement, the welfare implications can then be calculated by means of a computable general equilibrium (CGE) model, typically.

In their comprehensive survey on the state-of-the-art of NTM measurement, Anderson and van Wincoop (2004: 2) define trade costs as 'all costs incurred in getting a good to a final user, other than the marginal cost of producing the good itself'. This includes the following types of costs: (i) transportation costs, (ii) policy barriers (tariffs and NTBs), (iii) information costs, (iv) contract enforcement costs, (v) currency costs, (vi) legal and regulatory costs, and (vii) local distribution costs. Anderson and van Wincoop (2004) provide an ad-valorem tax equivalent estimate of trade costs in the order of 170 per cent for a representative rich country. These are broken down into a 21 per cent transportation costs, 44 per cent border related trade barriers and 55 per cent distribution costs. Of the 44 per cent border related trade barriers, roughly 8 per cent are associated with tariffs and NTBs, 7 per cent with language, 14 per cent with currency, 6 per cent with information costs and 3 per cent with security barriers. Given that average tariff levels in advanced industrialized countries are typically below 5 per cent, this estimate implies that NTBs add around 3–4 per cent to the price of a traded good (see Raza et al. 2014). However, the definition of NTBs in Anderson and van Wincoop (2004: 11) includes only price and quantity measures, e.g. quotas, quality measures (standards, licensing requirements, etc.), and in a broadened definition also threat measures (antidumping and countervailing measures). Thus it is seemingly focussed upon border barriers, i.e. barriers that arise at the point of entry into an economic territory and are discriminatory in nature.[1]

A particular complication of measuring NTMs as trade costs is the lack of direct evidence. Databases which provide information on non-tariff-barriers, like UNCTAD's TRAINS database, are incomplete and suffer from severe data-quality problems. In addition, they provide mainly information on incidence, and not on the trade restrictiveness of a particular instrument. Thus, trade economists have largely resorted to indirect methods of measuring the trade restrictiveness of NTBs. Here, trade costs are inferred from an economic model that links trade flows to observable variables and unobservable trade costs. The most widely applied approach uses the gravity model. The gravity model explains bilateral trade volume by a combination of factors that serve as attractors to trade – most notably the size of an economy as measured by GDP, and factors that make trade more difficult – most notably geographic distance, language or culture. NTMs enter the gravity equation typically in the form of a resistance term, i.e. it is assumed that both border and behind-the-border measures impede trade between two countries. Thus, the relative costs of NTMs can be estimated. Upon that basis, an ad valorem tax equivalent of NTMs can be calculated, which, however, is highly sensitive to the elasticity of substitution taken.

In order to come up with estimates of the trade restrictiveness of NTMs that are grounded in some empirical evidence, survey methods have been employed recently. In the case of the impact assessments of TTIP, the principal study commissioned by the EU Commission from Ecorys (Berden et al. 2009) conducted a survey among some 5500 business managers and industry experts. The respondents had to assess the trade restrictiveness of its sectoral bilateral trade by assigning a value of between 0 and 100. Upon that basis indices were constructed that were then used to estimate the impact of NTMs on trade and investment flows or, in other words, to calculate trade cost equivalents of existing NTMs. Ecorys (Berden et al. 2009: 23) arrive at an average trade cost estimate of NTMs across sectors of 17 per cent. This is a multiple of the 3–4 per cent estimate for policy barriers of the Anderson/van Wincoop (2004) paper, referred to above. Obviously, this has to do with the very wide definition of NTMs by the Ecorys study. NTMs are basically understood as "all non-price and non-quantity restrictions on trade [. . .]. This includes border measures (customs procedures, etc.) as well as behind-the-border measures flowing from domestic laws, regulations and practices . . ." (Berden et al. 2009: xiii).

In a further step, again with the help of experts, levels of actionability were established, i.e. assessments with regard to "the degree, to which an NTM or regulatory divergence can potentially be reduced . . ." (Berden et al. 2009: 15). Actionability levels were determined to range from 35 per cent to 70 per cent, with the average for the EU at 48 per cent and 50 per cent for the US. In a last step, these actionability levels were taken as inputs for the CGE scenario estimations of the economic impacts of TTIP, both in the Ecorys study (Berden et al. 2009), but also in later studies, in particular the CEPR (2013) study, also commissioned by the EU Commission. In the optimistic scenarios, a reduction of actionable NTMs of 50 per cent and 25 per cent was typically assumed.

Not surprisingly, the overall welfare effect, which is computed by the CGE simulations, is very sensitive to the assumed actionability level. The higher the actionability of NTMs, the higher the welfare gains. Actionability is defined as "the degree to which an NTM or regulatory divergence can potentially be reduced (through various methods) by 2018, *given that the political will exists to address the divergence identified*" (Berden et al. 2009: 15, emphasis added). Actionability thus depends on political will, which, however, is assumed as given. This definition is highly problematic, since the political process is effectively assumed away, and substituted for by an ad hoc assessment of a sample of mostly business-related experts, which, given their vested interests in the issues at stake, should be arguably expected to exhibit a certain tendency to both overestimate actionability levels and cost savings to companies. Thus, the determination of actionability levels is basically a more or less sophisticated guess of a group of persons with vested interests, and is not grounded in any kind of robust methodology.

By way of summary, the assessment of NTMs by mainstream trade economics is so far marked by a number of serious deficiencies. Firstly, the scope of NTMs remains unclear. While in the standard academic debate, NTMs have been defined as border measures referring to barriers such as quotas, quality measures (standards, licensing requirements, etc.), and in a broadened definition also to threat measures (antidumping and countervailing measures), the more recent literature extends that considerably. Here, behind-the-border measures, i.e. domestic laws and regulations are also included. Since behind-the-border measures are by definition non-discriminatory – at least on a *de jure* basis – this raises considerable theoretical problems. A significant part of the latter have to be considered as production costs and not as trade costs. If this were true, then it is questionable whether they should be included in a trade impact assessment at all. One could counter that trade in services as well as investment liberalisation, which have become an integral part of new generation FTAs, are *de facto* impeded by domestic laws and regulations, which differ between countries, regardless of whether they constitute production or trade costs. However, since firms encounter different NTMs in trade than in foreign direct investment (FDI), NTM impact assessments would have to account for that by distinguishing between NTMs related to trade and NTMs related to FDI. While NTMs related to trade would basically refer to border barriers, NTMs related to FDI would encompass behind-the-border measures, i.e. domestic laws and regulations.

This distinction notwithstanding, the economic argument for aligning FDI-related NTMs through FTAs remains blurry. While in the case of trade, mainstream economic theory suggests an increase in welfare, no general theory exists for international investment.[2] Thus it is an open theoretical question whether investment liberalisation through alignment and/or elimination of investment-related NTMs, aka domestic laws and regulations, increases economic welfare and growth. This question becomes the more pertinent, once we consider key areas of domestic law making, such as labour laws, environmental regulations or health and safety standards at work, where apart from the costs to business these regulations do have significant social benefits. Looking at NTMs as trade costs only thus risks ignoring these other relevant benefits.

The trade policy debate has addressed the problem of non-discriminatory behind-the-border measures in the context of investment agreements and services trade. In the framework of the WTO both the General Agreement on Trade in Services (GATS) and the Agreement on Trade-Related Investment Measures (TRIMS) aim at disciplining the use of domestic measures that impede trade. Article VI of GATS, for instance, introduces the concept of "measures of general application affecting trade in services", and stipulates inter alia that such measures "do not constitute unnecessary barriers to trade". For specific types of such measures, in particular qualification requirements and procedures, technical standards and licensing requirements, Article VI.4. of GATS provides for the development of "disciplines". These shall ensure that such measures are "based on objective and transparent criteria", and are "not more burdensome than necessary to ensure the quality of the service". In other words, multilateral guidelines shall be elaborated for specific domestic regulatory instruments that are *nota bene* non-discriminatory according to the definition of the WTO. With the exception of accounting services, no such disciplines have been elaborated since the entry into force of the General Agreement on Trade in Services (GATS) agreement in 1995. The main reason has precisely been political resistance by WTO members to the concept of the necessity test included in Article VI.4 as an excessive constraint on domestic regulatory autonomy. Similarly the Trade-Related Investment Measures (TRIMS) Agreement bans specific domestic regulations that countries have traditionally applied against foreign investments in order to foster national industrial development. Thus local content requirements, trade balancing requirements, foreign exchange restrictions and export restrictions (domestic sales requirements) are explicitly prohibited. Prominent authors such as Dani Rodrik (2007), Joseph Stiglitz (2005) and Robert Wade (2005) have repeatedly criticized such treaty obligations and argued that both developed and developing countries need sufficient policy space to manage the social and environmental consequences of a globalized economy and to steer a process of late industrial development, respectively.

With the new-generation FTAs encompassing both trade and investment liberalization, behind-the-border measures that include laws and regulations in key areas of public policy will inevitably become targeted by those social actors with a vested interest in the so-called "levelling of the playing field" for business across borders, that is transnational capital. Whether they will be discussed as costs to business only or seen as conferring benefits upon society will surely have a strong impact upon the future direction not only of trade policy, but of public policy more broadly.

Taking into account the benefits of regulation: cost–benefit analysis and beyond

In addition to the technical criticisms I have just outlined on the prevailing methodology used to assess the cost savings of regulatory alignment, a funda-mental concern here relates to the methodological approach in more general terms. First and foremost, most of the mainstream treatment of NTMs implicitly assumes that a substantial dismantling and alignment is possible without a change to the regulatory quality, i.e. the ability of a certain regulation or standard to safeguard a defined public policy goal. Only upon that basis, the Ecorys study (Berden et al. 2009) is, for instance, able to restrict itself to estimating the savings to companies, while completely neglecting the concomitant social costs. Consequently, the study arrives at small, but positive economic gains from the alignment of NTMs.

Overall, I think that using such an approach is not warranted, given that a considerable fraction of the gains derived from regulatory alignment happens – as in the Ecorys study (Berden et al. 2009) – in exactly those sectors, e.g. chemicals, cosmetics and pharmaceuticals, or food and beverages, where substantial and partly incommensurable differences in regulatory approaches and standards between countries exist. Any dismantling must have an effect on regulatory standards and thus infer a cost upon that society, which ends up with a lowered standard. As K.W. Kapp already observed in 1950 and conceptualized in the notion of "social costs of private enterprise", a change in a standard will always alter the distribution of costs and benefits between social actors, e.g. between firms and consumers. Thus, Kapp (1950, p. 15) wrote:

> In so far as social costs are the result of the minimization of the internal costs of the firm it is possible to regard the whole process as evidence of a redistribution of income. By shifting part of the costs of production to third persons or to the community at large producers are able to appropriate a larger share of the national product than they would otherwise be able to do.

And he continued by illustrating the argument with recourse to history:

> The political history of the last 150 years can be interpreted as a revolt of large masses of people (including small business) against social costs. It is doubtless true that the steady increase of protective social legislation, the enforcement of minimum standards of health and efficiency, the prohibition of destructive practices in many fields of production, the concern with air and water pollution, or even the efforts of farmers, businessmen and labor to peg the prices of products and services, reflect, at least in part, an attempt to restrain destructive methods of production and exploitation of resources.

As Kapp observed, in addition firms might be unevenly affected by regulatory change. The latter might, for example, favour big companies, while inferring an additional burden on small companies.

It must be stressed that for Kapp the whole issue of social costs was to be treated as "matters of political economy and political power" (ibid.). Instead of the policy suggestions flowing from cost–benefit analysis, of which Kapp was deeply sceptical, he insisted that issues of social costs thus do not lend themselves to some apparently easy technical fixes, but need to be resolved politically, as they represent core problems of what nowadays is referred to as public policy.

Thus, regulations that aim at safeguarding a certain public policy goal must be seen as the outcome of a process of social struggle and political negotiating, respectively. If that regulation is changed – either dismantled or aligned to some other standard, its effectiveness in serving the public policy goal will eventually be affected. This might infer a social benefit, if the new standard is higher than the old one, or a social cost, if the new standard is lower than the old one or has been eliminated without substitution. At a general level, social costs might come in the form of temporary adjustment costs, e.g. for harmonizing and implementing legislation, or be of a long-term nature to society, e.g. if standards for poisonous chemicals were relaxed and resulted in higher public health costs because of a higher incidence of allergies amongst the population.

That the alignment or elimination of NTMs will eventually result in a welfare loss to society, in so far as this elimination threatens public policy goals (e.g. consumer safety, public health, environmental safety) or corrects for market failure, has been recognized by the more recent literature. Schlueter et al. (2009)

stress that the welfare effects of standards and regulations are *a priori* unclear. Upon the basis of this recognition, Beghin et al. (2012: 360) propose a partial equilibrium cost–benefit framework to discern the trade and welfare effects of NTMs, domestically and internationally. Specifically, willingness-to-pay based on experimental consumer valuations is employed to account for the welfare loss of NTM removal. Upon that methodological basis, the same group of authors provides empirical welfare assessments for NTMs in food and agriculture (van Tongeren et al. 2010). However, the results derived severely hinge on data availability and are thus not conclusive.

In addition, certain regulations do not only promote welfare, but are directly conducive to international trade, e.g. labour and environmental standards under fair trade schemes. By applying the Trade Restrictiveness Index approach of Anderson and Neary (2005), Beghin et al. (2014) estimate that such trade-enhancing NTMs affect 12 per cent of HS 6-digit lines and that 39 per cent of these, i.e. 4.7 per cent of the lines, exhibit negative ad valorem equivalents, indicating a net trade-facilitating effect of these NTMs in the respective sectors. Unsurprisingly, such negative AVEs (ad-valorem equivalents) are observable for chemicals, pharmaceuticals and agri-foods. Similarly, Bratt (2014) estimates that about 46 per cent of the product lines affected by NTMs exhibit negative tariff equivalents (AVEs). Also Dean et al. (2009), using a price-based NTM quantification methodology, see partial positive correlations between NTM restrictiveness and country income, given that regulatory barriers can also reflect income sensitive demand for higher consumer protection for instance in food products. This casts considerable doubt on the predominant view that NTMs are exclusively trade impeding by nature. Strikingly, approaches to include these potential trade-facilitating effects of NTMs have not been included in the NTM estimations used in the standard impact assessments so far.

In contrast to the trade literature, cost–benefit analysis (CBA) has been employed widely in the economic assessment of public policy. In the US, for instance, federal legislative proposals are routinely assessed by way of CBA. The results of assessment exercises, such as those undertaken by US regulatory agencies would suggest that social benefits of regulations clearly outweigh their economic costs. A review of all economically significant US regulations over the period 2000–2012 conducted by the Office of Information and Regulatory Affairs (OIRA) has come to the conclusion that benefits outweighed costs in every year and did so by a factor of more than six on average over the whole period (OIRA 2010, cited in Myant and O'Brien 2014: 29).

This primarily owes to the fact that regulatory costs have been shown to be in general very small, even for ambitious projects such as the EU chemicals regulation REACH (Ackerman and Massey 2004), while the benefits of regulation for society are often very high, though difficult to express in purely monetary terms, or as Ackerman and Heinzerling (2004) have put it, they are in effect "priceless". But even if one subscribed to conventional CBA, the results of typical evaluation studies such as those undertaken by US regulatory agencies would suggest that social benefits of regulations clearly outweigh their economic costs.

It should thus be expected that a systematic consideration of the social benefits of regulation would substantially change the overall balance of any assessment of the costs and benefits of the removal or alignment of NTMs. In the best of cases, regulatory alignment in a trade agreement might lead to an improvement of regulatory standards. Since regulations are predominantly seen as a cost to business, in TTIP as well as most other trade agreements, I would, however, contend that risks for downward levelling of regulation should be expected to predominate. Given the high social benefits of regulation, even minor regulatory changes might dwarf the welfare gains of most new generation trade agreements or, even worse, shift the overall balance into the negative.

The methodological limits of mainstream approaches

In my discussion so far, I have laid open a fundamental flaw of the mainstream treatment of NTMs, namely that NTMs are typically seen as a cost item only. Though in the more recent literature it has been acknowledged that NTMs also infer benefits upon society, insofar as they correct for market failures, the analytical treatment has been focussed on CBA with the aim of estimating the monetary value of those benefits and costs. This raises some serious methodological and epistemological problems, to which I will now turn.

Neoclassical economics, of which CBA forms a part, is firmly rooted both in methodological individualism and utilitarianism. As such, basically every kind of regulation or administrative procedure is subjected to the kind of economic cost–benefit calculus outlined above. There is, for instance, no inherent limit in this approach to assess the economic costs and benefits of slave or child labour. Taking a less controversial example, from the neoclassical standpoint it is perfectly feasible to ask whether the fact that in most of Continental Europe annual paid leave amounts to 5–6 weeks, while in the US it is typically two weeks only, constitutes a cost and thus an impediment to international economic activity, aka a NTM. Similar points can be made about other labour standards, environmental regulations or tax policy. As a matter of fact, this approach has been extensively applied in key international policy documents, perhaps most notoriously in the *Doing Business Report* of the World Bank. For instance, the report has for many years categorized paid annual leave as follows: (i) excessively flexible (<15 days), (ii) balanced (15–21 days), (iii) semi-rigid (21–26 days), and (iv) excessively rigid (>26 days) (World Bank 2013). Thus, the implied policy recommendation is that a social optimum with regard to paid annual leave would lie somewhere in the order of 15–21 days. The problem here is not to concede that for workers in some countries this would constitute an improvement, or to criticize that this would weaken labour standards in some other countries. Instead, the crucial point is that mainstream economic theory implies that it is possible to express all the relevant dimensions of a phenomenon in monetary terms. Besides, an additional implication is that trade-offs can be handled by means of monetary compensation. In other words, it assumes the strong comparability or *commensurability* as well as the compensability of values (see Martinez-Alier et al. 1998). This is true regardless of whether CBA is applied to labour standards, environmental regulations, or health and safety regulations.

However, economic value expressed in monetary terms is just one of many dimensions of value that are typically present in a situation of social choice. Coming back to our example of paid annual leave, such other types of values could be the social value of devoting time to family life, the cultural value of engaging in cultural or religious activities in one's community, the political value of participating in some political activity, and so on. Thus, basing a decision on the duration of paid annual leave only on its cost to business would amount to methodological reductionism, since it leaves out other relevant dimensions. Of course, one could use willingness-to-pay to monetize the economic value workers attribute to an additional day of vacation and balance these with the cost to business. Would citizens accept such a CBA exercise as the exclusive basis for a political decision on the issue? I doubt it. Such decisions are strongly influenced by political interests, which in turn are shaped by collective systems of beliefs about what more recently has once again become discussed under the umbrella term of *the good life* (see Skidelsky and Skidelsky (2012) for an overview). CBA will thus potentially condense any kind of value dimensions into a monetary value, but this measure will not fully represent all the dimensions of social value inherent in typical collective choices.

If we accept this fundamental methodological point, two directions for applied research seem feasible. Either we concentrate on economic assessments by using CBA or similar methods, and leave it to the political process to bring in other social aspects that need to be contemplated as part of a collective decision process. Or we try to broaden our methodological approach so as to include these other dimensions of value more systematically.

The first option would constitute a step forward in comparison to the prevailing approach, insofar as it would imply a more "enlightened" form of methodological reductionism – of the sort "we economists know that we cannot grasp social phenomena in their full complexity by our standard methodology, but unfortunately we cannot do any better than that". A necessary complement of this approach would be, in my judgement, to explicitly call for a deliberative policy process where these other dimensions could be considered. Undoubtedly, from an episte-mological point of view, this approach is unsatisfactory, at least if the pretension of economic science is both to fully understand social reality and offer advice on rational economic policy-making. Besides, given the superior position of science as a source of legitimation in modern society, any standpoint that is substantiated by scientific knowledge enjoys an advantage over other standpoints in a public debate, thus biasing the *order of discourse* in the Foucaultian sense.

The second option would consist in finding an alternative methodological approach that would try to comparatively assess all value dimensions of a collective choice problem through some consistent procedure. This approach will have to be able to deal with the problems of incommensurability and of non-compensability of values. A method to use for that purpose is social multi-criteria evaluation (see, e.g., Munda 2008). Based on the concept of weak comparability of values it allows for making decisions even in the absence of a unitary standard of measurement (monetary or otherwise), i.e. in a context of plural values. Non-compensability refers to situations, in which certain values cannot be compensated, i.e. traded-off against some other value (Martinez-Alier et al. 1998). This is particularly pertinent where certain deeply held values have become enshrined as laws or human rights. Thus, for instance, the prohibition of slave or child labour must not be traded off by an FTA against some economic benefit. Multi-criteria evaluation allows for the operationalization of such situations of non-compensability. Alternatively, certain elements of social values might be considered superior to others, such that hierarchies of values might be defined. It might be feasible to define basic human rights, or in the ecological domain certain sorts of natural capital or eco-system services as critical and thus non-compensatory, while other social standards or ecological amenities are in principle considered compensatory.

Conclusions and policy recommendations

The relevance of the issue of social costs for the current trade policy debate should be self-evident. Indeed, more far-sighted trade policy-makers have recognized their importance already some time ago. For instance, former EU Trade Commissioner and WTO Director-General Pascal Lamy's (2004) proposal on "collective preferences" already addressed many of the issues I have taken up in this chapter. It argued that certain values societies hold are essentially incommensurable, i.e. cannot be traded off against some other trade benefit. Lamy wanted to spur a discussion on the scope of these collective preferences and their treatment in EU trade policy, since he expected these issues to become more important for trade governance in the future. Though it triggered some appreciative responses at the time (e.g. Charnovitz 2004), apparently interest in the discussion has subsequently abated.

Given the expansive nature of the current EU trade policy agenda with its emphasis on negotiating new generation FTAs, social costs will become a key issue of the trade policy discussion in the future. While the distribution of the benefits and costs of trade liberalization has never featured prominently in the debates of official policy circles, since the convenient though false assumption was that everybody will be better off by more trade, in the years to come this discussion will become both more important and complex: besides the traditional focus on the effects of trade liberalization on capital and labour, social costs will add a new dimension to this debate.

Thus *pro futuro*, official trade impact assessments like those of the European Commission will have to incorporate the manifold properties of NTMs both more systematically and by way of a more sophisticated methodological approach than at present. NTM is a catch-all phrase for a very diverse set of standards, regulations, laws and procedures. They range from very detailed technicalities to issues of major societal relevance. Conventional cost–benefit approaches have proved inapt to tackle the methodological challenges inherent in such exercises

(Ackermann 2008). Instead, they must be complemented by other approaches, for instance social multi-criteria analysis that are able to consistently deal with the problems of incommensurability, non-compensability and fundamental uncertainty, all of which are expected to appear in such an evaluation exercise. This is particularly pertinent for areas such as labour and social standards, environmental regulations and public health policies. With the scope of new generation FTAs increasingly becoming concerned with investment liberalisation, core areas of domestic regulation will become targeted under the label of behind-the-border measures.

With regulatory issues ranging among the top priorities of the current trade agenda, comprehensive as well as methodologically sound *ex-ante* regulatory impact assessments should thus become an integral part of future trade impact assessment exercises in the EU.

Notes

1 In contrast, behind-the-border barriers impose costs and constraints on economic activity in a non-discriminatory manner, regardless of the origin of the product.
2 Though one might argue that FDI increases the capital stock of a country and thus has a positive effect on growth, the definition of investment in the new generation trade agreements is much broader and also includes portfolio investment, i.e. investment into assets like securities, bonds and debentures of company, which are done for financial gain, usually have a short-term outlook and do not involve an active engagement with the management of the company. As recent experience has underlined, the speculative element usually involved in such transactions often leads to sudden inflows and outflows of capital and thus might exacerbate macroeconomic instabilities in the host country (see, e.g., Griffith-Jones et al. 2001).

References

Ackerman, F. (2008) *Poisoned for Pennies: The Economics of Toxics and Precaution*, Washington, DC: Island Press.

Ackerman, F. and Heinzerling, L. (2004) *Priceless: On Knowing the Price of Everything and the Value of Nothing*, New York: The New Press.

Ackerman, F. and Massey, D. (2004) The True Costs of REACH, A Study Performed for the Nordic Council of Ministers, TemaNord 2004: 557, Copenhagen, available from: www.ase.tufts.edu/gdae/Pubs/rp/TrueCostsREACH.pdf (26/08/2014).

Anderson, J.E. and Neary, P. (2005) *Measuring the Restrictiveness of Trade Policy*, Boston: MIT Press.

Anderson, J.E. and van Wincoop, E. (2004) "Trade Costs", *Journal of Economic Literature*, 42(3), 691–751.

Beghin, J., Disdier, A.-C. and Marette, S. (2014) "Trade Restrictiveness Indices in Presence of Externalities: An Application to Non-Tariff Measures", CESIFO Working Paper No. 4968, September 2014, Download at: https://ideas.repec.org/p/ces/ceswps/_4968. html (10/06/15).

Beghin, J., Disdier, A.-C., Marette, S. and van Tongeren, F. (2012) "Welfare Costs and Benefits of Non-Tariff Measures in Trade: A Conceptual Framework and Application", *World Trade Review*, 11(3), 356–375.

Berden, K., Francois, J., Thelle, M., Wymenga, P. and Tamminen, S. (2009) "Non-Tariff Measures in EU–US Trade and Investment – An Economic Analysis", in ECORYS, Study for the European Commission, Directorate-General for Trade, available from: http://trade.ec.europa.eu/doclib/docs/2009/december/tradoc_145613.pdf (24.03.2014).

Bratt, M. (2014) "Estimating the Bilateral Impact of Non-Tariff Measures (NTMs)", Working Paper WPS 14-01-1, University of Geneva.

Charnovitz, S. (2004) "An Analysis of Pascal Lamy's Proposal on Collective Preferences, GW Law Faculty Publications & Other Works", Paper 406, http://scholarship.law.gwu.edu/faculty_publications/406 (12/06/2015).

Dean, J.M., Signoret, J., Feinberg, R.M., Ludema, R.D. and Ferrantino, M.J. (2009) "Estimating the Price Effects of Non-Tariff Barriers", *The B.E. Journal of Economic Analysis & Policy*, 9(1), Art. 12.

EuroMemo Group (2014) "EuroMemorandum 2014", available from: www2.euro memorandum.eu/uploads/euromemorandum_2014.pdf (24.03.2014).

European Commission (2013a) "Impact Assessment Report on the Future of EU–US Trade Relations", Staff Working Document, SWD(2013) 68 final, Strasbourg, available from: http://trade.ec.europa.eu/doclib/docs/2013/march/tradoc_150759.pdf (26.03.2014).

European Commission (2013b) "Transatlantic Trade and Investment Partnership: The Economic Analysis Explained", available from: http://trade.ec.europa.eu/doclib/docs/2013/september/tradoc_151787.pdf (24.03.2014).

Felbermayr, G.J., Heid, B. and Lehwald, S. (2013) "Transatlantic Trade and Investment Partnership (TTIP): Who Benefits from a Free Trade Deal? Part 1: Macroeconomic Effects", in Bertelsmann Foundation, available from: www.bfna.org/sites/default/files/TTIP-GED%20study%2017June%202013.pdf (24.03.2014).

Felbermayr, G.J., Larch, M., Flach, L., Yalcin, E. and Benz, S. (2013) "Dimensionen und Auswirkungen eines Freihandelsabkommens zwischen der EU und den USA", in IFO Institute, report commissioned by the (former) German Federal Ministry for Economic Affairs and Technology.

Fontagne, L., Gourdon, J. and Jean, S. (2013) "Transatlantic Trade: Whither Partnership, which Economic Consequences?", CEPII, Policy Brief, 1, September.

Fontagné, L., Guillin, A. and Mitaritonna, C. (2011) "Estimations of Tariff Equivalents for the Services Sectors", CEPII, Working Paper 2011–24.

Francois, J., Jansen, M. and Peters, R. (2011) "Trade Adjustment Costs and Assistance: The Labour Market Dynamics", in M. Jansen, R. Peters and J.M. Salazar-Xirinachs (eds) *Trade and Employment: From Myths to Facts*, Geneva, pp. 213–52.

Francois, J., Manchin, M., Norberg, H., Pindyuk, O. and Tomberger, P. (2013) Reducing Transatlantic Barriers to Trade and Investment – An Economic Assessment, Final Project Report, Centre for Economic Policy Research, London.

GHK (2011) Mid-term evaluation of the European Globalisation Adjustment Fund: final report, submitted by GHK to DG EMPL, European Commission, Specific Service Order No. VC/2011/0207, 8 December.

Griffith-Jones, S., Montes, M.F. and Nasution, A. (eds) (2001) *Short-Term Capital Flows and Economic Crises*, Oxford: Oxford University Press.

Grumiller, J. (2014) "Ex-Ante Versus Ex-Post Assessments of the Economic Benefits of Free Trade Agreements: lessons from the North American Free Trade Agreement (NAFTA)", ÖFSE Working Paper No. 10, Vienna, available from: www.oefse.at/

publikationen/policy-notes/detail-policy-note/publication/show/Publication/ASSESS-TTIP-Assessing-the-Claimed-Benefits-of-the-Transatlantic-Trade-and-Investment-Partnership/ (01.02.2014).

Heid, B. and Larch, M. (2013) "International Trade and Unemployment: A Quantitative Framework", CESifo, Working Paper 4013.

Kalinova, B., Palerm, A. and Thomsen, S. (2010) "OECD"s FDI Restrictiveness Index: 2010 Update", OECD Working Papers on International Investment, 2010/03, Paris, available from: http://dx.doi.org/10.1787/5km91p02zj7g-en (24.03.2014).

Kapp, K.W. (1950) *Social Costs of Private Enterprise*, Cambridge, MA: Harvard University Press.

Laird, S. and de Córdoba, S.F. (2006) *Coping with Trade Reforms: A Development Country Perspective on the WTO Industrial Tariff Negotiations*, Basingstoke: Palgrave Macmillan.

Lamy, P. (2004) "The Emergence of Collective Preferences in International Trade: Implications for Regulating Globalisation", 15 September, www.google.at/url?sa=t& rct=j&q=&esrc=s&source=web&cd=1&cad=rja&uact=8&ved=0CCUQFjAAah UKEwiLl_KBporGAhXKWBQKHbH5ACI&url=http%3A%2F%2Ftrade.ec.europa. eu%2Fdoclib%2Fhtml%2F118929.htm&ei=ZON6VYvVH8qxUbHzg5AC&usg=AFQj CNEks3i3-XzOJAwWJzB-t1jQP10evA&bvm=bv.95515949,d.d24 (12.06.2015).

Lawrence, R. (1996) *Regionalisms, Multilateralism and Deeper Integration*, Washington, DC: The Brookings Foundation.

Martinez-Alier, J., Munda, G. and O'Neill, J. (1998) "Weak Comparability of Values as a Foundation for Ecological Economics", *Ecological Economics*, 26, 277–286.

Munda, G. (2008) *Social Multi-Criteria Evaluation for a Sustainable Economy*, Heidelberg: Springer.

Myant, M. and O'Brien R. (2014) "The TTIP"s Impact: Bringing in the Missing Issue", Working Paper 2015.1, Brussels: European Trade Union Institute.

Nölke, A. and Claar, S. (2012) "Tiefe Integration: konzeptuelle Grundlagen", *Journal für Entwicklungspolitik*, XXVIII(2), 8–27.

OECD (2005) *Employment Outlook 2005*, Paris: OECD.

Raza, W., Grumiller, J., Taylor, L., von Arnim, R. and Tröster, B. (2014) "ASSESS_TTIP: Assessing the Claimed Benefits of the Transatlantic Trade and Investment Partnership", Final Report, Vienna, March. http://guengl.eu/uploads/plenary-focus-pdf/ASSESS_TTIP. pdf

Rodrik, D. (2007) "How to Save Globalization from Its Cheerleaders", *The Journal of International Trade and Diplomacy*, Fall, 1(2), 1–33.

Schlueter, S., Rau, M.-L., Wieck, C., Humphrey, J., Colen, L. and Heckelei, T. (2009) "Analytical Framework for NTM-Impact Project", Working Paper 09/02, Projekt FP7NTM-IMPACT, December, download at: www.ntm-impact.eu (07/05/15).

Skidelsky, R. and Skidelsky, E. (2012) *How Much Is Enough? Money and the Good Life*, New York: Other Press.

Stiglitz, J. (2005) "Development Policies in a World of Globalization", in K. Gallagher (ed.) *Putting Development First: The Importance of Policy Space in the WTO and the International Financial Institutions*, London: Zed Books, pp. 15–32.

UNCTAD (2013) *World Investment Report 2013. Global Value Chains: Investment and Trade for Development*, Geneva: United Nations.

van Tongeren, F., Disdier, A.C., Komorovska, J., Marette, S., von Lampe, M. (2010) "Case Studies of Costs and Benefits of Non-Tariff Measures: Cheese, Shrimp and

Flowers", OECD Food, Agriculture and Fisheries Working Papers, No. 28, Paris: OECD Publishing.

Wade, R.H. (2005) "What Strategies are Viable for Developing Countries today? The World Trade Organization and the Shrinking of 'Development Space'", in K. Gallagher (ed.) *Putting Development First: The Importance of Policy Space in the WTO and the International Financial Institutions*, London: Zed Books, pp. 80–101.

World Bank (2013) *Doing Business Report 2014 – Understanding Regulations for Small and Medium-Size Enterprises*, Washington, DC: World Bank.

5 Inequity and unsustainability

The role of financialized masculinity[1]

Julie A. Nelson

Introduction

Our current global economy is characterized by excessive inequality—by vast inequalities in incomes, wealth, and access to resources and opportunities. It is also characterized by unsustainability. This is evident not only in the processes of climate change and environmental degradation, but also in a debasing of the social norms and institutions underlying successful commerce. Together, these are progressively undermining the physical and social foundations of human survival and flourishing. And I would argue that besides inequality and unsustainability, our economies—and our thinking about economies—are also being increasingly overwhelmed by financialization. That is, we have seen a sharp rise in the excessive or exclusive emphasis on financial outcomes, financial motivations, or financial institutions when thinking about economic issues. How can these problems be addressed?

Unless we *care* about these issues—that is, *care* about the poor, and about the environment, and about the quality of life—it is certain that nothing good will happen. But we need to be thoughtful about how we go about encouraging increased engagement. At a recent conference, I witnessed the presentation of a project aiming to interject notions of "care" into economics. The image used to illustrate "care" on the PowerPoint slides was of a white, middle-class mother and smiling baby. In terms of cultural stereotypes, this image is not surprising. Care, concern, nurturing, and attending to the feeding and care needs of daily life has long been stereotypically assigned to a feminine sphere. Yet when we think about the economy and economics, very different images come to mind. Common images used to illustrate "economics" are piles of currency, stock market graphs, or men in business meetings. Or we might think of an economist (the first to come to mind will likely be male) presenting a mathematical model, in a neutral and detached sort of way. If those are our mental images of "care" and "economy," let me suggest that melding them to create an image of a "caring economy" seems extremely unlikely.

We need to go deeper, and uncover the roots of the common belief that the economic sphere—culturally considered a masculine and monetized domain—is by its nature mechanical and radically incompatible with our deeper values and concerns. The chapter begins by describing this damaging hoax, tracing its historical and gendered dimensions, and describing its impact on both neoclassical and "radical" economic thinking. Rethinking the relationship between economics and care has implications for the economics discipline's ontological, epistemological, and behavioral assumptions, and for how we think about ways to achieve goals of prosperity, social justice, and environmental protection.

The hoax

There is a common conception that the "economic" sphere is technical, amoral, largely quantifiable, and mechanical, and exists independently of our more human and ethical concerns. Such a conceptualization is reflected in the widespread acceptance of the idea that there are certain "economic laws" driving economic processes. From a neoclassical point of view, for example, these may be "competitive market forces" or "profit-maximization by firms." A more Marxist commentator might point to "capital accumulation." Action on the basis of individual self-interest is often said to be the driving force of capitalism. The fact that much economic activity can be measured in units of currency appears to lend support to the idea that there exists a quantifiable, purely financial, dimension of life that is far removed from issues of meaning, ethics, and sociality.

The idea that economic life is separate from the rest of life is nothing more than a hoax that has been perpetuated by the economics discipline, which—as I will shortly discuss—adopted it as a way to satisfy pretentions to being considered a "hard science." This hoax has had many negative consequences, including:

*   A growing acceptance of the idea that selfish behavior is not only permissible, but even required, in capitalist commercial dealings—with a concomitant decline in actions arising from normal pro-social motivations such as responsibility and care.
*   Deference to a priesthood of economists, who, sheltered by the mathematical complexity of our models, are said to understand the economy in ways not possible for normal folk (including other social scientists, lawmakers, and regulators). Even the 2008 financial crisis failed to dislodge mainstream economics from its position of power.
*   A growing acceptance of an identification of business "success" with purely financial success, with corresponding neglect of all the social and environmental aspects of enterprise behavior.
*   Definitions and models of "economic development" and "economic welfare" that (with a few notable exceptions, such as in the work of Amartya Sen) are morally, socially, and ecologically short-sighted.

But the problems do not all stem from economists. The wide cultural success of this hoax has led to further problems, including:

*   *Critiques* of economistic or neoliberal approaches that work *within* the conventional economy/society dualism, and so—based on the assumption

that current systems actually are as economists describe them—fail to recognize many creative, helpful, and potentially attainable modifications and alternatives.

• *Critiques* of economistic or neoliberal approaches that, while not buying into the model of "economic man," still rely on his brother, "liberal man"—a creature for whom ethics is predominantly a matter of disembodied, universal rational principles.

My work has largely been in feminist economics. As an economist, I was trained in conventional, largely neoclassical but also policy-oriented economics. As a feminist, I entered the field detecting major biases and lacunae that seemed invisible to the vast majority of my colleagues. In the next two sections, I will describe how the hoax—that is, the belief that economies somehow exist apart from normal human and social life—came about, and at least one reason why it maintains cultural hegemony. Then I will return to the issue of the specific damages caused by the hoax, particularly (to avoid preaching to the choir) amongst critics of mainstream economic approaches.

The origin of the hoax

Mainstream economics is centered around neoclassical orthodoxy, in which a number of assumptions are considered too self-evident to be ever questioned. Three important assumptions are:

1   An ontological assumption: Economic life is fundamentally mechanical.
2   An epistemological assumption: The use of mathematical models (borrowed from mechanical physics), along with an avoidance of any discussion of values, endows economists' work with objectivity.
3   A behavioral assumption: People are self-interested and rational in their economic dealings.

An outsider might assume that the assumptions about mechanism, rationality, and self-interest came from economists' careful empirical study of actual economic phenomena. This demonstrates a misguided trust in economists, however, since the history of the development of these assumptions is quite otherwise.

Historical antecedents

John Stuart Mill's 1836 essay "On the Definition of Political Economy" was an historical milestone in the creation of the hoax. In this essay, Mill attempted to carefully distinguish economics from the physical sciences and technology, from ethics, and from a more general study of social behavior.[2] Political economy is distinguished from physical science, he wrote, because it is about "phenomena of *mind*" (Mill 1836, 12, 29, emphasis in original) rather than about physical laws. Among the mental sciences, it is further distinguished by the particular "part of man's [*sic*] nature" (36) with which it deals. Conscience, duty, and other feelings relevant to a person's dealings with other individuals were consigned by Mill to the realm of ethics (34). Principles of human nature that have to do with life in society were consigned by Mill to the realm of "speculative politics" (35). With issues concerning physical bodies, ethics, and social interactions split off and assigned to other disciplines, political economy would deal with what was left. It should, Mill wrote, deal with "man [*sic*] . . . solely as a being who desires to possess wealth, and who is capable of judging of the comparative efficacy of means for obtaining that end" (38). Voila! Here emerges rational, autonomous, self-interested "economic man."

Why did Mill believe that he had to separate out a very thin slice of human nature for analysis by each of the various fields? He believed that this was required by the nature of *science*. Significantly, his model for science was geometry. Political economy, Mill thought, could only proceed as a "pure" and "abstract" science, resulting in general truths and timeless laws, if it posited a minimal set of starting principles. Political economy and geometry, he claimed, both "must necessarily reason . . . from assumptions, not from facts" (1844/1874, 46). Political economy presupposes "an arbitrary definition of man" for the same reason that "[g]eometry presupposes an arbitrary definition of a line, 'that which has length but not breadth'" (46). That is, Mill's fundamental assumption of material self-interest was not derived from observation, but from the presumed requirements of scientific methodology. That is, the illusion of objectivity and the assumption of self-interest—and came not from a broad evaluation of evidence, but from Mill's conscious intention to align economics with geometry and clearly distinguish it from everything social and ethical.

Mill, to his credit, in principle left his premises open (64). He argued that no political economist would ever be "so absurd as to suppose that mankind" is really described by only the parts of human nature selected for study in political economy (38). He explicitly presented his assumptions of self-interest and rationality as arbitrary and partial, chosen not for comprehensiveness but for the goal of creating conclusions by logical deduction. In any application, he said, political economy would need to be complemented by the insights of other sciences that had focused on other parts of human nature and other circumstances (58), and also by practical knowledge of specific experiences (68).

Unfortunately, however, what remained and flourished in later economic thought was not Mill's modesty concerning the *ad hoc* premises and limited applicability of the geometry-like discipline he proposed, but rather his idea that political economy must become an axiomatic-deductive and mathematical enterprise in order to be "scientific." This approach received a big boost in the late nineteenth century when neoclassical economists (including Edgeworth, Jevons, Walras, and Pareto) found that they could formalize Mill's idea of the "desire for the greatest amount" of wealth in terms of maximization of mathematical profit and utility functions. Alfred Marshall's systematization of the neoclassical approach was instrumental in its wider acceptance. In the 1930s, economist Lionel Robbins (1935) offered his precedent-setting definition of economics as the science of *choice-making* in the face of unlimited wants and scarce resources. Through such an historical process, the original broader meaning of economics in terms of processes of household management, wealth creation, and distribution increasingly faded, to be replaced by the currently dominant, narrower emphasis that approaches policy design from the direction of the formal modeling of choice and abstract market exchange.

An explanation of persistence

There still remains the question of *how* such a way of thinking—which vastly narrows the scope of economics, its toolbox, and its potential for productive engagement with problems of real human interest—gained such a near stranglehold on economics. Feminist theorists and others who have studied the role played by gender in the rise of modern science offer one explanation for which there is considerable historical and psychological evidence (Harding 1986; Keller 1985).

The term "gender" does not refer to biological sex, but to the social constructions that cultures make on the base of sexual dimorphism. Of particular interest for our purposes is what we might call *cognitive gender*, or the way that our Western minds tend to organize a variety of disparate concepts on the basis of the dualism "male/female." Most people in Euro-American cultures will, for example, think of dogs as somehow masculine and cats as somehow feminine (even though of course both species come in both sexes). Recent psychological research (Wilkie and Bodenhausen 2012) has confirmed that many modern people, like the ancient Pythagoreans (Lloyd 1993, 3), tend to associate odd numbers with masculinity and even numbers with femininity. Psychological research shows that cognitive gender schemas are important ways in which we "organize incoming information and integrate it—through no conscious act of will—into clusters" (Most et al. 2007, 288) and that these gender associations pervade perceptions about academic fields (Whitehead 1996).

Very often this dualistic metaphorical structure is also hierarchical. The term "virile," for example, refers to a masculine trait with a positive connotation, while the term "effeminate" carries negative valence. Masculinity is traditionally associated with strength, and femininity with weakness. When John Stuart Mill set up geometry as the model for economics, he drew on the Cartesian tradition in the philosophy of knowledge. According to Descartes, the cosmos is split into a *res cogitans* (a thinking something which has no spatial extension) and a *res extensa* (a spatial something which has no psychic qualities). The mind is considered to be the active, valuable part with which "rational man" identifies, reigning over the passivity of matter and the body. In characterizing "rational man" by traits of mind, activity, rationality, detachment, and a search for generalities, all the human characteristics not included in this picture were split off—and projected onto women. James Hillman has written, "The specific consciousness we call scientific, Western and modern is the long sharpened tool of the masculine mind that has discarded parts of its own substance, calling it 'Eve,' 'female' and 'inferior'" (quoted in Bordo 1986, 441). The counterpoint to "rational man," Elizabeth Fee has pointed out, is "woman [who] provides his connection with nature; she is the mediating force between man and nature, a reminder of his childhood, a reminder of the body, and a reminder of sexuality, passion, and human connectedness" (Fee 1983, 12).

Of course, if we examine the key assumptions and methodology of orthodox neoclassical economics, we find that it has been systematically defined by an elevation of stereotypically "masculine" ideals of detachment, "hard" and provable knowledge, and mathematical abstraction, and a neglect or denigration of "feminine" associations of connection, ethics, uncertainty, and concrete, grounded understandings (McCloskey 1985; Nelson 1992; Jennings 1993; Nelson 1996). To include more of the latter would, given dominant cultural understandings of gender and value, be felt as equivalent to accepting "emasculation." The hoax is supported by the fear of being called a sissy.

My point is not to reify these gender dualisms or attributions of value, but rather to bring them out from an unconscious level into the light of awareness where they can be examined. I do not wish in any way to endorse the idea that women are "by nature" more emotional, intuitive, or connected—or, à la Larry Summers' comments (Bombardieri 2005), less able in mathematics and science. Rather, the point is that these dualisms reflect a cognitive habit that deeply permeates our Western and modern way of thinking. In pointing out how cognitive habits reinforce the aspirations of economists to false "scientificity," I also do not mean to overlook the fact that such an abstract, ostensibly objective and neutral discipline of economics clearly supports some special interests. By sidetracking a discipline that might otherwise concern itself with phenomena such as concentrations of power, injustice, and exploitation into less status-quo-challenging pursuits, the hoax is of use to those who want to hold onto wealth and power.

The result is a splitting of reality in half: aspects of human existence associated with embodiment, with sociality, with moral judgment and with any kind of connection or interdependence are—a priori, and with not even a pretense to confirmation by empirical observation—shunted aside by economics. This is, of course, a radically reality-denying move, by a field that at the same time aspires to be objectively reality-describing; and a heavily normative move—valuing, for example precision of analysis over richness of analysis, and rationality over emotion—by a field that denies any normative leanings.[3] The notion that objectivity is somehow guaranteed by a position of abstraction and detachment has been challenged by numerous philosophers of science (e.g., Keller 1985; Longino 1990; Sen 1992; Kitcher 2011). A much more sensible notion of objectivity defines reliable knowledge as that which passes the test of evaluation by larger communities.

The damages done

Many readers are already deeply familiar with the damages that the conventional economistic, disembedded, highly biased approach has caused in areas of development and environmental policy, as well as other applications. But the widespread cultural acceptance of the fundamental assumptions of this approach—namely, that economic processes are mechanical and asocial, and that persons and businesses operating in the commercial realm must always act out of rational self-interest—means that the approach has also, in often unnoticed and unquestioned ways, permeated the thinking of many of its critics. Let me give two examples.

Financial structures

The influence of the hoax is highly evident, for example, in Jürgen Habermas's influential distinction between what he calls the "lifeworld" arena of communicative action and the "system" arena driven by unconscious, objectifying forces (Habermas 1981). The lifeworld, Habermas claims, is the area of truly social public and private life, and the arena of norms, aesthetics, and conscious and deliberative action. Systems, on the other hand—in which Habermas includes both economies and state bureaucracies—are "steered by" the nonhuman media of money or power (Habermas 1981, 164). Within the latter, people are dehumanized—"stripped of personality structures and neutralized into bearers of certain performances" (308).

Recently, there has been much discussion about the "the financialization of the economy" (Epstein 2006; Denning 2014). But notice how the image of the "personality-stripped" robotic profit-maximizer, or equally robotic industrial worker—stereotypically, images of *men*—conveys a notion of financialized *masculinity*.

A key element in Habermas's theory is a belief that money is a neutral, asocial medium. But let us examine this belief. Habermas claims that because money is backed up by "gold or means of enforcement" (1981, 270), it therefore does not require social, communicative agreements or legitimation (272). In fact, however, there hasn't been an international gold standard since the early 1930s, and money has long been a quintessential social construction: It has value precisely and only because (or when) people believe it has value. Those close to the actual management of national or regional monetary systems are, in fact, deeply concerned with issues of beliefs, expectations, credibility, reputation, legitimacy, and the problems of collective decision-making (King 2004). As with money, so too with other financial assets: During the financial crisis of 2008, trillions of dollars' worth of assets suddenly evaporated, simply because of a change in the socially influenced beliefs of people as to whether or not the various collateralized debt obligations or credit default swaps had value. As to the economistic assumption that people are stripped of from their human values and emotions when enacting their economic "performances" . . . consider again the incidents leading up to the financial crisis, or the emotions that accompanied going over the brink.[4] Money and markets are thoroughly human and social creations.

Beware, then of strategies that suggest that a separation of "purely economic" or "technical" issues such as national financial structures or international economic agreements from "social" concerns of human development. They are intimately linked. Naomi Klein (2007, Chap. 10), for example, documents how just such a separation of "technical issues" concerned with central banking and trade agreements from other political struggles occurred during the transition of power to the African National Congress in South Africa. As a result, the ANC was left with its hands tied in regard to jobs, land redistribution, and the rest of its more obviously "social" program. And the sort of knowledge required to begin participating such discussions is not—as some in the self-appointed economic priesthood may argue—an understanding of graduate-level mathematics and the latest in ultra-sophisticated modeling techniques. There is often much less content to economic models than outsiders are led to believe. Rather, the most important requirements are a good knowledge of history, a familiarity with institutions and current events, and a willingness to persistently engage with empirical evidence and with issues generally portrayed as unsexy, boring, and "too complicated."

Business and government

Another example of criticism that puts far too much faith in conventional economic thinking are claims, such as these by Gar Alperovitz, that "the logic and dynamics" of the capitalist system, with its "profit-maximizing imperatives" makes it impossible for business executives to consider the social good in their decision-making (Alperovitz 1995, 3). While such claims are so common that they may seem entirely unobjectionable, they in fact are rooted precisely in the economistic hoax. They are examples, again, of a narrowly financialized masculinity.

The belief that firms must always sacrifice social responsibilities in favor of profits does not originate in the study of actual, historical business practices; nor is it based in law; nor can it be said to be generally forced on businesses by competitive markets (given that competition is not the only, or even necessarily the strongest, force acting on businesses) (Nelson 2006; Bratton 2011; Nelson 2011b; Stout 2012). It instead originates from the mechanical metaphor used in neoclassical economics, and, even more precisely, from ideologues of the far-right University of Chicago school of economics (Nelson 2011b). Businesses are, in fact, social organizations within which people have to cooperate, have to get along, and to which people bring their whole complex bundle of values and aspirations—for good or ill. Serious scholars are increasingly noticing that a regard for ethics is absolutely required for economic functioning (even though the teaching of economics may simultaneous serve to undercut it) (e.g., Stout 2011).

Yet the belief in single-minded profit maximization has become so culturally pervasive that it is turning into a self-fulfilling prophecy. The more we teach that the role of business is to profit-maximize at all costs, the more we allow "the system made me do it" as an excuse for all sorts of unethical corporate social (yes, "social" *includes* "economic") behavior. And the more we may neglect thinking creatively about possible positive roles that businesses could play in economic life.

Such an unwarranted cynicism about business is often also paired with an equally unwarranted faith in the beneficence of governments, non-governmental organizations, and nonprofits. Partha Dasgupta, for example, in his writings about economic development, sets out a hard-and-fast dichotomy between the market sphere, in which he claims that self-interest is appropriate and "we should not worry about others," and the public sphere, in which concern for others is appropriate (2005, 247; 2007, 151). One need not be a public choice theorist to wonder if the public and non-profit spheres are capable of bearing the full ethical burden on their own. They are human and social organizations, too—with all the fallibility that implies.

The problem of "liberal man"

So, let us assume that we agree we need to include consideration of ethics in discussions of economics, at least, whether or not I have convinced you that they are also part of economics "proper." What, then, do we mean by ethics? While most philosophers do not adopt the model of rational, autonomous, self-interested, hedonically-drive "economic man," those influenced by Enlightenment thought still tend to base their theories on what we might call "liberal man." "Liberal man" is an autonomous, rational thinker, who uses principles of reason to determine the proper rules for living among his peers. This image is, however, also part of a larger hoax, and limits the creativity of our responses to economic crises.

Neuroscience

Contemporary cognitive neuroscience suggests that focusing on principles, rules, and reasons may be a fundamentally misleading way of approaching questions of moral judgment and moral action. Emotion and socialization play a much larger role than we have commonly believed. In studies using brain imaging, observation of people with specific brain damage, and other techniques, psychologists have found that moral judgment is—initially at least, and often entirely—more a matter of affective moral response than of moral reasoning (Greene et al. 2001; Haidt 2001; Greene and Haidt 2002). Moral reasoning, rather than being part of the process of coming to a judgment, is more often—as a practical and empirical matter—involved in possible *post hoc* justifications of a judgment already arrived at intuitively. That is, we often sense the "rightness" or "wrongness" of something, and then may work to come up with reasons for what we feel. This is not to say that introspective moral reasoning plays *no* role—people may in some circumstances consciously reflect on their intuitive judgments, and then change their mind. In practice, however, this seems to occur relatively rarely.

For questions of positive moral *action*—as opposed to moral judgment—emotional responses such as empathy, sadness, and shame seem to be particularly important, while the role of moral reasoning is particularly weak. Emotion is a motivator: One can be an expert on the many ways of formulating principles of justice, but if one does not *care* about acting justly, all the principles in the world will have no effect on behavior (Warren 2000; Haidt 2001, 112).

The fear, of course, on the part of those who are loyal to a purely rationalist view of ethics is that once one lets emotions in, "anything goes," and universal agreement on principles is lost. But this is a misconception, for two main reasons.

First, the idea that reason-based arguments can be relied on to create unassailable moral decisions is itself misleading: Even when principles can be clearly stated, it is often the case that more than one principle can apply to a particular matter. Reasonable people often, then, in good faith, disagree about the relative importance of different ethical principles. Second, the emotional aspects of moral judgments are not merely whims experienced, subjectively and randomly, by individuals. Rather, they tend to be formed out of the experience and knowledge of larger cultures.

Cultural variation

Jonathan Haidt (2001, 817), for example, defines moral judgments as "evaluations (good vs. bad) of the actions or character of a person that are made with respect to a set of virtues held to be obligatory by a culture or subculture." Gerd Gigerenzer suggests that moral intuitions are a sort of unconscious "moral grammar," built up within particular social environments and having emotional goals, and taking the form of gut feelings or rules of thumb (2007, 185). In various cultures, some moral intuitions will be nurtured more than others, and some principles will be considered more acceptable and binding than others. Individualistic principles, such as those embodied in "liberal man" and concerned with individual goals, reciprocity, and non-harming form only one of three clusters of moral intuitions that researchers have identified cross-culturally. The second cluster revolves around community, loyalty, in-groups, hierarchy, and wise leadership. The third emphasizes divinity and purity (Haidt 2006, 188; Gigerenzer 2007, 187). Unlike individual goals that can be traded off, issues related to community and purity are usually perceived of as in some way non-negotiable and absolute—or, as put by Gigerenzer, "not up for sale" (2007, 206).

The shaping of norms

Furthermore, investigation into the culture-specific aspects of moral judgments gives some insight about how they are shaped. "[C]ultural knowledge is a complex web of explicit and implicit, sensory and propositional, affective, cognitive, and motoric knowledge," writes Haidt (2001). Consider, for example, why soldiers practice marching in formation for hours, often chanting at the same time. I had always assumed this was merely a matter of practicing moving efficiently from Point A to Point B until my attention was drawn to "motoric" knowledge and the bodily enculturation of moral values by this literature. Drawing on work by neuroscientist Andrew Newbury, Haidt points out that repetitive motor activities and chanting have been used throughout history to create "resonance patterns" among people and that lead to feelings of group harmony and cohesion (2006, 237). Similarly, behavioral scientists, including economists, have found that the creation of apparently substantively meaningless group identifications among experiment subjects (e.g., assignment to a "team" that never works together) can create in-group feelings.

Besides highlighting the cross-cultural variability and social and embodied roots of ethical norms, recent research has also highlighted the importance of framing effects in eliciting ethical (or unethical) behavior. Framing a decision as being merely "business" or "legal" or otherwise "technical" tends to draw our attention away from its moral aspects (Bazerman and Tenbrunsel 2011). There is even preliminary evidence that putting people in an analytical rather than feeling frame of mind—for example, having people do calculations in advance of being asked to make a choice—can lead to a fading of ethical concerns and ethical emotions such as guilt (Zhong 2011). Of course, if this research is correct, this makes the economistic hoax even more powerful: To the extent people associate economics with calculation, the somatic indicators we generally rely on to alert ourselves to ethical concerns may become even more suppressed.

Relations of asymmetric mutuality

Another problem with the liberal man image that is particularly relevant to justice issues is the way it highlights relationships among autonomous peers who can engage in reciprocal behaviors, while neglecting to give any guidance about relationships characterized by significant and continuing differences in wealth, power, knowledge, leadership ability, or specialized responsibilities, in which autonomy is compromised and reciprocity is not possible. Within the "liberal man" view, hierarchy is generally considered to be oppressive, with egalitarianism (in at least some dimensions), democracy, and participation the goal. That is, among peers, reciprocity should reign.

But if this is our only view of morality and justice, then we are left unable to deal with the real, distinct, and sometimes unavoidable differences that characterize actual human societies. Liberal man is clearly not a five-year-old child. Nor, traditionally, was the child's female caregiver considered part of the society of liberal men. Teacher/student, doctor/patient, current generation/future generation, and boss/worker are all relationships in which there is a fundamental imbalance of power, but in which we may yet hope that dimensions of care, helpfulness, and mutual respect may prevail. An analysis of moral judgment arising from norms of connection, as highlighted by feminist work on the existence of an "ethics of care" alongside an "ethics of justice" (Nelson 2011a) may be more helpful in examining the relevant ethics for economic life than an analysis based on a false imagined equality of position.

One image of asymmetric, yet caring, economic activity that might be helpful is that of "diligent husbandry" (Nelson 2016). Grounded in agrarian and pastoral practice, "husbandry" refers to careful cultivation, tending, and management. Think of a yeoman farmer who carefully nurtured the growth of his crops, or the nomads herding and tending their cattle. Picture this "husbandman" knowing intimately the challenges of drought and flood, the lore concerning breeding and protection, and the shape of the landscape. The "husbandman" both works hard to bring forth the necessities of life for the family and community to which he belongs, and respects the natural forces at play and the non-human beings in his care. Now imagine that attitude transferred to the workplace, and to the executive suite, and to the CEO. This rich iconic image of attentiveness in productive activities is in stark contrast to the stripped-down images of homo economicus and the "incentivized" CEO—images that have arisen from the deleterious financialization of masculinity.

While both men and women can "husband" businesses, the somewhat masculine cultural association of this "husbandman" image has its positive aspects. Our cultures already associate—and often over-associate—women with care. What we have been missing is a strong image of masculine care. The "husbandman" holding a sheep in his arms is a much more cogent and accessible image of "economics and care" than is a mash-up of images of babies and the stock market.

Conclusion

Is there a purely mechanical and technical "economic" side to questions of prosperity, justice, and sustainability? This essay has argued that the answer is "no": Economic life has always been thoroughly human, social, and ethically significant, even if the economics profession has over the last century-plus tried to convince us otherwise. I have attempted to outline the dangers implicit in confusing the images of "financialized man," of neoclassical "economic man"—or even of philosophical "liberal man"—with actual socially embedded and embodied human beings.

Instead of believing that economies are mechanical, we need to recognize that they are part and parcel of society. My preferred definition of economics is "The study of the ways societies organize themselves to provide for the survival and flourishing of life," though it should also be added, "or fail to do so." Instead of relying on math, we need to recognize that openness to critique from wider communities is the hallmark of scientific objectivity. Instead of assuming self-interest, we need to recognize the complexity of human motivations, and the essential role of care in economic life.

The implications of this are quite challenging. Dropping the hoax brings down the disciplinary walls among economics, development, ethics, psychology, sociology and the like. We need more people who will seriously engage with specific, complicated economic issues of real-world importance, using whatever tools of study and action are most helpful. This means going beyond the much easier (and therefore popular) paths of consigning difficult economic analysis to someone else's bailiwick, or understanding economies in terms of stale theories about economic "laws," or perhaps cultivating a position as a morally superior critic of a presumably ethically bereft capitalism. It means thinking seriously about the moral possibilities as well as the moral failings of all different types of social organizations, including businesses, governments, and NGOs, and about the ethical dimensions of relationships that inherently vary along dimensions of culture and power. It means rethinking not only economics, but also ourselves.

Notes

1 This chapter is partially based on a talk given at the European Association for Evolutionary Political Economy (EAEPE) Summer School on July 6, 2015 in Rome, Italy.
2 One could, of course, begin this history of important themes in economics earlier, perhaps with Adam Smith. Mill's essay is highlighted here for the sake of brevity.
3 Exposing the distortions caused by such dualistic thinking has been one of the major projects of feminist economics since the early 1990s (Ferber and Nelson 1993; Ferber and Nelson 2003). This analysis will not be repeated here.
4 There is also a growing literature in "behavioral economics" exploring the emotional and social dimensions of motivations (e.g., Fehr and Falk 2002).

References

Alperovitz, Gar (1995). "Sustainability and the System Problem." *The Good Society* 5(3): 1, 6–10.

Bazerman, Max H. and Ann E. Tenbrunsel (2011). *Blind Spots: Why We Fail to Do What's Right and What to Do About It*. Princeton, NJ, Princeton University Press.

Bombardieri, Marcella (2005). "Summers' Remarks on Women Draw Fire." *Boston Globe,* January 17.

Bordo, Susan (1986). "The Cartesian Masculinization of Thought." *Signs: Journal of Women in Culture and Society* 11(3): 439–456.

Bratton, William W. (2011). "At the Conjunction of Love and Money: Comment on Julie A. Nelson, Does Profit-Seeking Rule Out Love? Evidence (or Not) from Economics and Law." *Washington University Journal of Law and Policy* 35: 109–115.

Dasgupta, Partha (2005). "What do Economists Analyze and Why: Values or Facts?" *Economics and Philosophy* 21: 221–278.

Dasgupta, Partha (2007). *Economics: A Very Short Introduction*. Oxford, Oxford University Press.

Denning, Steve (2014). Why Financialization Has Run Amok. *Forbes*, www.forbes.com/sites/stevedenning/2014/06/03/why-financialization-has-run-amok/.

Epstein, Gerald A. (ed.) (2006). *Financialization and the World Economy*. Cheltenham, Edward Elgar.

Fee, Elizabeth (1983). "Women's Nature and Scientific Objectivity." In M. Lowe and R. Hubbard (eds.) *Women's Nature: Rationalizations of Inequality*. New York, Pergamon Press: 9–27.

Fehr, Ernst and Armin Falk (2002). "Psychological Foundations of Incentives." *European Economic Review* 46(4–5): 687–724.

Ferber, Marianne A. and Julie A. Nelson (eds.) (1993). *Beyond Economic Man: Feminist Theory and Economics*. Chicago, University of Chicago Press.

Ferber, Marianne A. and Julie A. Nelson (eds.) (2003). *Feminist Economics Today*. Chicago, University of Chicago Press.

Gigerenzer, Gerd (2007). *Gut Feelings: The Intelligence of the Unconcious*. New York, Penguin Books.

Greene, Joshua and Jonathan Haidt (2002). "How (and Where) Does Moral Judgment Work?" *Trends in Cognitive Sciences* 6(12): 517–523.

Greene, Joshua D., R. Brian Sommerville, et al. (2001). "An fMRI Investigation of Emotional Engagement in Moral Judgment." *Science* 293(Sept. 14): 2105–2108.

Habermas, Jürgen (1981). *The Theory of Communicative Action*. Boston, Beacon.

Haidt, Jonathan (2001). "The Emotional Dog and Its Rational Tail: A Social Intuitionist Approach to Moral Judgment." *Psychological Review* 108(4): 814–834.

Haidt, Jonathan (2006). *The Happiness Hypothesis: Finding Modern Truth in Ancient Wisdom*. New York, Basic Books.

Harding, Sandra (1986). *The Science Question in Feminism*. Ithaca, NY, Cornell University Press.

Jennings, Ann L. (1993). "Public or Private? Institutional Economics and Feminism." In *Beyond Economic Man*. M. A. Ferber and J. A. Nelson. Chicago, University of Chicago Press: 111–129.

Keller, Evelyn Fox (1985). *Reflections on Gender and Science*. New Haven, CT, Yale University Press.

King, Mervyn (2004). "The Institutions of Monetary Policy." *American Economic Review* 94(2): 1–13.

Kitcher, Philip (2011). *Science in a Democratic Society*. Amherst, NY: Prometheus Books.

Klein, Naomi (2007). *The Shock Doctrine: The Rise of Disaster Capitalism*. New York, Metropolitan Books.

Lloyd, Genevieve (1993). *The Man of Reason: 'Male' and 'Female' in Western Philosophy*. Minneapolis, MN, University of Minnesota Press.

Longino, Helen (1990). *Science as Social Knowledge: Values and Objectivity in Scientific Inquiry*. Princeton, NJ, Princeton University Press.

McCloskey, Donald N. (1985). *The Rhetoric of Economics*. Madison, WI, University of Wisconsin Press.

Mill, John Stuart (1836). "On the Definition of Political Economy; and On the Method of Philosophical Investigation in That Science." *London and Westminster Review* Vol. IV and XXVI(1): 1–29.

Mill, John Stuart. (1844/1874). "Essay V: On the Definition of Political Economy; and on the Method of Investigation Proper to It." In *Essays on Some Unsettled Questions*. London: Longmans, Green, Reader and Dyer Co.

Most, Steven B., Anne Verbeck Sorber, et al. (2007). "Auditory Stroop Reveals Implicit Gender Associations in Adults and Children." *Journal of Experimental Social Psychology* 43(2): 287–294.

Nelson, Julie A. (1992). "Gender, Metaphor, and the Definition of Economics." *Economics and Philosophy* 8: 103–125.

Nelson, Julie A. (1996). *Feminism, Objectivity and Economics*. London, Routledge.

Nelson, Julie A. (2006). *Economics for Humans*. Chicago, University of Chicago Press.

Nelson, Julie A. (2011a). "Care Ethics and Markets: A View from Feminist Economics." In M. Hamington and M. Sander-Staudt (eds.) *Applying Care Ethics to Business*. Dordrecht, Springer: 35–53.

Nelson, Julie A. (2011b). "Does Profit-Seeking Rule Out Love? Evidence (or Not) from Economics and Law." *Washington University Journal of Law and Policy* 35(69): 69–107.

Nelson, Julie A. (2016). "Husbandry: a (Feminist) Reclamation of Masculine Responsibility for Care." *Cambridge Journal of Economics* 40(1): 1–15.

Robbins, Lionel (1935). *An Essay on the Nature and Significance of Economic Science*. London, Macmillan.

Sen, Amartya (1992). *Objectivity and Position*. Lawrence, KS, University of Kansas.

Stout, Lynn (2012). *The Shareholder Value Myth: How Putting Shareholders First Harms Investors, Corporations, and the Public*. San Francisco, Berrett-Koehler.

Stout, Lynn A. (2011). *Cultivating Conscience: How Good Laws Make Good People.* Princeton, NJ, Princeton University Press.

Warren, Karen J. (2000). *Ecofeminist Philosophy: A Western Perspective on What It Is and Why It Matters.* Lanham, MD, Rowman & Littlefield.

Whitehead, Joan M. (1996). "Sex Stereotypes, Gender Identity, and Subject Choice at A-level." *Educational Research* 38(2): 147–160.

Wilkie, J. E. B. and G. V. Bodenhausen (2012). "Are Numbers Gendered?" *Journal of Experimental Psychology: General* 141(2):206–210.

Zhong, Chen-Bo (2011). "The Ethical Dangers of Deliberative Decision Making." *Administrative Science Quarterly* 56: 1–25.

Part II

Empirical evidences of inequality

6 Intergenerational inequality

Transmission channels, direct and indirect mechanisms and evidence for European countries

Michele Raitano

Introduction

The literature on social mobility and intergenerational inequality investigates the link between individuals' outcomes when adult (e.g. education, occupation, income) and the characteristics of their family background, and assesses whether and how much socio-economic inequalities persist in subsequent generations. From a policy perspective an increase in social mobility – i.e. a weakening of the connection between social positions of parents and children – is usually to be hoped for on both equity and efficiency grounds because it can improve equality of opportunity and the way human resources are allocated to their best use.

The index usually adopted in the economic literature to measure intergenerational inequality is the intergenerational elasticity β that measures the association between parents' and children's incomes and is estimated by regressing children's log income on parental income (Bjorklund and Jäntti 2009). According to this index, empirical studies agree on the following taxonomy for European countries (e.g. Corak 2006 and 2013; d'Addio 2007): Nordic countries are the most mobile, followed by Germany and by other central European countries with France in the worst position of these, whereas UK and Southern countries are the least mobile.

However, the β elasticity is merely a synthetic measure of the correlation between the earnings of two subsequent generations and it does not provide comprehensive information on the process behind such a correlation and on possible differences of this process across countries. Actually, the transmission of inequalities from one generation to the next is a complex process that can be due to several transmission mechanisms – i.e. it can be due to the interplay of genetic, economic, cultural and social factors – and could unfold at different points in individual lives, e.g. in the early infancy, at school or university and during the working career.

Following the "human capital view" suggested by Becker and Tomes (1979, 1986), the persistency of income inequality across generations is usually attributed to the reduced investment in human capital of individuals coming from disadvantaged backgrounds. Put differently, the association between parents' and children's earnings would be mainly due to a lower investment in human capital by those coming from a poor background. Given the positive return on such investment, this would reduce future earnings of the less-advantaged children, thus producing the intergenerational transmission of inequality. However, as concerns the process lying behind the intergenerational persistence of incomes across generations, this approach does not make a clear distinction between the effects that family background has, on the one hand, on the level of educational attainment and then on earnings (i.e. the 'indirect effect') and, on the other hand, on achievements in the labour market that are independent of educational attainments (i.e. the 'direct effect').

Various factors can instead determine a direct influence of background on children's earnings. For instance, countries with highly heterogeneous schooling systems could endow students with very different qualities of human capital according to their parental background or, in other countries, family connections could play a major role in determining occupational achievements and earnings, independently of education. Conversely, a good public education could create a high and homogeneous human capital floor for all citizens, thus mitigating a direct family background effect on the working career. Likewise, public policies reducing non-competitive rents in the labour market could help to build a more meritocratic environment, thus reducing the role played by family networks in determining children's outcomes.

As highlighted by empirical analyses based on the 2005 wave of the European Union Statistics on Income and Living Conditions (EU-SILC), the distinction between direct and indirect influences seems crucial for explaining cross-country differences in the correlation between parents' characteristics and children's earnings inequality (Franzini and Raitano 2009; Franzini et al. 2013; Raitano and Vona 2015a and 2015b): countries characterized by a high level of the intergenerational elasticity β (e.g. Italy and the UK) are indeed characterized by a large and significant influence of parental background on children's earnings also when children's education is taken into account; conversely, in countries characterized by a lower level of the intergenerational elasticity β (e.g. Denmark and Finland) the association between parental characteristics and children's earnings is wholly mediated by educational attainment, since no significant correlation between parental background and children's earnings emerges when children's education is taken into account.

Following this line of research, in the final part of this chapter I make use of micro-data provided in the 2011 wave of the EU-SILC and compare the features of the process of intergenerational association in five major European countries – Norway, Germany, France, Italy and the UK – that, according to the economic literature (e.g. Blanden 2013; Corak 2013), are characterized by different levels of intergenerational inequality and belong to different welfare regimes (respectively, Nordic, Continental, Southern and Anglo-Saxon).[1] The comparison is carried out first by analysing the association between the proxy of family background and children's educational attainments in the five countries and then measuring the association between family background and children's earnings. In order to distinguish the aforementioned 'direct' and 'indirect' effects in my estimates I also control for children's education and occupation, with the goal of assessing whether direct mechanisms emerge and, especially, whether major differences between countries exist as regards mechanisms affecting the transmission of inequalities between parents and children.

More in detail, this chapter is organized as follows. In the second section I list the possible channels that determine the association between parental characteristics and children's outcomes, while in the third section I present my conceptual framework where indirect and direct mechanisms – i.e. mediated or not by human capital accumulation – are explicitly distinguished. Therefore, in the fourth section I briefly discuss the measurement issues of intergenerational inequality in economic studies. Finally, I proceed with my empirical analysis by presenting the used dataset (fifth section) and showing main findings (sixth section). The final section concludes by summarizing the main implications of my results.

Channels of intergenerational transmission of inequalities

An association between parental characteristics and children's outcomes when adult emerges when parental characteristics affect some children's traits that can determine these outcomes. For instance, an association between parents' background and children's earnings emerges when parents are able to affect children's traits correlated to earnings, e.g. the endowment of hard and soft skills or children's capacity to benefit from ties related to the social network which parents belong to.

The economic literature points out the existence of four possible channels through which parents can affect children's traits correlated to their future prospects (Meade 1973; d'Addio 2007; Bowles and Gintis 2002; Franzini and Raitano 2009): (i) genetic, (ii) economic, (iii) cultural/familiar, (iv) social.

The genetic channel refers to the genetic inheritance of cognitive and non-cognitive abilities. However, is has to be stressed that the unavoidable intersection between *nature* and *nurture* make it almost impossible to distinguish a pure effect due to biological factors.

The economic channel concerns the direct impact of household income and wealth on the menu of choices available to children. The literature pays a great attention to those mechanisms that, through family economic variables (income and wealth), may determine the future standards of children's lives. Following Becker and Tomes (1979, 1986) models, the economic literature usually interprets the intergenerational persistence as related to the role of household income and wealth in compensating liquidity constraints that, in the presence of imperfect capital markets, can limit the investment in human capital. In general, coming from a wealthy household enlarges the options set of an individual. For instance, especially when effective universal unemployment benefits are not provided and capital markets are largely imperfect, those coming from a richer background can wait for a better match in the labour market or have a comparative advantage in starting up an activity as a self-employed. Furthermore, wealth may directly pass across generation through gifts and inheritance, especially when inheritance taxes are low.

The cultural/familiar channel is related to the role of the domestic environment in shaping the choices, preferences, tastes and behaviours of children. For instance, a better cultural home environment can provide better incentives to continue to study, awarding a higher non-monetary value to education. Furthermore, house-mates' characteristics strongly influence children's non-cognitive traits, i.e. their soft skills (risk aversion, propensity to team jobs, discipline or leadership, which are increasingly rewarded in the labour market (Bowles and Gintis 2002; Goldthorpe and Jackson 2008).

Finally, the social channel refers to the influence of the social environment (e.g. the neighbourhood where children grow up, the social network which the household belongs to) on individuals' abilities, preferences, choices and opportunities. This channel also includes those mechanisms that make easier the marriage between similar (for socio-economic and cultural aspects) partners, i.e. the so-called assortative mating.

Due to the interplay of the four channels the process of intergenerational transmission is really complex. On the one hand, these channels affect children's traits during various steps of their life (the genetic influence happens at birth, the other influences emerge along the life of the offspring, i.e. during the first infancy, the childhood or the various phases of the educational and the occupational path). On the other hand, the mechanisms related to these channels often interact with each other through several negative or positive feedbacks, thus creating a sort of cumulative influence on the child development (e.g. an unpleasant familiar and social environment can enhance the role of liquidity constrains in reducing the probability to continue studying). In line with a picture of a complex path with many steps, whose outcomes significantly affect subsequent ones, the inter-generational reproduction of inequalities is indeed considered by some scholars as a cumulative process in which small effects on every single outcome can also engender a large cumulative final effect, thus exerting a deep influence on individuals' chances according to their origins[2].

The intergenerational transmission process is not interrupted in a particular point of time. For instance, economic, familiar and social channels may influence children's prospects even after the completion of studies, affecting both the access to the labour market and the following working career (especially when the func-tioning of the labour market is scarcely meritocratic and is influenced by informal relationship). However, as mentioned, the economic literature mainly focuses on a single mechanism of transmission, i.e. on the role exerted by income constrains in determining human capital accumulation. Anyhow, following the pioneering study by Meade (1973), a recent, often multidisciplinary, literature has started to give a relevant weight to all channels of intergenerational transmission and to focus on all steps of the process of intergenerational transmission of inequalities, rather than on school achievements only.[3]

Direct and indirect mechanisms of intergenerational transmission

The traditional economic view of intergenerational inequality focuses on the key role played by family background in the accumulation of human capital. Hence, differences in earnings and occupational attainments are usually viewed as a consequence of differences in human capital (usually proxied by educational attainments in empirical studies). The association between parental characteristics and children's human capital has indeed been considered to be dependent on several factors: liquidity constraints in the presence of imperfect financial markets (Becker and Tomes 1979, 1986), costless transmission of genetic traits and endowments (Becker and Tomes 1979, 1986; Bjorklund et al. 2006), extra-schooling investments by more advantaged parents (Duncan and Murnane 2011), peer effects (Benabou 1996) and all these factors make easier the access of well-off children to better-quality schools (Blanden and Machin 2004). However, beyond human capital, family ties can also play a major direct role in determining children's occupational achievements and earnings. Apart from an indirect influence through human capital accumulation, a direct influence of parental background on children's occupations and earnings can indeed occur through membership of privileged social networks (Granovetter 1995), the transmission of employers (Corak and Piraino 2011) or soft skills (Bowles and Gintis 2002).

A more general conceptual framework is then required to inform an analysis that aims at explaining cross-country differences in intergenerational inequality. Following Franzini et al. (2013), in this chapter I do not view education as the exclusive (indirect) mechanism of the intergenerational transmission of inequality, because, as summarized in Figure 6.1, family background, in addition to education, can also 'directly' influence children's earnings, i.e. differently affecting earnings of similarly educated workers according to their parental background.[4]

Distinguishing 'direct' and 'indirect' influences of family background on children's prospects in the different stages of their lives seems appealing for highlighting differences in intergenerational inequality across countries. For instance, a low level of intergenerational inequality could be due to a weak influence of parental features in every phase of children's life or to the absence of any influence of family background on children's prospects in a specific stage. And these differences can be due to institutional differences across countries.

Therefore, consistently with this framework, in the final part of this chapter I will present original estimates of the association between children's earnings and parental characteristics, also including among the regressors the two main mediating factors through which the intergenerational transmission of advantages can occur, i.e. children's education and occupation. We expect to find, everywhere, a strong relationship between parental characteristics and children's educational attainments and, hence, a significant association between children's earnings and

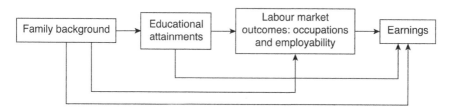

Figure 6.1 Mechanisms of intergenerational transmission of inequalities

parental background when children's education is not taken into account. If only indirect influences matter, we expect that the association between children's earnings and parental characteristics will no longer be positive and significant when children's education is taken into account. Conversely, if a positive and significant association remains when children's education – and also occupation – are controlled for, a direct influence of parental background on offspring earnings would emerge in addition to the effect acting through parental investment in children's education.

How to measure and interpret intergenerational inequality?

Studies on social mobility follow two main approaches: the sociological approach classifies individual statuses according to social classes (usually defined in terms of jobs and occupations) and investigates whether similarities in classes among parents and children emerge; the economic approach assesses social positions by means of monetary indicators (usually earnings or total incomes) and focuses on the transmission of income inequalities among subsequent generations.

As mentioned, the index adopted by almost all economic studies to measure intergenerational inequality is the intergenerational elasticity β that is estimated through OLS by regressing children's log income on parental income (Bjorklund and Jantti 2009):

$$y_c = \alpha + \beta y_p + \varepsilon \tag{1}$$

where y_c and y_p are, respectively, log of children's and parents' incomes, α is the mean income of children generation and ε is a residual.

Thus, the intergenerational elasticity β measures how much of parents' income gap persists among children (e.g. $\beta=0.5$ tells that, on average, half of the gap in parents' incomes persists among sons). Theoretically the value of β is unlimited; however, following a reverse to the mean process, all studies show a positive, but incomplete, process of intergenerational transmission, thus $0 < \beta < 1$.

However, this indicator is too much synthetic, as it points out only the mean level of intergenerational transmission – assuming an underlying linear relationship – without informing about the features of the process in the different points of the income distribution. Policy implications are instead very different if, for instance, the same β is linked to a high mobility in all quintiles apart from the last one (i.e. if a sort of entry barrier in the richest group emerges) or if it is linked to a low probability to escape from the poorest quintile (i.e. if a poverty trap emerges).

Apart from that, it has to be stressed that estimating the intergenerational elasticity β is a very demanding task due to some methodological problems related to the ages when parental and children's incomes have to be observed and due to the characteristics of the needed data.

A correct estimate should take into account permanent incomes (i.e. earnings along the whole working life) of both parents and children. Therefore, longitudinal data tracking individuals for many decades would be needed. This kind of dataset is currently available nowhere. In actual studies the β elasticity is estimated by observing parents' and children's income distribution in, at most, a few years (and, more often, in single years). However, empirical analyses (e.g. Haider and Solon 2006; Bjorklund and Jannti 2009; Nybom and Stuhler 2016) show that the estimates of the β elasticity are significantly affected by the number of years of observation of incomes (the so-called 'attenuation bias') and by the age of children when their incomes are observed (the so-called 'life-cycle bias').

In other terms, the estimation of the 'true' relationship between permanent incomes of succeeding generations can be biased both by the fact that only a part of individual life is observed and by the specific phase of individual life observed. Wide longitudinal data is not usually available to address the issue of the life cycle, so most empirical studies suggest considering men aged approximately 35–49 – because at those ages the differences between current income and permanent income would be minimized – while for women a simple rule does not emerge, as women display more variety in their life-cycle income profiles (Bohlmark and Lindquist 2006; Haider and Solon 2006). On the contrary, if too young children were considered (i.e. aged less than 30) the β elasticity would be strongly underestimated since the various mechanisms behind the intergenerational correlation have not had enough time to act. For instance, pioneer studies on income intergenerational mobility in the US (e.g. Becker and Tomes 1986) found a very low β, confirming the idea of the US as a land of opportunities. Anyway, these studies were biased from having considered a too young sample of sons. On the contrary, when the same analysis has been repeated considering older sons a very high level of intergenerational inequality was found in the US (Solon 2002; Jannti et al. 2006).

The estimation of income intergenerational inequality is also limited by the availability of proper panel data and it has been carried out only in the few countries where long panel datasets recording, at least for some years, incomes for both parents and children are available (Nordic countries, the US and the UK). However, methodologies based on a two-stage, two-sample instrumental variables procedure (2S2SLS; Bjorklund and Jannti 1997) allow researchers to estimate the β elasticity even when longitudinal data are not available, but repeated cross-section surveys including retrospective information about parental characteristics are available (as in Italy and Spain).

Meta-analysis of existing studies (Corak 2006 and 2013) show that the estimated values of the β elasticity largely differ across countries (Figure 6.2). The lowest values emerge in Nordic European countries and in Canada, the highest in the UK, the US and Italy (where estimates based on the 2S2SLS procedure have been carried out; Mocetti 2007 and Piraino 2007).

In order to estimate the link between parental incomes and offspring outcomes, as mentioned, very long panel data are needed, but only a few countries provide such data. This, among other things, heavily limits international comparisons that are based on studies often using not homogenous datasets. However, from an empirical perspective, the process of intergenerational transmission of

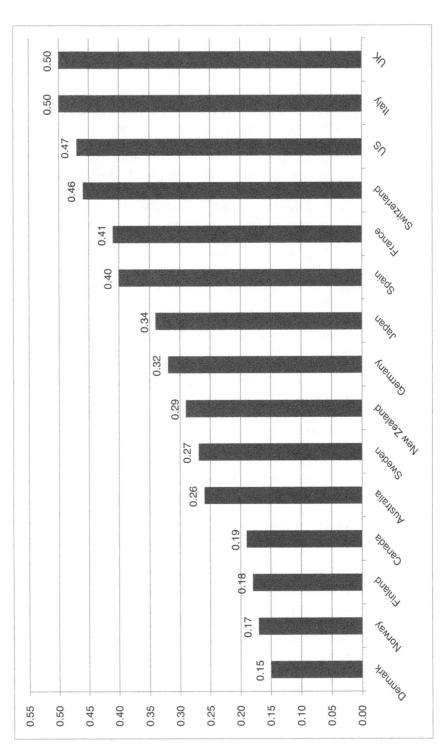

Figure 6.2 Estimates of the intergenerational income elasticity β in selected OECD countries

Source: Elaborations on data provided in Corak (2006 and 2013)

advantages can be analysed also through cross-sectional data containing retrospective information about individual family background. Retrospective surveys, being based on recalls by the interviewed, are not accurate for collecting data on parental incomes – thus they cannot be used for computing the β intergenerational income elasticity – but they could include qualitative questions about family socio-economic conditions that could be used as good proxies of incomes for assessing the association between parental characteristics and children's incomes. When panel data are not available, Jenkins and Siedler (2007) indeed suggest that qualitative retrospective information can be a very fruitful way to study intergenerational inequality.

Two waves (2005 and 2011) of the EU-SILC survey include a specific section about intergenerational mobility where many aspects of family background when the respondent was aged around 14 are recorded: i.e. number of siblings, parents' educational attainments, activity statuses and occupations, proxies of financial distress. Therefore, EU-SILC data permit an international comparison of the association among several individual outcomes (firstly, incomes) and background variables, even if they do not allow researchers to compute intergenerational income elasticities because parents' incomes are not collected. Moreover, EU-SILC data enable to study the impact of parental characteristics at various stages of children's lives, making it possible to analyse the direct and indirect relationships between family background and children's outcomes previously highlighted in Figure 6.1.

Recent studies based on EU-SILC 2005 data, and comparing some EU countries (e.g. Franzini and Raitano 2009; Franzini et al. 2013; Raitano and Vona 2015a and 2015b), have shown that, in all European countries, parental characteristics (proxied by dummies on parental education, occupation or financial distress when young) affect children's educational attainment, thus pushing an indirect background effect, whereas in only a few European countries – Italy, Spain and the UK, i.e. those characterized by higher intergenerational inequality and by residual welfare states – a direct influence of family status on children's earnings emerges. Indeed, in these three countries parental background exerts an impact on children's earnings independently of their education and occupation. Moreover, in a short paper analysing the links between parents' occupations and children's earnings in the welfare regimes of EU15 countries, Raitano (2009) has noticed that, unlike the other welfare regime clusters where the intergenerational transmission process is mainly mediated by educational attainment, parental background has a significant direct effect on children's earnings in Southern and Anglo-Saxon regimes.

However, it has to be pointed out that the existence of a correlation between parents' characteristics and children's incomes when children's educational attainment is controlled for is not enough for concluding that this correlation is not related to human capital accumulation. Indeed a residual correlation on top of that acting through educational attainment could be due both to unobservable children's skills associated with parental background[5] and to still less meritocratic mechanisms related to the functioning of family ties and networks (Raitano and Vona 2015a). Therefore, on empirical grounds, it is exceedingly difficult to distinguish whether a better background is more associated with higher human capital than with a better endowment of social networks.

Taking these caveats in mind, I now proceed to show the results of an original empirical estimate of the association between parents' characteristics and children's earnings carried out by using the EU-SILC 2011 data.

Data and main variables

As mentioned, the aim of the final part of this chapter is to shed some light on what lies behind the association between parents' characteristics and offspring's incomes, by looking into the data referring to European countries on the basis of a conceptual framework whose main feature consists in challenging the common view according to which the intergenerational transmission of inequality takes place almost exclusively through education. Indeed, I consider that family background can influence offspring's earnings not only through education but also in a more direct way, i.e. differently affecting, through various mechanisms, earnings of similarly educated workers according to their parental background.

To achieve this aim, I use the recent release of EU-SILC 2011 data. Compared with the earlier studies carried out by using EU-SILC 2005, this chapter presents two main novelties: (i) as a proxy of family background status, it uses the variable recorded in EU-SILC 2011 for the first time to identify the father and mother who had supervisory responsibility in their job when the children were aged around 14; (ii) unlike EU-SILC 2005, EU-SILC 2011 provides a homogeneous definition of gross annual earnings for all countries (in EU-SILC 2005 in Southern countries earnings were only recorded net of taxes), thus allowing a direct comparison across the various countries of the size of the estimated coefficients of the association between parental background and offspring earnings.

As mentioned, as a proxy for family background, I then use the variable collected in EU-SILC 2011 recording whether the father and the mother of the respondent had a supervisory responsibility in their job (i.e. if they supervised a group of other employees other than apprentices). My proxy of background is then a dummy whose value is 1 (High background, henceforth) when at least one parent had a supervisory responsibility, 0 (Low background, henceforth) when neither the father nor the mother had a supervisory responsibility.

Then, using information about the dummy about parents' supervisory responsibility when working as a proxy of the characteristics of parental background, I inquire whether family background affects children's prospects, assessing these prospects through two outcomes: educational attainments and gross annual labour incomes (from employment and self-employment), also controlling in some specifications for educational and occupational achievements. Education is coded through three dummy variables about the highest qualification attained: at most lower secondary (ISCED 1–2), upper secondary or post-secondary non-tertiary (ISCED 3–4), tertiary (ISCED 5). Occupation is coded through nine dummy variables based on the one-digit ISCO 2008 classification.

In line with suggestions in the empirical literature (Grawe 2006; Haider and Solon 2006), I restricted my sample to men aged 30–49 and earning positive wages, in order to avoid biased estimates of individuals' long-run earnings. Considering only this subsample has several advantages: (i) it is reasonable to assume that, for prime age workers, the influence of the home environment has almost totally displayed its effects; (ii) individuals in the central part of their working life are less affected by high turnover, earnings volatility and retirement choices than in their early or later stages; (iii) estimates based on the female labour force could be heavily affected by selection biases (especially in Southern countries), due to the dependency of female participation to the labour market on preferences influenced by the family of origin and on joint decisions at the household level (on which family background still exerts an impact through 'assortative mating').

I compare five European countries – Norway, Germany, France, Italy and the UK – which belong to different welfare regimes and are characterized by different values of the β elasticity according to the most reliable estimates (Corak 2006 and 2013). My sample comprised 16,923 observations who report positive labour incomes in the EU-SILC 2011 and answered to the section of the questionnaire about characteristics of the family of origin.

Empirical findings

Parental background and educational attainments

The association between family background and children's educational attainment is analysed by means of ordered probit models run for each country. The dependent variable in the regressions is the level of education (lower secondary, upper secondary, tertiary), while background is proxied by the dummy on supervisory responsibility ('Low background' is the reference category) and age and age squared are included as covariates in the estimates.

A strongly significant influence of parental background on children's education emerges everywhere: compared with those coming from a low background, those coming from a high background are indeed characterized by a significant (at 99.9 per cent level) higher probability to attain a higher degree.[6] Figure 6.3 shows the predicted distribution of children's education according to parental background in the five countries. Predicted distributions clearly depend on the different distribution of workers by education in the five countries. However, in all countries the sons of parents without supervisory responsibilities, compared with the sons of supervisors, are characterized by a much lower share of tertiary graduates.

Therefore, in all countries a significant association between sons' education and family background emerges. As pointed out in previous sections, this association could suggest that intergenerational income inequality is mainly due to mechanisms acting during the educational period. In other words, the transmission of intergenerational inequalities, i.e. lower wages earned by workers coming from

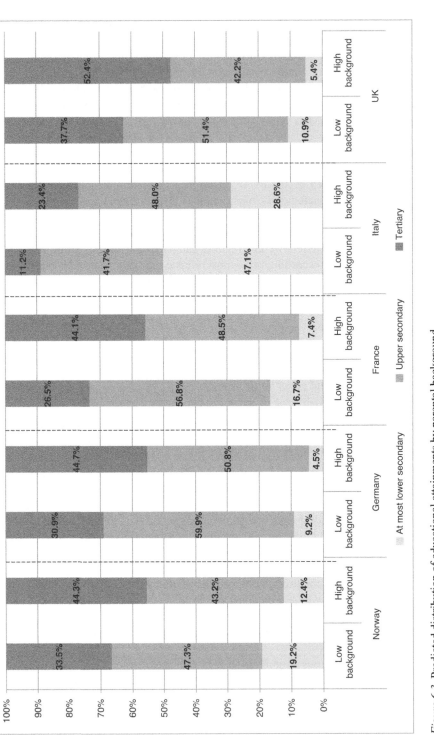

Figure 6.3 Predicted distribution of educational attainments by parental background

Note: predicted values obtained by ordered probit estimates on individual education. Control variables are age and age squared.

more disadvantaged households, would only depend on the strong role played by 'cultural' and liquidity constraints in affecting educational outcomes on which future earnings significantly depend. Consequently, proper measures for improving social mobility would just refer to educational policies, e.g. to enrolment in pre-primary education, postponing tracking among vocational and general programmes, financing loans for students coming from disadvantaged backgrounds, in order to increase their participation in tertiary education. For assessing this statement I have to confirm that a further direct effect of family background does not emerge.

Indirect and direct influences of parental background on earnings

The goal of this section is to investigate how strong, if any, a "direct" influence of family background on sons' earnings is, i.e. whether background still has a residual influence on earnings after controlling for background-related factors such as education and occupation.

To this aim, three different OLS models were estimated, where the dependent variable is the log of annual gross incomes from employment and self-employment. In the first model, only parental background and sons' age and age squared are included among the regressors. In the second and third models, respectively, sons' education and sons' education and occupation are added. Therefore, once sons' achievements in terms of education and occupation are controlled for, coefficients of parental background dummies measure the residual association between background and earnings.[7] Figures 6.4–6.6 show the estimated coefficient and the 95 per cent confidence intervals of my proxy of parental background in the three aforementioned models (low background is the reference category, thus the coefficient shows the advantage for those coming from a good background).

As the first step in my analysis (Figure 6.4, without controlling for mediating outcomes, i.e. education and occupations), in all countries those coming from a high background are advantaged by significantly higher earnings compared to those coming from a low background, even if the sizes of the estimated coefficient differ and are consistent with the usual country ranking in terms of intergenerational income inequality. The advantage for those coming from a good background is indeed much lower in Norway (even if the standard error is very high due to the limited sample size in EU-SILC 2011 and this enlarges the confidence interval) and Germany than in France, Italy and the UK.

Adding children's education substantially reduces the advantage of coming from a high background (Figure 6.5). What is more important, striking differences among countries emerge once educational attainments are controlled for. The estimates do not indicate the existence of a statistically significant direct effect of background in Norway and Germany. Conversely, controlling for education, those coming from a low background are still characterized by a large and significant earnings gap compared to those coming from a high background in France, Italy and the UK.

Therefore, my estimates suggest that the transmission of earnings inequality occurs mainly throughout the educational channel in Norway and Germany, given

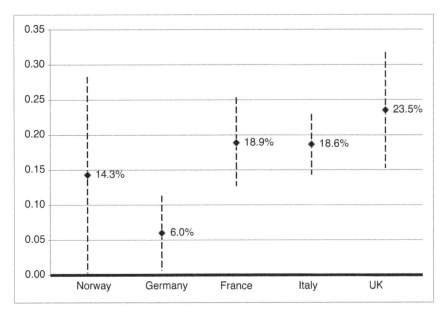

Figure 6.4 OLS estimated coefficient of the association between parental background and children's earnings (95 per cent confidence interval)

Note: Control variables A are age and its square. Low background is the reference category.

Source: Elaborations on EU-SILC 2011

that the direct association between children's earnings and parental background is not significant when sons' education is included among the covariates.

However, it has to be remarked that EU-SILC records educational attainment using the ISCED classification; neither proxies of the quality of education (e.g. the mark or the attended university) nor the field of study are collected. A residual correlation of family background on earnings, controlling for sons' ISCED level, could then partially mask an association between background and unobservable features of the educational process, which labour market attainments depend on.

Actually, according to the routinization hypothesis proposed by Acemoglu and Autor (2011), what counts more in terms of earnings gaps is the task content of each job. Therefore, if workers are paid according to their effective skills rather than to their mere educational attainment, and if a better parental background allows children to be endowed with better abilities and receive a better quality of education, the crucial factor affecting earnings is not the formal degree, but the occupation that is achieved in the labour market due to the effective skills and abilities indicated by the workers to the employers. As a consequence, the direct effect shown in Figure 6.5 could be due to the missed consideration of effective individual skills, enabling those coming from a better background to achieve better occupations.

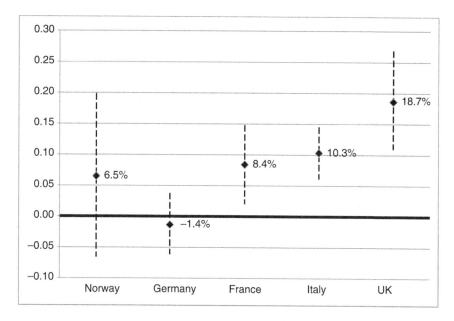

Figure 6.5 OLS estimated coefficient of the association between parental background and children's earnings controlling for children's education (95 per cent confidence interval)

Note: Control variables are: age and its square and three dummies on educational attainments. Low background is the reference category.

Source: Elaborations on EU-SILC 2011

In order to better disentangle the direct influence of background, I also add children's occupation among the covariates (Figure 6.6). The estimated coefficients of the association between background and earnings are now not significant in Norway, Germany and France, but remain large and statistically significant in Italy and the UK, where a large and significant income premium for those coming from a high background compared with those coming from a low background is confirmed also when controlling for both children's education and occupation.

Conclusions

In this chapter, after having reviewed the main mechanisms of intergenerational transmission of inequality pointed out by the economic literature, I have contributed to the empirical literature on cross-country differences in intergenerational inequality by investigating the role of various transmission mechanisms. More specifically, I have compared five European countries belonging to different welfare regimes for which we expect a variation in the importance of these mechanisms, reflecting differences in welfare policies, culture, labour markets and educational systems.

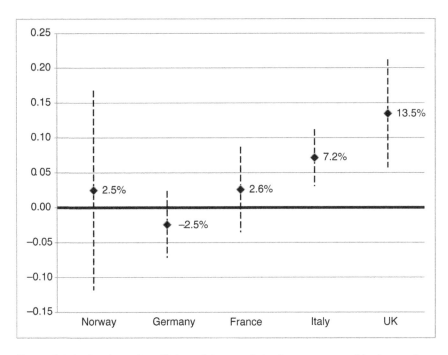

Figure 6.6 OLS estimated coefficient of the association between parental background and children's earnings controlling for children's education and occupation (95 per cent confidence interval)

Note: Control variables are: age and its square, three dummies on educational attainments and nine dummies on occupations (coded at ISCO-07 one digit level). Low background is the reference category.

Source: Elaborations on EU-SILC 2011

The common belief is that the Nordic countries, characterized by generous welfare states, regulated wage setting and well-functioning public education offer equal chances to all. Consistently with Esping Andersen (2015), social democratic regimes, compared with conservative or liberal regimes, can more effectively equalize the opportunity structure providing homogeneous and good education to all children, independently on their origins, thus reducing the strength of direct mechanisms of intergenerational transmission of disadvantages related to the differences in the quality of education effectively attained by those coming from different backgrounds. Accordingly, Bratsberg et al. (2007) argue that, in Nordic countries, good public education has created a high and homogeneous human capital floor for all citizens and has been essential to mitigate the direct effect of family background on the working career.

Conversely, in countries characterized by highly heterogeneous schooling systems, like the UK, well-off children can improve their earnings' prospects by accessing top schools and universities, whose access is very often related to parental incomes (Blanden and Machin 2004). Furthermore, family ties can play a major role in determining occupational achievements and earnings, especially in countries belonging to the Southern European welfare regime, where labour markets are often considered less meritocratic (Checchi et al. 1999; Guell et al. 2007).

My findings have confirmed these expectations since the estimated relationship between parental background and children's earnings differs widely across groups of European countries. Furthermore, major differences concerning the residual association between family background and earnings point to the existence of a 'direct' intergenerational effect not mediated by other factors in Anglo-Saxon and Southern countries, while in Nordic and Continental countries background effects are almost entirely mediated by indirect effects acting through formal education and through sorting into occupational groups. Actually, my findings show that a statistically significant direct association of parental background and children's earnings disappears when the main channels of inequality transmission, i.e., education and occupation, are considered in Norway, Germany and France while a large direct background effect persists in Italy and the UK.

As argued also by Franzini et al. (2013), the evidence that family background can also exert a direct influence on children's wages, independently of education, defies the explanatory capacity of what can be called the 'human capital view' of inequality persistence, according to which education is the main, if not the unique, channel of intergenerational inequality transmission.

The empirical evidence presented in this chapter has confirmed for all European countries that family background has a strong impact on education. But the importance of other, more 'direct' influences, at least in some countries, seems to defy the general validity of this view. Therefore improving educational equality of opportunity would not be enough to foster social mobility. Indeed, it seems important to explore in depth the analysis of the mechanisms regulating, in each country, access to the job market and subsequent careers.

In particular, a direct influence of parents' characteristics on individuals' wages could depend on the following aspects that can act together: (i) the impact of family background on the unobservable quality of education (well-off students can have access to better schools and universities – or at least perceived as better by the employers – and this will increase their future wages); (ii) the influence of family and social background on children's soft skills; (iii) a higher opportunity cost of searching for the most appropriate job, that encourages less advantaged individuals 'to be satisfied' with the first job they find, without waiting for the one providing the best prospects; (iv) the impact of parental background and family networks on workers' careers. The relative importance of these mechanisms is likely to vary substantially across countries. For instance, in the UK, heterogeneous school quality and high skill premia could reinforce the mechanism related to the quality of education, while in Southern countries a non-transparent labour market selection could reinforce the strength of family networks. However, data limitations do not allow an identification of these two mechanisms in a cross-country comparison. Anyhow, the evidence of a direct influence of family background on earnings – beyond the indirect one acting through educational attainments – suggests the need for a deeper analysis of the mechanisms regulating, in each country, access to different types of schools and universities and, primarily, access to the labour market and the subsequent career, in order to highlight the main factors explaining the performances of the different countries.

Notes

1 For the debate on welfare regimes see Esping Andersen (1990), Ferrera (1996) and the survey of Arts and Gelissen (2002).
2 See, e.g., Mayer (2002), Di Prete and Eirich (2006), Jenkins and Siedler (2007).
3 See, for instance, the studies included in the volumes edited by Bowles et al. (2005), Corak (2004) and Morgan et al. (2006).
4 Being almost impossible to measure the "quality" of education, in Figure 6.1 I assume that the educational step could exert a further direct impact on income in addition to the one determined by qualifications.
5 Education being the same, children who are better off often benefit from a higher-quality education (Bratsberg et al. 2007) and from more extra-schooling activities (Duncan and Murnane 2011). They outperform other children on test scores at age 15 (Fuchs and Woessmann 2007), are advantaged in early-age skill formation (Cunha and Heckman 2008) and have a more profitable endowment of soft skills (Bowles and Gintis 2002; Goldthorpe and Jackson 2008).
6 Detailed results of the estimates are available upon request from the author.
7 Detailed results of the estimates are available upon request from the author.

References

Acemoglu, D. and Autor, D. (2011) 'Skills, tasks and technologies: implications for employment and earnings', *Handbook of Labor Economics*, 4(B), 1043–1171.

Arts, W. and Gelissen, J. (2002) 'Three worlds of welfare capitalism or more? A state-of-the-art report', *Journal of European Social Policy*, 12(2), 137–158.

Becker, G. and Tomes, N. (1979) 'An equilibrium theory of the distribution of income and intergenerational mobility', *Journal of Political Economy*, 87(6), 1153–1189.

Becker, G. and Tomes, N. (1986) 'Human capital and the rise and fall of families', *Journal of Labor Economics*, 4(3), S1–S39.

Benabou, R. (1996) 'Equity and effectiveness in human capital investment: the local connection', *Review of Economic Studies*, 63, 37–64.

Bjorklund, A. and Jäntti, M. (1997) 'Intergenerational income mobility in Sweden compared to the United States', *American Economic Review*, 87(5), 1009–1018.

Bjorklund, A. and Jäntti, M. (2009) 'Intergenerational income mobility and the role of family background', in W. Salverda, B. Nolan and T. Smeeding (eds) *Oxford Handbook of Economic Inequality*, Oxford: Oxford University Press.

Bjorklund, A., Lindahl, M. and Plug, E. (2006) 'The origins of intergenerational associations: lessons from Swedish adoption data', *The Quarterly Journal of Economics*, 121(3), 999–1028.

Blanden, J. (2013) 'Cross-country rankings in intergenerational mobility: a comparison of approaches from economics and sociology', *Journal of Economic Surveys*, 27(1), 38–73.

Blanden, J. and Machin, S. (2004) 'Educational inequality and the expansion of UK higher education', *Scottish Journal of Political Economy*, 51(2), 230–249.

Bohlmark, A. and Lindquist, M. (2006), 'Life-cycle variations in the association between current and lifetime income: replication and extension for Sweden', *Journal of Labor Economics*, 24(4), 879–900.

Bowles, S. and Gintis, H. (2002) 'The inheritance of inequality', *Journal of Economic Perspectives*, 16(3), 3–30.

Bowles, S., Gintis, H. and Osborne Groves, M. (eds) (2005) *Unequal Chances: Family Background and Economic Success*, New York: Russell Sage.

Bratsberg, B., Røed, K., Raaum, O., Naylor, R., Jäntti, M., Eriksson, T. and Österbacka, E. (2007) 'Nonlinearities in intergenerational earnings mobility: consequences for cross-country comparisons', *Economic Journal*, 117, C72–C92.

Checchi, D., Ichino, A. and Rustichini, A. (1999) 'More equal but less mobile? Education financing and intergenerational mobility in Italy and in the US', *Journal of Public Economics*, 74(3), 351–393.

Corak, M. (ed.) (2004) *Generational Income Mobility in North America and Europe*, Cambridge: Cambridge University Press.

Corak, M. (2006) 'Do poor children become poor adults? Lessons from a cross country comparison of generational earnings mobility', *IZA Discussion Paper*, no. 1993.

Corak, M. (2013) 'Income inequality, equality of opportunity, and intergenerational mobility', *Journal of Economic Perspectives*, 27(3), 79–102.

Corak, M. and Piraino, P. (2011) 'The intergenerational transmission of employers', *Journal of Labor Economics*, 29(1), 37–68.

Cunha, F. and Heckman, J. (2007) 'Formulating, identifying and estimating the technology of cognitive and noncognitive skill formation', *Journal of Human Resources*, 2, 738–82.

d'Addio, A.C. (2007) 'Intergenerational transmission of disadvantage: mobility or immobility across generations? A review of the evidence for OECD Countries', *OECD Working Paper*, 2007/7.

Di Prete, T. and Eirich, G. (2006) 'Cumulative advantage as a mechanism for inequality: a review of theoretical and empirical developments', *Annual Review of Sociology*, 32, 271–292.

Duncan, G. and Murnane, R. (2011) 'Introduction: the American dream, then and now', in G. Duncan and R. Murnane (eds) *Whither Opportunity? Rising Inequality, Schools, and Children's Life Chances*, New York: Russell Sage.

Esping Andersen, G. (1990) *The Three Worlds of Welfare Capitalism*, Princeton, NJ: Princeton University Press.

Esping Andersen, G. (2015) 'Welfare regimes and social stratification', *Journal of European Social Policy*, 25(1), 124–134.

Ferrera, M. (1996) 'The southern model of welfare in social Europe', *Journal of European Social Policy*, 6(1), 17–37.

Franzini, M. and Raitano, M. (2009) 'Persistence of inequality in Europe: the role of family economic conditions', *International Review of Applied Economics*, 23(3), 345–356.

Franzini, M., Raitano, M. and Vona, F. (2013) 'The channels of intergenerational transmission of inequality: a cross-country comparison', *Rivista Italiana degli Economisti*, XVIII(2), 201–226.

Fuchs, T. and Woessmann, L. (2007) 'What accounts for international differences in student performance? A re-examination using PISA data', *Empirical Economics*, 32(2), 433–464.

Goldthorpe, J. and Jackson, M. (2008) 'Education-based meritocracy: the barriers to its realization', in A. Lareau and D. Conley (eds) *Social Class: How Does it Work?*, New York: Russell Sage Foundation Press.

Granovetter, M. (1995) 'Afterword', in M. Granovetter (ed.) *Getting a Job: A Study of Contacts and Careers*, Chicago: Chicago University Press.

Grawe, N. (2006) 'Life-cycle bias in estimates of intergenerational earnings persistence', *Labour Economics*, 13(5), 551–570.

Guell, M., Rodriguez-Mora, J. and Telmer, C. (2007) 'Intergenerational mobility and the informative content of surnames', *CEPR Discussion Papers*, no. 6316.

Haider, S. and Solon, G. (2006) 'Life-cycle variation in the association between current and lifetime earnings', *NBER Working Papers*, no. 11943.

Jannti, M., Bratsberg, B., Roed, K. Raaum, O., Naylor, R., Osterbacka, E., Bjorklund, A. and Eriksson, T. (2006) 'American exceptionalism in a new light', *IZA Discussion Paper*, no. 1938.

Jenkins, S. and Siedler, T. (2007) 'The intergenerational transmission of poverty in industrialised countries', *DIW Discussion Paper*, no. 693.

Mayer, S. (2002) *The Influence of Parental Income on Children's Outcomes*, New Zealand Ministry of Social Development Report, Knowledge Management Group, Wellington.

Meade, J. (1973) *The Inheritance of Inequality: Some Biological, Demographic, Social, and Economic Factors*, The Proceedings of the British Academy, vol. 59, pp. 3–29, Oxford: Oxford University Press.

Mocetti, S. (2007) 'Intergenerational Earnings Mobility in Italy', *The B.E. Journal of Economic Analysis & Policy*, 7(2), 1–25.

Morgan, S., Grusky, D. and Fields, G. (eds) (2006) *Mobility and Inequality: Frontiers of Research from Sociology and Economics*, Stanford, CA: Stanford University Press.

Nybom, M. and Stuhler, J. (2016) 'Heterogeneous income profiles and lifecycle bias in intergenerational mobility estimation', *Journal of Human Resources*, 51(1), 239–268.

Piraino, P. (2007) 'Comparable estimates of intergenerational income mobility in Italy', *The B.E. Journal of Economic Analysis & Policy*, 7(2), 1–27.

Raitano, M. (2009) 'When family beats welfare: background effects in EU15 countries clusters', *Intereconomics*, 44(6), 337–342.

Raitano, M. and Vona, F. (2015a) 'Measuring the link between intergenerational occupational mobility and earnings: evidence from 8 European Countries', *Journal of Economic Inequality*, 13(1), 83–102.

Raitano, M. and Vona, F. (2015b) 'Direct and indirect influences of parental background on children's earnings: a comparison across countries and genders', *The Manchester School*, 83(4), 423–450.

Solon, G. (2002) 'Cross-country differences in intergenerational income mobility', *Journal of Economic Perspectives*, 16, 59–66.

7 Financialised capitalism and inequality

Shareholder-value-driven firms, marketised household balance sheets and bubbly financial markets

Nicholas Black and Ismail Ertürk

Introduction

Although the scholarly interest in financialised capitalism pre-dates the 2007 crisis and the consequent Great Recession (see, for example, Lapavitsas 2011), the role in the 2007 crisis, of complex global interconnectedness of financial institutions through credit derivatives (see, for example, Fligstein and Habinek 2014) and of giant too-big-to-fail banks with balance sheets equivalent to multiples of country GDPs (see, for example, http://fessud.eu/the-project/) have unleashed a torrent of academic output on financialisation since the 2007 crisis (see, for example, reviews in Engelen and Konings 2010; Treeck 2009; Zwan 2014). However, this rather belated critical interest in the transformation of banking from intermediation for productive economy to trading of risk embedded in an originate and distribute business model (see, for example, Ertürk and Solari 2007 and Engelen et al. 2011) tends to distract from the malign distributive and allocative consequences of shareholder-value-driven firm behaviour, including banking firms, in financialised capitalism. As Andrew Haldane (2015), the Chief Economist of the Bank of England, argues, shareholder-value-driven firms are serious structural obstacles to the revival of post-crisis economies nullifying the desired effects of loose monetary policy.

In this chapter we will discuss financialisation both as a financial phenomenon and as a dominant form of corporate governance in present-day capitalism. The chapter is organised as follows: the first section will follow this introduction and provide the material context of financialisation by describing the size of financial markets and household balance sheets in relation to real economy. Since the early 1980s with deregulation of financial services, liberalisation of financial markets, globalisation of finance and the technological advances in trading financial instruments the size of finance has grown to multiples of global GDP. The size of household financial balance sheets too has grown significantly with the rise of neo-liberalism as welfare benefits have been replaced by market-based risk arrangements like defined contribution pensions and consumer credit to augment falling real wages. In the second section we will discuss financialised firm behaviour and shareholder-value ideology that justifies high levels of executive pay.

In the third section we will demonstrate how financialisation has led to increasing inequality by providing data on ten high-income economies. The concluding section will summarise the key arguments of this chapter.

Wall of money: financialisation as rise of financial economy in relation to real economy

One of the key aspects of financialised capitalism is the exponential growth and the towering size of financial markets in relation to the real economy (see, for example, Ertürk et al. 2008). Figure 7.1 shows stock of bank credit, bonds and equities between 1990 and 2011 in ten high-income economies. In all of these ten economies, by 2011, the total size of credit and equity markets was bigger than the real economy measured by gross domestic product (GDP). In the so-called liberal market economies (LMEs) of the United Kingdom and the United States, in which according to the varieties of capitalism literature we should expect more financial activity (see, for example, Hall and Soskice 2001), the size of credit and equity markets were already several times of GDP in 1990 and grew to 3.5 and 4.5 times of GDP by 2011 in spite of the financial crisis of 2007. However, financialisation has been and is a universal phenomenon and some of the so-called coordinated market economies (CMEs) in which, according to the varieties of capitalism approach, the size of finance is related to the productive activities in the economy, exhibit similar tendencies to the LMEs. For example in Denmark, Spain and Sweden the size of credit and equity markets are almost equal scale to the UK and the US. Of course the institutional characteristics of financial markets vary in all these countries and bank credit plays a bigger role than equity markets in these CME countries. Germany and Italy, on the other hand, are less financialised among this group of countries by the size of their financial markets. But this is in relative terms as in both countries the size of credit and equity markets is about 1.5 times of GDP and in Germany before the dot.com crisis of 2001 it reached almost 2.5 times of GDP and in Italy it has consistently grown over the period. Even without taking into consideration the size of the global derivatives and currency trading markets the data in Figure 7.1 demonstrates the globally consistent nature of capitalism where finance is much bigger than the real economy. In this chapter we are not going to cover the literature and discussion on the reasons for the rise of financialisation. As mentioned above, Engelen and Konings (2010), Lapavitsas (2011), Treeck (2009) and Zwan (2014) provide a literature review on this aspect of financialisation. In this chapter we are interested in the governance characteristics and distributional consequences of financialisation.

Financialisation is not only a macroeconomic phenomenon that is observed in financial markets but also affects household balance sheets and wealth. Table 7.1 shows the size of household balance sheets in the same countries covered in Figure 7.1.

In all ten countries financial assets as percentage of national income grew significantly between 1990 and 2011 in spite of sharp declines after the 2007 financial crisis. Housing assets too grew in value reflecting the general increase in

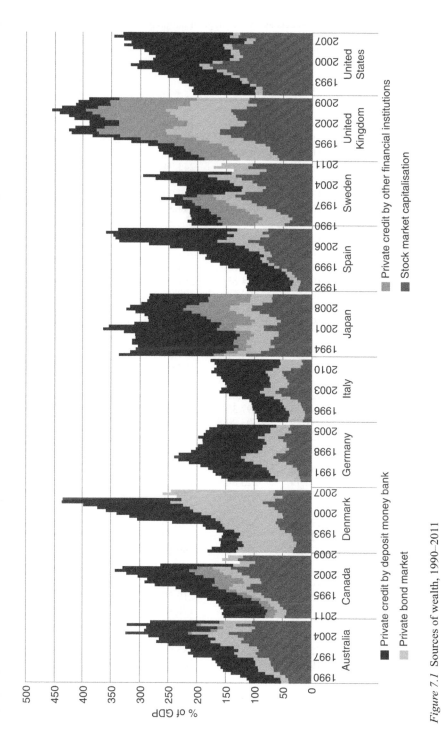

Figure 7.1 Sources of wealth, 1990–2011

Source: World Bank Financial Structure Database

Table 7.1 Household balance sheets as a percentage of national income

	Net private wealth A + (B − C)	Net financial wealth (B − C)	Non-financial assets (A)	Financial assets (B)	Liabilities (C)	Housing assets
Australia						
1990	403.87	102.07	301.81	160.98	58.91	233.43
1995	422.97	114.10	308.87	186.28	72.18	250.57
2000	443.46	118.33	325.13	215.09	96.76	268.80
2005	540.68	116.46	424.22	243.94	127.48	365.18
2007	580.91	143.32	437.59	280.55	137.23	379.44
2008	565.49	130.59	434.90	269.90	139.31	376.86
2011	527.37	100.36	427.00	244.36	144.00	372.55
Canada						
1990	294.36	143.04	151.31	214.35	71.31	119.05
1995	346.29	183.06	163.24	261.06	78.00	131.07
2000	365.48	217.26	148.23	294.04	76.78	117.89
2005	372.60	197.77	174.83	281.89	84.12	139.02
2007	401.54	209.05	192.50	298.99	89.94	153.24
2008	382.75	184.87	197.88	278.95	94.08	156.68
2011	406.36	191.92	214.44	300.54	108.62	170.37
Denmark						
1990	221.12	44.21	176.91	151.94	107.73	134.09
1995	246.81	75.18	171.63	183.06	107.88	129.86
2000	317.47	115.41	202.06	228.84	113.43	164.09
2005	359.40	120.59	238.82	256.89	136.30	200.89
2007	438.47	141.13	297.35	295.05	153.92	255.64
2008	415.29	111.39	303.90	272.94	161.55	259.66
2011	387.86	132.65	255.20	303.58	170.93	218.05
Germany						
1990	302.42	81.23	221.19	147.70	66.47	180.82
1995	309.67	85.79	223.88	156.33	70.54	185.82
2000	353.90	113.65	240.26	199.21	85.56	202.89
2005	380.93	129.11	251.82	210.67	81.56	215.66
2007	372.50	128.60	243.91	201.76	73.16	209.53
2008	380.01	128.74	251.27	200.39	71.65	216.03
2011	384.34	131.88	252.46	199.16	67.28	217.82
Italy						
1990	442.08	169.7	272.37	193.06	23.36	218.38
1995	504.75	188.64	316.12	219.20	30.56	257.56
2000	539.05	239.09	299.96	278.49	39.40	245.94
2005	608.35	238.98	369.38	290.90	51.92	311.68
2007	645.83	241.29	404.53	299.87	58.58	345.09
2008	651.64	223.39	428.25	285.66	62.27	366.26
2011	655.40	198.44	456.95	267.39	68.95	392.27
Japan						
1990	698.80	183.92	514.88	272.63	88.71	337.90
1995	602.27	205.49	396.78	305.89	100.40	269.15
2000	596.47	247.17	349.30	350.39	103.22	247.38
2005	573.92	286.78	287.13	384.64	97.86	206.77

	Net private wealth A + (B – C)	Net financial wealth (B – C)	Non-financial assets (A)	Financial assets (B)	Liabilities (C)	Housing assets
2007	578.44	292.13	286.31	386.99	94.86	209.39
2008	586.53	289.29	297.24	385.22	95.93	218.73
2011	592.13	303.99	288.14	403.82	99.83	215.35
Spain						
1990	488.18	88.74	399.44	134.50	45.76	351.37
1995	464.52	108.57	355.96	154.19	45.62	320.97
2000	510.91	128.61	382.30	187.67	59.06	343.71
2005	742.90	107.32	635.58	191.67	84.35	585.95
2007	841.91	110.29	731.62	210.36	100.07	677.89
2008	820.81	92.69	728.12	196.47	103.78	675.23
2011	771.35	92.27	679.08	200.12	107.85	630.30
Sweden						
1990	229.85	66.01	163.84	131.78	65.77	148.87
1995	218.21	71.18	147.03	123.96	52.78	134.68
2000	284.74	127.45	157.29	182.17	54.72	141.11
2005	339.09	133.27	205.82	206.39	73.12	185.65
2007	358.03	138.98	219.04	216.48	77.50	199.21
2008	364.99	126.48	238.52	208.47	81.99	216.46
2011	394.21	138.60	255.61	232.94	94.34	230.26
United Kingdom						
1990	389.19	144.44	244.75	218.15	73.71	215.26
1995	371.78	191.95	179.83	267.07	75.12	157.43
2000	520.27	289.99	230.28	373.06	83.07	206.28
2005	523.58	222.52	301.07	330.44	107.92	278.28
2007	540.66	216.56	324.10	333.59	117.03	300.73
2008	521.29	203.27	318.03	323.37	120.10	293.81
2011	541.77	230.42	311.35	342.53	112.11	284.62
United States						
1990	376.53	146.51	230.02	235.28	88.77	176.26
1995	383.78	181.36	202.41	269.58	88.22	158.84
2000	457.05	244.82	212.23	338.55	93.73	165.35
2005	489.10	198.81	290.29	319.46	120.65	232.79
2007	509.43	217.83	291.59	351.21	133.38	224.88
2008	455.17	190.03	265.13	327.52	137.49	197.35
2011	426.24	212.05	214.20	335.25	123.20	156.39

Source: The World Wealth and Income Database

global real estate prices except in the US and Japan. The value of housing assets is included in our analysis of household financialisation because as the post-crisis macro-prudential regulatory framework acknowledges real estate is used as collateral by financial institutions to expand credit in the economy (see Borio 2010; Claessens et al. 2013; BIS 2014). In Japan the value of household housing assets declined from 337.9 per cent of national income in 1990 to 215.35 per cent in 2011 reflecting the chronic deflationary forces in Japanese economy that were set in motion in the early 1990s following the crash in asset markets. Consequently the net wealth of Japanese household declined from 698.8 per cent of national income in 1990 to 592.13 per cent in 2011 as gains in financial assets failed to compensate losses in non-financial assets especially the housing assets. But nevertheless Japanese households have the third largest net wealth after Spain and Italy in these ten high-income economies. Although the value of housing assets in the US declined to 156.39 per cent of national income in 2011 from 176.26 per cent in 1990, reflecting the burst of the housing bubble there in 2007 and setting off the financial crisis, the value of financial assets and net wealth grew over the period from 146.51 per cent and 376.53 per cent of national income to 212.05 per cent and 426.24 per cent respectively. Households in Denmark are the most indebted at 170.93 per cent of national income whereas German households have the least debt at 67.28 per cent of national income. Again just like the findings in Figure 7.1 on financial markets the data in Table 7.1 on household balance sheets confirm that the 2007 financial crisis has not stopped the process of financialisation. In relation to the real economy, globally the size of the financial economy has grown significantly and is multiple times the size of the former.

Financialised firm behaviour

Financialisation is not simply a phenomenon of macro-economic quantities measured in terms of the size of financial markets and household balance sheets as multiples of real economy. Before the 2007 crisis researchers like Froud et al. (2006), Lazonick and O'Sullivan (2000) and Stout (2002) focused on firm behaviour in financialised capitalism. Maximisation of shareholder value in firms with dispersed ownership has been widely offered by both mainstream corporate finance books and consultancy firms as the solution to the agency problem in present-day capitalism where ownership and control of capital in corporations are separated. Froud et al. (2006) discusses the mainstream finance-inspired work of consultancy firms that sold to and implemented shareholder-value practices in stock-market-listed corporations. Lazonick and O'Sullivan (2000) explore the historical rise of shareholder-value maximisation principle as the dominant corporate governance practice in the US corporations where distributing profits to shareholders through high dividends and share buybacks is preferred to retaining profits for long-term investments. Share price is influenced immediately by current cash payments to shareholders. Retaining profits to invest, on the other hand, does not have the same immediate effect on share price. Therefore firms that are expected to invest capital in growth-generating projects instead prioritise share price that is the key measure of corporate success in stock-market-based economies like the US.

As the financialisation literature demonstrates capital markets have largely failed in efficient allocation of capital because corporate governance mechanisms and investor behaviour in financialised capitalism have been mostly dysfunctional almost since the 1990s causing regular stock-market bubbles and crashes with significant output and job losses. International Corporate Governance Network

(ICGN), which has 600 members in over 50 countries representing institutional investors with global assets under management in excess of US$26 trillion, itself acknowledged such dysfunctionality of corporate governance mechanisms after the 2008 financial crisis.

> Some commentators have criticised shareholders for failing to hold boards to account. It is true that shareholders sometimes encouraged companies, including investment banks, to ramp up short-term returns through leverage. They were not always as close as they could have been to companies they owned.
>
> (ICGN 2008)

In a financialised economy corporations compete in the stock market to deliver shareholder value and banks that caused the 2007 financial crisis are no exceptions to this financialised form of competition, even under state ownership as the case of Royal Bank of Scotland in the UK shows. The principle of shareholder-value maximisation is uncritically accepted by the UK government who bailed out RBS at a record cost to the taxpayer of £46 billion in 2008. The remuneration package of the chief executive officer Stephen Hester included £6.4 million worth of long-term incentives that were linked to increase in share price (BBC, 22 June 2009). The UK government saw the taxpayers as shareholders in the 80 per cent state-owned RBS and believed that a pre-specified increase in share price was a more justifiable performance target than recouping the total taxpayer's cost of £46 billon spent in bailing out RBS. In a financialised economy where the hegemonic corporate governance form requires firms seeking maximisation of shareholder value and the remuneration of the managers is linked to the achievement of this objective then return on shareholders' funds becomes the key financial metric to measure firm performance. Consequently, return on equity has become a universal metric to measure financial performance in all publicly listed banks. Both academics like Engelen et al. (2011) and regulators like the Bank of England's economist Haldane (2009) agree that high unrealistic return on equity targets in shareholder-value-driven banks that compete in stock markets encouraged excessive risk taking by management. Engelen et al. (2011) show that in the banking sector there is a consensus rate of 15 per cent return on equity that banks universally aim to achieve. Since management compensation in financialised banks is determined by share price in the stock market where the equity analysts' and activist hedge fund shareholders' opinions on bank strategy are crucially important, actual risk-taking behaviour is not likely to be influenced by the regulators' views on risk. Academics like Bebchuk and Spamann (2009) who study corporate governance and optimal executive remuneration contracts draw regulators' attention to this fundamental gap in regulators' thinking about risk in banking:

> Moreover, as long as management's incentives are tied to those of shareholders, management might have an incentive to increase risks beyond what is intended or assumed by the regulators, who might often be one step behind

banks' executives. Regulators should attempt to make management incentives work for, rather than against, the goals of banking regulation.

(Bebchuk and Spamann 2009, p. 5)

Distributional consequences of and inequality in financialised capitalism

The Friedman doctrine (1962) enshrines shareholder-value-driven capitalism by proposing that maximising the returns for shareholders ought to be the guiding purpose behind all firms. Essentially, this legitimises a socio-economic system of market-based transactions that discipline firms that do not allocate their resources efficiently by making them uncompetitive and restricting their ability to win more resources (Friedman 1962). As such, all firms have to participate in the portfolio society where financial evaluation is everything in order to survive and acquire capital (Davis 2009a). This hegemonic societal belief has even become the dominant definition of corporate governance which centres around aligning the interests of executives as agents of principal shareholders (Shleifer and Vishny 1997). Or in other words, firm behaviour is about the controllers of finance (executives) serving the suppliers of finance (shareholders and creditors) by using the firm (labour and assets) to maximise the returns for capital (Fama 1980; Fama and Jensen 1983b; Fama and Jensen 1983a). As a consequence, the well-being of labour, communities and customers is only important to the extent to which it can impact on the firm's ability to create shareholder value. Under this ideological view of corporate behaviour it is not unexpected that distributional consequences with increased income and wealth inequality have not been challenged by political and business elites.

Shareholder-value-driven capitalism is a movement that began in the 1970s and 1980s in the US and UK (Deakin 2005). It marks the transition point between the dominance of manufacturing firms being replaced by the dominance of financial market (Boyer 2000). Before the 1970s large manufacturers were depicted as the vanguards of progressive labour practices and they were responsible for creating high-wage jobs; they were pillars of society by offering secure employment with real pay increases (Davis 2009b). These large manufacturers owned the supply chain and implemented bureaucratic human resource (HR) systems that rationalised pay and employment standards across all of society (Davis and Cobb 2010). As such, the distributive consequences of this Fordist capital regime were low levels of income inequality, real wage growth and economic stability (Vidal 2013).

However, inflation, competition and slow economic growth began to squeeze profits in the 1970s which led to the creation of shareholder-value-driven capitalism (Fligstein and Shin 2007). In order to better serve the interests of providers of capital firms began a massive relocations of manufacturing activity as well as an entire reorganisation of labour markets (Harvey 2010). This created the situation where firms were no longer socially embedded and the interests of capital were disconnected from labour (Murphy and Willmott 2015). Instead, the only connection was the rhetoric of trickle-down economics which claims that value captured at the top flows down to the bottom of society, which is found to have not worked (Piketty 2014). The development of shareholder-value orientation of firms is most pronounced in Anglo-Saxon countries, but both Nordic and Continental Europe countries are also following suit (Zalewski and Whalen 2010). Indeed, financialised capitalism is a global phenomenon (Epstein 2005) and several major developed countries are experiencing comparative falls in production values in the manufacturing sector relative to the finance, insurance, real estate and business services sector.

The rise of the post-industrial society is linked to income inequality through the changing employment demands of firms which has resulted in the growth of both highly skilled and low-skilled occupations over the past few decades (Nolan 2003). As such, the distributive consequences of financialised capitalism are a higher degree of polarisation between different occupational hierarchies (Goos and Manning 2007). A service-based economy is more prone to income inequality because non-academic qualifications tend to lead to low job prospects; workers who would have been in the past working on the factory floor, as skilled craftsmen or production workers, are now flipping hamburgers (Levy and Murnane 1992). A manufacturing-based economy provides an alternative route for the less academically able to acquire skills and find good employment opportunities. In contrast, a service-based economy in financialised capitalism encourages income inequality as those who obtain academic qualification flourish because of the needs of a post-industrialised economy. For instance, in the US the need for routine manual and cognitive tasks has decreased, whereas the need for non-routine cognitive tasks has increased (Levy and Murnane 2003). The study also claims that from 1970 to 1997 the shifting education demands can explain 60 per cent of the estimated relative demand shift favouring the college labour market and the creation of highly paid jobs. This idea also has empirical support as one study showed that the polarisation of jobs can explain 33 to 51 per cent of the increase in the log 50–10 income differential, and 54–79 per cent of the increase in the log 90–10 income differential (Goos and Manning 2007).

The type of production value firms create in shareholder-value-driven capitalism is dependent on what creates the best return for capital; the consequences such as the type of employment creating income inequality is unimportant. Financial markets are not some neutral force but are the product of neoliberal ideology which is rebalancing power relations in present day capitalism in favour of a small elite by dismantling the social embeddedness of firms (Murphy and Willmott 2015) and legitimising the situation where the benefit from economic growth evades most citizens and only the elite becomes richer (Klein 2007). Essentially, financialised capitalism is creating income inequality by prioritising the interests of capital despite the fact that in ten high-income countries in Table 7.2 there has been a growth in the average annual wage between 1990 and 2011 in 2015 prices. It is also worth noting that from 1990 to 2011 the longitudinal trajectory of all these countries is relatively constant and the 2008 financial crisis had little impact on the amount of income firms distribute to their employees except in the UK.

Table 7.2 Average annual wage per employee

2015 constant prices	1990	1995	2000	2005	2007	2008	2011
Australia (AUD)	59,117	61,880	68,808	72,473	74,985	75,559	79,556
Canada (CAD)	45,861	46,119	51,375	54,203	57,268	58,352	60,119
Denmark (DKK)	315,237	327,617	349,758	384,531	395,947	401,385	413,404
Germany (EUR)		32,920	34,034	34,447	34,416	34,634	35,522
Italy (EUR)	28,047	27,129	28,396	29,219	29,391	29,423	29,388
Japan (JPY)	4,008,651	4,108,129	4,089,953	4,081,507	3,999,329	4,011,457	4,128,636
Spain (EUR)	24,543	26,017	25,927	25,923	26,163	27,216	28,156
Sweden (SEK)	263,444	262,291	308,670	332,846	351,908	356,763	365,776
United Kingdom (GBP)	25,655	26,762	31,057	34,207	35,867	34,835	33,338
United States (USD)	43,446	44,634	51,295	53,811	55,780	55,560	56,540

Source: OECD Stat

Table 7.3 Percentage change in average annual wage per employee and GDP, 1990–2011

	Wages	*GDP*	*Ratio*
Australia	34.6	114.1	1-to-3.30
Canada	31.1	127.1	1-to-4.09
Denmark	31.1	46.5	1-to-1.50
Germany*[1995]	7.9	30.5	1-to-3.87
Italy	4.8	53.4	1-to-11.13
Japan	3.0	57.3	1-to-19.11
Spain	14.7	123.6	1-to-8.41
Sweden	38.8	57.7	1-to-1.49
United Kingdom	29.9	68.2	1-to-2.28
United States	30.1	62.5	1-to-2.08

Sources: OECD Stat and Penn World Table

The growth in wages, however, has not caught up with the growth in real GDP. As Table 7.3 shows, across all these countries the growth of real GDP is faster than the growth of wages per person. As such, employees are receiving a lower fraction of benefits from the expanding economy and this is growing on a yearly basis. Firms in all these ten countries distribute less to labour and contribute to increasing inequality.

The performance of stock markets in all of the major high-income countries except Japan, which has not recovered from the collapse of its stock market in the early 1990s, between 1990 and 2001, as it can be seen in Figure 7.2, supports the shareholder-value-creation rhetoric of financialised firms. Despite the major stock-market crashes of 2001 and 2007 share prices have at least doubled in five

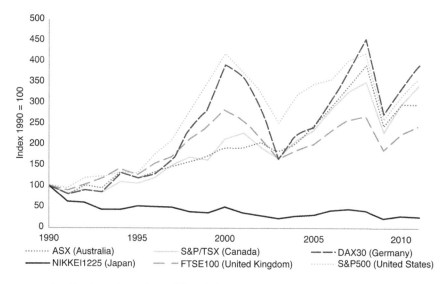

Figure 7.2 Stock-market values, 1990–2010

Table 7.4 Percentage change in wealth as a percentage of national income, 1990–2007

	Net private wealth	Net financial wealth	Non-financial assets	Financial assets	Liabilities	Housing assets
Australia	43.8	40.4	45.0	74.3	132.9	62.5
Canada	36.4	46.1	27.2	39.5	26.1	28.7
Denmark	98.3	219.2	68.1	94.2	42.9	90.6
Germany	23.2	58.3	10.3	36.6	10.1	15.9
Italy	46.1	78.6	48.5	55.3	150.8	58.0
Japan	−17.2	58.8	−44.4	41.9	6.9	−38.0
Spain	72.5	24.3	83.2	56.4	118.7	92.9
Sweden	55.8	110.5	33.7	64.3	17.8	33.8
United Kingdom	38.9	49.9	32.4	52.9	58.8	39.7
United States	35.3	48.7	26.8	49.3	50.3	27.6

of these countries. However shareholder-value-driven capitalism confuses value capture with value creation and normalises firms transferring any value to a small percentage of holders of financial assets and to executives with equity-linked remuneration packages at the expense of employees as well as other stakeholders without ownership of financial assets.

The distributive consequences of shareholder-value-driven capitalism are then such that, as Table 7.1 demonstrates, individuals who own non-financial or financial assets receive more benefit from the socio-economic system than those who do not (Piketty 2014). Prior to the financial crisis, there were significant increases in all forms of private wealth in relation to GDP – excluding Japan as explained above (see Table 7.4). Essentially, individuals gain more wealth benefit from the growth of asset values than of wages. Those who own financial assets and to a slightly lesser extent housing assets have had the largest growth in wealth.

A few years after the impact of the 2008 financial crisis the values of wealth have res-established themselves in most of these countries with the exception of Australia, Denmark and the United States (see Table 7.5). In Australia the drop is due to financial assets not recovering whereas in Denmark and the United States the drop is due to housing assets not recovering. These bursts of bubbles in asset markets in financialised capitalism are regular thus creating a great deal of precariousness in individuals' well-being.

Since the ownership of financial and housing assets tends to concentrate in the hands of non-wage earners of national income, wealth inequality increases in financialised capitalism. The deteriorating wealth inequality due to the ownership patterns in financial and housing assets accompanies the deteriorating income inequality (see Table 7.6) due to a lower share of GDP growth being paid as wages as discussed above in a shareholder-value-driven financialised capitalism (Lazonick and O'Sullivan 2000). For example, the CEO–worker pay multiple in the US was in 1965 only 20-to-1 but it has since risen to a staggering 303-to-1 in 2014 (Mishel and Davis 2015). In the US and the UK the pay of executives has

Table 7.5 Percentage change in wealth as a percentage of national income, 1990–2011

	Net private wealth	Net financial wealth	Non-financial assets	Financial assets	Liabilities	Housing assets
Australia	30.6	–1.7	41.5	51.8	144.4	59.6
Canada	38.0	34.2	41.7	40.2	52.3	43.1
Denmark	75.4	200.0	44.3	99.8	58.7	62.6
Germany	27.1	62.4	14.1	34.8	1.2	20.5
Italy	48.3	393.2	67.8	38.5	195.2	79.6
Japan	–15.3	65.3	–44.0	48.1	12.5	–36.3
Spain	58.0	4.0	70.0	48.8	135.7	79.4
Sweden	71.5	110.0	56.0	76.8	43.4	54.7
United Kingdom	39.2	59.5	27.2	57.0	52.1	32.2
United States	13.2	44.7	–6.9	42.5	38.8	–11.3

Table 7.6 Income share of the top 1 per cent

	1990	1995	2000	2005	2007	2008	2010/2011
Australia	5.64	6.19	7.54	7.50	7.67	7.43	7.68
Canada	9.34	9.97	12.78	13.09	13.72	13.06	12.22
Denmark	5.17	5.03	5.73	5.78	6.12	6.05	6.41
Germany		8.84		11.85	12.93	13.89	12.81
Italy	7.78	8.13	9.09	9.35	9.86	9.66	
Japan	8.05	7.30	8.22	9.42	9.64	9.71	9.51
Spain	8.37	7.88	8.65	8.80	9.03	8.74	8.53
Sweden	4.38	5.25	5.97	6.28	6.91	7.09	7.02
United Kingdom	9.8	10.75	13.51	14.22	15.44		12.93
United States	12.98	13.53	16.49	17.68	18.33	17.89	17.47

Source: The World Wealth and Income Database

been increasing exponentially since the 1970s and executives commonly receive compensation packages worth millions of pounds/dollars (Conyon and Murphy 2000; Erturk et al. 2004; Frydman and Saks 2010). This exponential increase in the pay multiple between CEO compensation and average wage is not justified by performance as the literature finds no empirical support for equivalent value creation by the top management (see, for example, Ezzamel et al. 2008; Tosi et al. 2008; Willmott 2010). Value creation is not the same as value wealth creation (Willmott 2010) and firms operating under the premise of shareholder value is legitimising a dysfunctional capital accumulation regime (Vidal 2013). While proponents of neoliberalism might argue it is impossible for firms to underpay their employees by invoking the imagery of market forces in labour market, markets are simply the aggregate consequences of organisational behaviours (Rubery 1997; Rubery and Grimshaw 2003). All firms competing under the premise of shareholder-value-driven capitalism will homogeneously engage in the same organisational behaviours that will create a convergence in their distributive outcomes. It is purportedly the product of market forces because all firms are engaging in the same organisational behaviours. Hence, firms are collectively using their power to control wages for profit maximisation causing labour to compete against each other in a race to the bottom while executives compete against each other through lucrative remuneration packages in a race to the top (Kalleberg 2011).

The setting of executive remunerations is a key part of the corporate governance literature and there has been a huge academic interest in this area over the past decade (Gillan 2006). The corporate governance literature is normally split into two schools of thought for explaining the rise in executive pay – the efficient contracting hypothesis and the managerial hypothesis. Competitive pay argues that market-based contracts or optimal pricing contracts have forced corporate executive salaries to increase (Gabaix and Landier 2008) whereas the managerial hypothesis argues that corporate executives engaging in rent-seeking behaviour has caused income inequality (Bebchuk and Fried 2003). There is empirical evidence supporting and opposing both schools of thought and neither discourse can explain the rise of income inequality satisfactorily in line with empirical evidence for an extended period of time (Frydman and Jenter 2010).

The traditional debate of whether executive remunerations (e.g. base salaries, annual bonuses, stock options and long-term incentive plans) are linked to corporate performance (Chahine and Goergen 2012), however, places too much emphasis on top management's role in organisations. Indeed, such debates tend to be counter-productive and place too much emphasis on equating corporate performance of organisations – which are worth billions of dollars, employ tens of thousands of people and are multinational – to a handful of corporate executives. The contribution that these individuals make is theoretically over-exaggerated and wall-of-money supported stock-market bubbles in financialised capitalism play a significant role in creating economic success measured by share price (Garvey and Milbourn 2006). However, most empirical evidence supports that there is no link between corporate performance and executive remunerations (Tosi et al. 2008), but even if there was, this does not mean that their pay is socially justified and they should capture the disproportionate rewards of economic growth. They cannot be individually responsible for it and despite CEOs being able through their rhetoric to influence share prices, it does not affect the bottom line and create tangible value (Froud et al. 2008). The debate of whether executive remuneration is linked to corporate performance presupposes that they are individually responsible for creating that superior performance which is extremely difficult to argue given how complex large corporations are.

Conclusion

This chapter discussed the phenomenon of financialisation by providing data on two aspects of the growing size of financial economy in relation to the real economy. In ten high-income economies at varying degrees the size of financial markets has grown significantly to multiples of GDP. The institutional characteristics of individual countries determine the scale and the most significant contributing financial intermediation market in the financialisation process. Financialisation, however, is not only a financial market phenomenon. It is reflected in the size of household balance sheets as well. Financial assets, liabilities and housing assets on household balance sheets have grown consistently in major high-income economies between 1990 and 2011. Financialised capitalism is not simply a macroeconomic phenomenon. Firm behaviour where agents – managers – are driven by the shareholder-value maximisation objective in a capitalism that is defined by the separation of control and ownership of capital is an equally important aspect of financialised capitalism as such behaviour prioritises financial motives and financial measures of corporate success. Consequently managers are given equity-linked remuneration packages to align their interests with those of shareholders. Labour loses out in this process as wages are controlled to distribute more of the cash generated to the shareholders and stock markets reward wage controls. Top management's share of the income has increased and the multiple of CEO pay to average wage has unjustifiably reached dizzying heights causing significant deterioration in income and wealth inequality in financialised capitalism. Formation of bubbles in asset markets and dysfunctional corporate governance arrangements in financialised capitalism jointly produce increasing inequality and precariousness for wage earners without ownership of financial and housing assets.

References

BBC News (2009) 'RBS boss set for £9.6m pay deal' [Online]. Available at: http://news. bbc.co.uk/go/pr/fr/-/1/hi/business/8112199.stm.

Bebchuk, L. A. and Fried, J. M. (2003) 'Executive compensation as an agency problem', *Journal of Economic Perspectives* 17(3): 71–92.

Bebchuk, L. A. and Spamann, H. (2009) 'Regulating bankers' pay', Harvard John M. Olin Center for Law, Economics, and Business. Discussion Paper No. 641, www.law.harvard. edu/programs/olin_center/.

BIS (Bank for International Settlement) (2014) 'Debt and the financial cycle: domestic and global', BIS 84th Annual Report. Available at: www.bis.org/publ/arpdf/ar2014e. htm.

Borio, C. (2010) 'The financial cycle and macroeconomics: what have we learnt?', *BIS Working Papers* No. 395, available at: www.bis.org/publ/work395.htm.

Boyer, R. (2000) 'Is a finance-led growth regime a viable alternative to Fordism? A preliminary analysis', *Economy and Society* 29(1): 111–145.

Chahine, S. and Goergen, M. (2012) 'CEO compensation and stock options in IPO firms', in R. S. Thomas and J. G. Hill (eds) *Research Handbook on Executive Pay*, Cheltenham: Edward Elgar Publishing.

Claessens, S., Ghosh, S. R. and Mihet, R. (2013) 'Macro-prudential policies to mitigate financial system vulnerabilities', *Journal of International Money and Finance*, 39: 153–185.

Conyon, M. J. and Murphy, K. J. (2000) 'The prince and the pauper? CEO pay in the United States and United Kingdom', *The Economic Journal* 110(467): 640–671.

Davis, G. F. (2009a) *Managed by the Markets: How Finance Re-Shaped America*, Oxford: Oxford University Press.

Davis, G. F. (2009b) 'The rise and fall of finance and the end of the society of organizations', *The Academy of Management Perspectives*, 23(3): 27–44.

Davis, G. F. and Cobb, J. A. (2010) 'Corporations and economic inequality around the world: The paradox of hierarchy', *Research in Organizational Behavior*, 30: 35–53.

Deakin, S. (2005) 'The coming transformation of shareholder value', *Corporate Governance: An International Review*, 13(1): 11–18.

Engelen, E., Ertürk, I., Froud, J., Johal, S., Leaver, A., Moran, M., Nilsson, A. and Williams, K. (2011) *After the Great Complacence: Financial Innovation and Politics of Financial Reforms*, Oxford: Oxford University Press.

Engelen, E. and Konings, M. (2010) 'Financial capitalism resurgent: comparative institutionalism and the challenges of financialization'. In G. Morgan et al. (eds) *The Oxford Handbook of Comparative Institutional Analysis*, Oxford: Oxford University Press, pp. 601–624.

Epstein, G. A. (2005) *Financialization and the World Economy*. London: Edward Elgar Publishing.

Ertürk, I., Froud, J., Johal, S. and Williams, K. (2004) 'Corporate governance and disappointment', *Review of International Political Economy*, 11(4): 677–713.

Ertürk, I., Froud, J., Johal, S., Leaver, A. and Williams, K. (2008) *Financialization at Work: Key Texts and Commentary*. London: Routledge.

Ertürk, I. and Solari, S. (2007) 'Banks as continuous reinvention', *New Political Economy*, 12(3): 369–388.

Ezzamel, M., Willmott, H. and Worthington, F. (2008) 'Manufacturing shareholder value: the role of accounting in organizational transformation', *Accounting, Organizations and Society* 33(2): 107–140.

Fama, E. F. (1980) 'Agency problems and the theory of the firm', *The Journal of Political Economy*, 88(2): 288–307.

Fama, E. F. and Jensen, M. C. (1983a) 'Agency problems and residual claims', *Journal of Law and Economics*, 26(2): 327–349.

Fama, E. F. and Jensen, M. C. (1983b) 'Separation of ownership and control', *Journal of Law and Economics*, 26(2): 301–325.

Fligstein, N. and Habinek, J. (2014) 'Sucker punched by the invisible hand: the spread of the worldwide financial crisis, 2007–2010', *SocioEconomic Review*, 12(4): 1–29.

Fligstein, N. and Shin, T. (2007) 'Shareholder value and the transformation of the US economy, 1984–2001', *Sociological Forum*, Wiley Online Library, 399–424.

Friedman, M. (1962) *Capitalism and Freedom*, Chicago, University of Chicago Press.

Froud, J. et al. (2006) *Financialization and Strategy: Narrative and Numbers*, London: Routledge.

Froud, J., Johal, S., Leaver, A. and Williams, K. (2008) 'GE under Jack Welsch: narrative, performance and the business model', in I. Erturk, J. Froud, S. Johal, A. Leaver and K. Williams (eds) *Financialization at Work: Key Texts and Commentary*, London: Routledge, pp. 343–356.

Frydman, C. and Jenter, D. (2010) 'CEO compensation', *Annual Review of Financial Economics*, 2(1): 75–102.

Frydman, C. and Saks, R. E. (2010) 'Executive compensation: a new view from a long-term perspective, 1936–2005', *Review of Financial Studies*, 23(5): 2099–2138.

Gabaix, X. and Landier, A. (2008) 'Why has CEO pay increased so much?', *The Quarterly Journal of Economics*, 123(1): 49–100.

Garvey, G. T and Milbourn, T. T. (2006) 'Asymmetric benchmarking in compensation: Executives are rewarded for good luck but not penalized for bad', *Journal of Financial Economics*, 82(1): 197–225.

Gillan, S. L. (2006) 'Recent developments in corporate governance: an overview', *Journal of Corporate Finance*, 12(3): 381–402.

Goos, M. and Manning, A. (2007) 'Lousy and lovely jobs: the rising polarization of work in Britain', *The Review of Economics and Statistics*, 89(1): 118–133.

Haldane, A. (2009) 'Small lessons from big crisis' [Online]. Available: .www.bankof england.co.uk/publications/speeches/2009/speech397.pdf

Haldane, A. (22 May 2015) 'Who owns a company?', speech delivered at University of Edinburgh Corporate Finance Conference, Edinburgh. Available at www.bankofengland. co.uk/publications/Pages/speeches/2015/833.aspx (accessed on 20 July 2015).

Hall, P. A. and Soskice, D. (eds) (2001) *Varieties of Capitalism: The Institutional Foundations of Comparative Advantage*, Oxford: Oxford University.

Harvey, D. (2010) *The Enigma of Capital and the Crisis This Time*, London: Profile Books.

ICGN (International Corporate Governance Network) (2008) 'Statement on the Global Financial Crisis', 10 November, www.iasplus.com/en/binary/resource/0811icgn.pdf/ view (accessed on 10 July 2015).

Kalleberg, A. L. (2011) *Good Jobs, Bad Jobs: The Rise of Polarized and Precarious Employment Systems in the United States, 1970s to 2000s*, New York: Russell Sage Foundation.

Klein, N. (2007) *The Shock Doctrine: The Rise of Disaster Capitalism*, London: Allen Lane.

Lapavitsas, C. (2011) 'Theorizing financialization', *Work, Employment & Society*, 25(4), 611–626.

Lazonick, W. and O'Sullivan, M. (2000) 'Maximizing shareholder value: a new ideology for corporate governance', *Economy and Society*, 29(1): 13–35.

Levy, D. L. (2008) 'Political contestation in global production networks', *Academy of Management Review*, 33(4): 943–963.

Levy, F. and Murnane, R. J. (1992) 'US earnings levels and earnings inequality: a review of recent trends and proposed explanations', *Journal of Economic Literature*, 30(3): 1333–1381.

Levy, F. and Murnane, R. J. (2003) 'The skill content of recent technological change: an empirical exploration', *The Quarterly Journal of Economics*, 118(4): 1279–1333.

Mishel, L. and Davis, A. (2015) 'Top CEOs make 300 times more than typical workers', Economic Policy Institute, Issue Brief #399.

Murphy, J. and Willmott, H. (2015) 'The rise of the 1%: an organizational explanation', in M. Lounsbury (ed.) *Elites on Trial (Research in the Sociology of Organizations)*. Bingley: Emerald Group Publishing Limited, 25–53.

Nolan, P. (2003) 'Reconnecting with history: the ESRC future of work programme', *Work, Employment & Society*, 17(3): 473–480

Piketty, T. (2014) *Capital in the Twenty-First Century*, Cambridge, MA: Harvard University Press.

Rubery, J. (1997) 'Wages and the labour market', *British Journal of Industrial Relations* 35(3): 337–366.

Rubery, J. and Grimshaw, D. (2003) *The Organization of Employment: An International Perspective*, Basingstoke: Palgrave Macmillan.

Shleifer, A. and Vishny, R. W. (1997) 'A survey of corporate governance', *The Journal of Finance*, 52(2): 737–783.

Stout, L. A. (2002) 'Bad and not-so-bad arguments for shareholder primacy', *Southern California Law Review*, 75: 1189–1210.

Tosi, H.L., Jr., Katz, J. and Comez-Mejia, L. (2008) 'Testing the pay/performance relation', in I. Erturk, J. Froud, S. Johal et al. (eds) *Financialization at Work: Key Texts and Commentary*, Routledge: London, 120–133.

Treeck, T. van (2009) 'The political economy debate on "financialization" – a macro-economic perspective', *Review of International Political Economy*, 16(5): 907–944.

Vidal, M. (2013) 'Postfordism as a dysfunctional accumulation regime: a comparative analysis of the USA, the UK and Germany', *Work, Employment & Society*, 27(3): 451–471.

Willmott, H. (2010) 'Creating "value" beyond the point of production: branding, financial-ization and market capitalization', *Organization*, 17(5): 517–542.

Zalewski, D. A. and Whalen, C. J. (2010) 'Financialization and income inequality: a post Keynesian institutionalist analysis', *Journal of Economic* Issues, 44(3): 757–777.

Zwan, N. van der (2014) 'State of the art: making sense of financialization', *Socio-Economic Review*, 12: 99–129.

8 Regional inequalities and foreign direct investments

The case of Hungary

Miklós Szanyi

Introduction

"The mysteries of the trade become no mystery, but are, as it were, in the air" Alfred Marshall wrote a long time ago Alfred Marshall in his seminal book *Principles of Economics* (Marshall, 1890, p. 271).[1] This sentence has been cited very frequently (4,020 hits in a simple Google search for the sentence), and in fact has also been considered by policy makers and influential institutions like the World Bank or the European Commission (see Krugman, 1991; Venables, 2002). Spatial concentration of economic activity has attracted the attention of classical economics. Centres of active economic development and welfare continued to attract various businesses with the advance of capitalist economic and social development. Some of these centres began to specialize in certain industrial activities. Dutch porcelain from Delft, fine lacework from Brussels, and many other products were world famous and demonstrated specialization. Other locations on the other hand concentrated on a wider range of business activities. Hence, regional concentration is an old phenomenon. Spatial concentration of specialized economic activities has been largely supported by knowledge spillovers – sources of increasing return on scale.[2]

Recently the aspect of supporting the exchange of ideas and innovation – the main sources of spillover effects – became priority in economic analysis and policy alike. In many cases this element is separated from other components of the "mystery" and treated with some kind of obsession as a panacea to spur economic growth. This is expressed in policies supporting innovation and regional economic growth, like the European Union's Lisbon Strategy and the new Europe 2020 plan. The obvious failure of the Lisbon Agenda raises the question of whether policies adequately set the target, or if the increasing returns' complex nature and background has been properly understood and addressed. Another popular view attributed large importance to multinational business in delivering the desired spillover effects to local business. The main argument would be that they possess the largest pool of technological and managerial knowledge that could be used and implemented to some extent in their cooperation networks including associated local companies. Most recent research called attention to the importance of territorial capital that creates adequate absorption capacity of knowledge (OECD, 2001; Casi and Resmini, 2012). Without this spillover effects and agglomeration process cannot unfold.

The emergence of multinational firms in a given region can also boost local business thus contributing to higher economic growth. Several studies tried to prove the existence of spillover effects and measure their impact (e.g. Görg and Greenaway, 2004; Lengyel et al., 2011; Iwasaki et al., 2012; for an interesting meta-analysis of the related literature see Iwasaki and Tokunaga, 2014). However, due to various methodological reasons and the high complexity of determinants of spillovers and of regional growth empirical evidence remained rather mixed (Szanyi, 2002). This fact gave fuel to critical approaches towards foreign direct investment (FDI) in Central Europe, such as the dependent market economy (DME) model of Nölke and Vliegenhart (2009).

What stands clear is the growth-enhancing contribution of the activity of new multinational investments themselves (Antalóczy and Sass, 2005). Sources of economic growth have been manifold in the transition process of Hungary, but two main sources stood out. The first was the establishment of de novo business facilities through FDI (much less through the activity of local capital owners). This was expressed in the establishment and growth of new industries like electronics and automotive industry, the two main manufacturing branches that are largely run by multinational firms' affiliates in Hungary. The other main growth engine was public investments and related construction work. The concept of this chapter is interested mainly in the spatial consequences of the FDI-led growth pattern.

A conservative approach to the impact of multinational business on regional economic growth may omit indirect impacts (spillovers) but concentrate on the effect of foreign investments themselves. The main question in this context is whether foreign investments are directed to certain locations by existing spatial differences in factor endowments and levels of development, or foreign invest- ments themselves create spatial differences. This seems to be a "chicken and egg" type question that cannot be answered in general terms but rather case by case. What is suggested by the new economic geography is that once the process has launched it may become self-sustaining through positive externalities until for some reason growth sources become exhausted and stagnation or even economic decline follows (Krugman, 1998). Another important question is about the role of federal and local governments' policies influencing this process. Can these poli- cies effectively support the creation and improvement of local factors of economic growth? Can spatial economic development be drifted from its "natural path" and approach a new higher level and sustainable on the long run development path?

The main aim of this chapter is to provide some evidence on the questions about the relationship of foreign direct investments (FDI) and regional differences in development levels and the concentration of business activity. Hungary is the selected country which was a forerunner in the attraction of FDI after the political and economic transition of 1989. Hungary is an interesting test environment also, because during the communist era spatial structure of the economy was strongly influenced by government decrees. Much effort was made to establish an industrial base in traditional agricultural areas and less developed regions. The Hungarian evidence also sheds some light on the durability of this administratively shaped regional economic structure. FDI played a crucial role in the restructuring and modernization of the Hungarian economy during the past 25 years. It is a highly interesting question if the investments built on traditional (historic) endowments, opportunities of the communist-era large-scale development programmes or found entirely new locations for their operation. We can test the effects of capital-attraction policies of Hungarian governments. Comparisons are made on the timely development and the relationship of foreign investments and regional economic growth. While previous research found a strong correlation between FDI and regional growth in Hungary (Antalóczy and Sass, 2005; Lengyel et al., 2011), the relationship seemed to loosen somewhat during the 2000s.

The establishment of the FDI-led development model in Hungary

Hungary is a small open economy, which started the transition process from socialism to the market economy in 1989. The establishment of minority foreign ownership in the form of joint ventures was already legally allowed in 1972, and a US$400 million large stock of investments had been accumulated until 1989. Moreover, regular contacts with world markets and foreign firms allowed the accumulation of some network capital in the Hungarian economy that became

Table 8.1 Inward FDI in Hungary (net inflow, reinvested profits, loans, € bn)

	FDI change	Capital inflow	Reinvested profits	Loans
1995	3,695.7	3,562.7	−163.6	296.5
1996	2,625.0	1,745.9	397.3	481.8
1997	3,681.1	2,010.2	1,155.0	515.9
1998	2,988.1	1,371.8	1,009.2	607.1
1999	3,106.3	1,434.9	1,054.2	617.3
2000	2,998.4	1,509.6	1,135.0	353.8
2001	4,390.7	1,096.3	1,478.7	1,815.7
2002	3,185.1	1,156.7	1,911.4	116.9
2003	1,887.5	−664.1	1,787.6	764.0
2004	3,438.7	1,081.6	2,227.4	129.6
2005	6,172.1	3,966.2	1,917.9	288.0
2006	5,454.4	1,475.3	1,358.6	2,620.4
2007	2,852.1	844.0	2,274.5	−266.4
2008	3,086.8	2,301.4	895.1	−109.8
2009	1,289.1	2,821.6	−191.8	−1,340.8
2010	1,231.6	2,814.0	−186.1	−1,396.3
2011	1,557.5	430.0	1,225.9	−98.4
2012	3,942.1	1,915.9	1,462.0	564.1
2013	1,871.8	2,202.7	1,491.0	−1,821.9
2014	4,504.5	87.3	3,682.7	734.5

Source: Hungarian National Bank

an important lever of Hungary's internationalization process. More significant volumes of FDI started to arrive in the country after 1991 when the privatization process was directed towards sales to foreign investors. When the privatization process decelerated at the end of the 1990s large-scale greenfield investments started to upheld yearly FDI inflow levels in the range of €3–4 billion. Later on the expansion of existing capacities gained momentum. This is shown by the increasing share of reinvested profits in the source structure of FDI stock increment (Antalóczy et al., 2011).

Hungarian FDI statistics demonstrate the outstanding role of foreign investments. During the years of the transition process most of the largest multinational companies established a direct presence in Hungary in the form of an affiliated company. A foreign presence has been especially strong in the automotive and electronics industries in manufacturing, in retail trade, banking and financial services, telecommunication and media. These are typically the most globalized businesses. The establishment of Hungarian affiliates in them reflects the fact of successful integration of the Hungarian economy in global production networks. One clear evidence of this development is the increasing and rather high share of intra-company transactions in foreign trade (Fridmuc et al., 1999) or the analysis of Hungarian affiliates' role in global value chains (Sass and Szalavetz, 2014).

The economic situation of Hungary at the beginning of the transition process was determined by a number of specific factors (Szanyi, 2003). Firstly, the country was heavily indebted; cash revenues were required to cover debt services and possibly reduce debt. Secondly, the economic reform process during the last two decades of socialism produced valuable contact network and experience with doing business on international markets with multinational companies. This prior managerial knowledge could be readily utilized already in the early phase of transition. Thirdly, the Hungarian government put great emphasis on improving national competitiveness through restructuring and technological development in the economy. This process could be most efficiently launched with the involvement of multinational firms. Fourthly, privatization and especially sales to foreign owners was regarded as an important element of institution building.[3] The mode of entry of FDI in privatization transactions strongly influenced the spatial patterns: investments arrived in traditional industrial centres. Later, when FDI gained momentum and follow-up investments of first- and second-tier suppliers of multinational firms also arrived, spatial concentration of FDI further increased (Antalóczy and Sass, 2005).

Parallel with the privatization process an investment-attraction policy was applied (Antalóczy et al., 2011). It aimed at the attraction of big business in most globalized industries like electronics or the automotive industry. The applied policy tools were fiscal (tax allowances), financial (budget subsidies) and other specific regulatory incentives. In the first period (1988–1995) of FDI attraction policy in Hungary mainly fiscal incentives played important role. Large-scale investments (sometimes bound to privatization purchases) received long-time tax holidays that could be renewed with further investments. Hungary successfully attracted a large portion of FDI investing in the Visegrad countries (V4).

From 1996 till 2003 a more transparent system was in effect that defined some general policy aims to be achieved with the help of FDI (large-scale investments). These aims included structural elements with preferred sectors and regional focus alongside employment and export targets. Besides the fiscal incentives new regulatory changes played an important role: the establishment of industrial free trade zones (IFTZs). Firms operating in these zones were exempt from customs duties as well as the value added tax.[4] Not only new fiscal incentives were available, but IFTZs significantly reduced the costs of bureaucratic procedures. Based on advantageous IFTZ regulation regional investment hubs developed. Pilot FDI projects attracted traditional suppliers to invest in Hungarian IFTZs. In some counties large-scale changes of economic structure occurred. On the other hand, FDI became regionally concentrated and typically also isolated from local business.

One of the last problems of Hungary's EU accession negotiations was the streamlining of FDI incentives with EU competition policy regulations. FDI incentives had to be transformed into the general European state aid system. Development goals had to be articulated more precisely, fiscal and financial support were to be fitted into the aid intensity principle, IFTZs were to be abolished altogether. Due to the changes the importance of financial means increased, and emphasis of the supports shifted towards more general objectives that aimed the improvement of competitiveness in general, not specifically addressed to single investment projects. Since the most important elements of investment support were still bound to investment size, aid was still largely addressed to big multinational business. Nevertheless, Hungary's leading role in capital attraction faded out. Yet, by this time the Hungarian economy was driven by the activity of multinational firms.

The strong influence of multinational companies in the Hungarian economy can be illustrated by several figures. They have contributed much to national investments creating a massive body of highly productive manufacturing and services base.[5] The spread of FDI is very much visible too. In certain hot spots like Komárom, Győr and Székesfehérvár, various parts of the larger Budapest agglomeration new industrial districts have been created or old ones renovated. Foreign companies produced 53 per cent of GDP in 2013, employed every fourth employee and contributed 46 per cent of gross capital formation (Central Statistical Office, 2015). Their share in retail trade, banking and financial services, telecommunication, the automotive industry and electronics is exceptionally high. Since foreign firms, especially those in manufacturing, are partners in international value chains they by definition are export oriented. Over 80 per cent of total manufacturing export is delivered by the foreign-owned sector.

We can evaluate the strong presence of multinational business in various ways. We can approach from the standpoint of development trends of the whole transition period up till now. Compared with the starting point the current economic structure of Hungary is more developed with a high share of high- and upper medium-tech manufacturing production and highly efficient services sector. It is not likely that this extraordinary change in economic structure would have been achieved without

Table 8.2 Share of foreign-owned companies in sales, employment and gross investments in Hungary (selected economic branches, per cent)

Sales		2008	2012
	Manufacturing	64.9	69.0
	Energy supply	74.4	67.5
	Trade	44.6	45.4
	Infocommunication	62.7	67.7
	Total non-financial	50.1	53.3
	Financial	53.8	70.1
Employment			
	Manufacturing	44.0	47.7
	Energy supply	51.5	51.9
	Trade	21.5	24.0
	Infocommunication	29.8	37.0
	Total non-financial	23.8	26.1
	Financial	46.9	45.1
Gross investments			
	Manufacturing	67.8	78.3
	Energy supply	61.6	65.0
	Trade	49.4	41.3
	Infocommunication	74.2	79.0
	Total non-financial	49.6	55.3

Source: Central Statistical Office

the strong investment activity of foreign firms.[6] On the other hand, we can see also clear drawbacks. For example, the strong presence of multinational firms produced a dual structure in V4 economies. Foreign firms have relatively few contacts to local companies along their main production activity. Local suppliers usually do not enter their value chain.

The reasons of this are manifold. Firstly, existing technological cooperation links in the value chain are not likely be replaced by new entrants because of the high costs of entry. Secondly, local firms attained technological capabilities, financial and logistics capacities for cooperating with global business only gradually. At the moment of FDI penetration of the V4 economies local firms were not fit for cooperation (Antalócy et al., 2011). Nevertheless, the scope of essential contribution by local firms to the global value chains started to increase after 2000. Due to the 2008/9 crisis and recession thereafter cost-cutting considerations became even more important that moved multinational firms towards more intensive local sourcing. V4 countries launched support programmes to enable local firms to cooperate with multinational companies (Kalotay and Sass, 2012). The other dimension of the dual structure is spatial duality. I deal with this problem in the remaining part of the chapter.

Much of the FDI literature tried to identify investment-attraction factors but usually on a national rather than a regional level. Among studies concentrating on regional observations Villaverde and Maza (2015) regressed yearly regional FDI inflow and regional GDP ratios of EU regions. They concluded that investments were concentrated in highly developed European regions (Ile de France, Brussels, Stockholm) with the top 30 regions receiving 52 per cent of total investments of the 2000–2006 period. Among the regressed variables economic potential, labour-market characteristics, technological progress and competitiveness were the most significant. Interestingly, all Hungarian regions received considerable amounts of investment, four of them above their absorption potential. But the robustness of the model was not very impressive, maybe because large parts of FDI represented mergers and acquisitions of developed regions' firms. These were transactions that were mainly influenced by capital market developments and not by the determinants of "classic" FDI. A further interesting observation was made concerning the implementation of economic and administrative regions. When the authors corrected the calculations, counting also progress in neighbouring regions, the robustness increased. Similar "adjustment" of the administratively fixed borders of European regions was suggested in an earlier publication (Szanyi, 2008).

In a similar approach in search for determinants of regional FDI flows Casi and Resmini (2010) used the total number of FDI-related companies in their estimations, arguing that attraction factors influenced investment decisions regardless of the size of the investments. They found similar results: most investments were realized in regions of core-Europe, the most developed regions in the 2005–07 period. Most important determinants were market potential, market growth, labour cost and the existence of agglomerations. Their findings do not provide useful information to the local economic impact of FDI; however, the importance of existing clusters and agglomerations corroborates well with some other empirical findings (see, e.g., Lengyel et al., 2011) and also with the roots of agglomeration theory from Marshal to Krugman.

The other approach in the research of FDI and regional growth relationships tried to address the question more directly using regional data of both FDI inflow and economic activity. The traditional argument on growth enhancing positive externalities, direct (competition, employment) and indirect (spillover) effects were to be proved on the level of regions. Casi and Resmini (2012) found little convincing evidence on the growth-enhancing effect of FDI at the level of European regions. The correlation between total FDI stock and gross value added rate was weak. The lack of correlation was explained by the different level of absorption capacity of the regions. Many European regions could not effectively utilize the growth-enhancing potential of FDI due to the high level of corruption, closed social capital and low level of relational capital (lack of cooperation). The role of territorial capital in the relationship of FDI and regional growth, and the unfolding of spillover effects, was also emphasized by Lengyel and Szanyi (2011).

Casi and Resmini (2012) found significant difference in growth effects of various types of investments. FDI in the services sector seemed to have a stronger and more widespread effect on regional growth than manufacturing investment. This later was effective in regions with strong specialization on the same activity. Peripheral regions were driven mainly by FDI in manufacturing while core (and higher developed) regions with more diversified economic structure benefited more from FDI in services. This finding supported those pieces of literature that differentiated among different types of spillover effects based on varying qualities of knowledge in different types of firms and varying qualities of absorption capacities depending on regional specialization patterns. (For a comprehensive analysis of this topic see Lengyel et al., 2011.) This finding may also lead us to the conclusion that FDI may increase rigidity of economic structures by increasing the importance of existing businesses in a given region. The case of Hungary is typical for this type of development: much of the FDI received after 1989 went to regions and industries that seemed to have strong local underpinnings. As we will see in the detailed analysis this process contributed to growing regional inequalities: more developed regions with a stronger industrial production base received the bulk of FDI which then ignited further growth effects locally, while less developed regions remained largely untouched and produced a lower level of economic growth. This observation also highlights the limits of capital-attraction policies that could not make FDI spread more evenly in the country despite strong efforts.

Regional inequalities of economic activity and FDI

The core part of this chapter is based on an analysis of Hungarian statistical data for the period 2000–2014. Antalóczy and Sass (2005) conducted a comprehensive analysis on the relationships of FDI concentration and economic concentration in Hungarian counties for the period 1990–2002. In this section I continue and expand the analysis for more recent years. Before going into the details of the analysis the chosen database needs some explanation. Firstly I have to emphasize the problem of limited accessibility of data. The Central Statistical Office provides in line with EU requirements FDI stock and flow data only within a rather limited scope: the number of projects/companies and invested capital is accessible.[7] In some sporadic publications the CSO also publishes other highly interesting figures on foreign companies' share in production, employment, investments and exports, but time series are no longer accessible. This is very unfortunate, since this data could best describe the direct economic impact of FDI. Thus, my analysis is also restricted to the usage of invested capital stock as a measure of FDI.

Another important methodological problem arises with the administrative and economic meaning of regions. Administrative regions of the EU do not coincide with economic regions. Moreover, economic hotspots of Hungary have a more limited geographic outreach concerning employment or regular production supplies. Therefore I use data on Hungarian counties rather than regions with the note that in certain aspects even counties are too large observation units. On the other hand, in many cases neighbouring counties may be also economically bound to some of the growth poles of the country (Szanyi, 2008). Finally, some explanations for the selected years: 2000 was chosen as starting point mainly because up till around that year massive FDI inflows in the form of new investments strongly altered economic structure. There have also been major new investments in the 2000s, though not on the same scale. FDI stock was increased by the expansion of existing capacities. These were therefore follow-up investments and not genuine ones that could alter the spatial pattern of investments. There were only a few cases of new factories opened by incumbent companies in new locations. More frequently they reduced the number of outlets and concentrated activities on main hubs. 2006 was chosen as the exact middle of the time span 2000–2012, and also because this was the last year of strong economic growth in Hungary.[8] 2012 was finally the last year for which the CSO published a full range of data, although much data for 2013 and 2014 was also available by the time of the preparation of the study.

As shown in Figure 8.1, the counties Vas, Győr-Moson-Sopron, Komárom-Esztergom and Fejér had a roughly average or above average development level in 2012. Budapest stood out with an extremely high per capita GDP production level. Figure 8.4 contains more information on the large differences among regions. Per capita GDP figures for Budapest were twice as high as the national average and were increasing in the 2000–2012 period. Moreover, Budapest as a growth pole had huge weight in economic activity. Economic concentration in Budapest was very high during the 1990s and also increasing up till today (Figure 8.2 and Table 8.3). On the other hand, Nógrád, Szabolcs-Szatmár and Békés counties had a much below average per capita GDP as well as very small weight in economic activity. Pest county includes the larger agglomeration of Budapest, hence its relatively high share in GDP reflects this proximity. However, due to the high level of inhabitancy (many commute to work from the county to Budapest) the per capita ratio is lower than average.

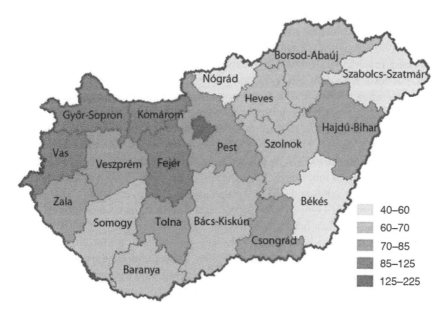

Figure 8.1 Hungarian counties' level of development (percentage of average per capita GDP, 2012)

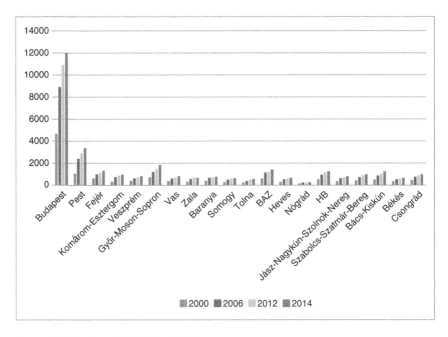

Figure 8.2 Regional GDP, 2000–2014

The figures in Table 8.3 show the dynamics of regional activity too. We can see that the share of Budapest and Pest county continuously increased throughout the 2000s, following similar trends in the 1990s (Antalóczy and Sass, 2005). 2014 showed a remarkable decline for Budapest's share which was taken over mainly by Győr-Moson-Sopron county's impressive growth. Bács-Kiskun county also scored significantly better. These changes may be at least partly explained by the activity of certain multinational firms. The recovery of the European automotive industry reached affiliates of Audi in Győr-Moson-Sopron county and Mercedes in Bács-Kiskun county. The decline in Budapest may be also attributed to the still sluggish performance of FDI-dominated financial services industry centred there. Economic growth of most regions was highest in the 2000–2006 period, and more sluggish between 2006 and 2012. We can see new recovery after 2012, albeit with the lead role of Győr-Moson-Sopron and Bács-Kiskun counties: a different geographic pattern than before with a more modest contribution from Budapest. On the flip side of the coin we can observe very weakly performing counties whose economic decline started in the 1990s and continued during the 2000s (Nógrád, Békés, Baranya, Veszprém). To sum up: regional inequalities in the production of GDP and also in per capita GDP measures increased until 2012. By 2014 counties lagging behind could not improve their status; however, the up till then outstanding Budapest did not further increase its distance from other regions. Instead, some other counties, not necessarily those with a higher per capita GDP

Table 8.3 Shares in national GDP (per cent)

	2000	2006	2012	2014
Budapest	34.88	36.88	38.13	37.23
Pest	8.03	9.98	10.12	10.48
Fejér	4.85	4.13	3.98	4.12
Komárom-Esztergom	2.55	3.17	3.08	3.01
Veszprém	3.10	2.63	2.53	2.61
Győr-Moson-Sopron	5.51	5.04	5.18	5.71
Vas	2.92	2.59	2.42	2.60
Zala	2.51	2.38	2.41	2.13
Baranya	3.02	2.83	2.52	2.41
Somogy	2.27	2.05	2.03	1.98
Tolna	2.01	1.60	1.80	1.76
Borsod	4.72	4.77	4.26	4.40
Heves	2.28	2.20	2.03	2.13
Nógrád	1.21	1.06	0.89	0.88
Hajdu-Bihar	3.99	3.96	4.11	3.92
Jász-Nagykun-Szolnok	2.74	2.61	2.51	2.47
Szabolcs-Szatmár-Bereg	3.33	3.06	3.13	3.10
Bács-Kiskun	3.83	3.59	3.68	3.90
Békés	2.70	2.23	2.08	2.08
Csongrád	3.51	3.15	3.11	3.05

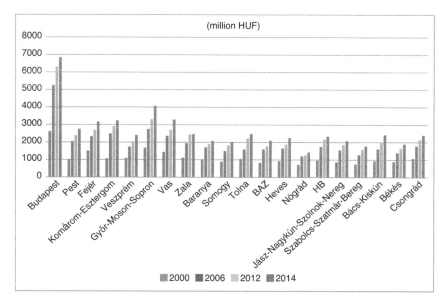

Figure 8.3 Per capita regional GDP, 2000–2014

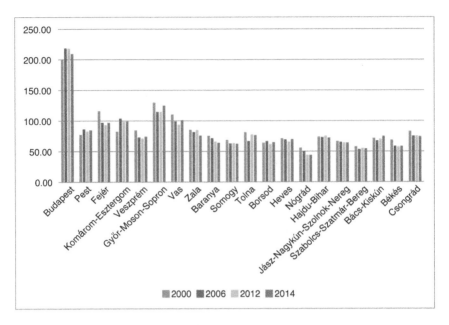

Figure 8.4 Per capita GDP in percentage of national average

level, could somewhat reduce their distance from Budapest or the national average. Yet, fluctuations of earlier years' GDP data does not allow us to conclude that there is a longer-term change in spatial patterns in sight.

In order to figure out the potential role of multinational business in the spatial pattern of economic growth in Hungary I first introduce basic FDI figures in the next charts. Total FDI stock has been even more concentrated geographically than GDP production throughout the 1990s and 2000s. The most important investment locations have been the most developed counties and mainly Budapest. Antalóczy and Sass (2005) called attention to the fact that concentration on Budapest could be larger in the statistical figures than in real economic activity, since many foreign affiliates registered the main office in Budapest and carried out activities also in other locations. They could not measure the impact of this bias, but reported a better fit of FDI-GDP growth regression analysis when calculated data without the figures of Budapest. In the preparation of this chapter I also made calculations with and without Budapest data and found no significant difference. Therefore, all calculations in this chapter include the complete data including Budapest except the last one that compares FDI stock and GDP growth.

Budapest's outstanding role is reflected in the high share in FDI stock that reached almost 60 per cent in 2000; meanwhile the capital city's share in GDP was 38 per cent. Also, the share of Győr-Moson-Sopron county in FDI stock permanently exceeded the share in GDP (10–18 per cent vs. 5.5–6 per cent between 2000 and 2014). Consequently, counties with lower GDP received even lower amounts of FDI. This is a most interesting phenomenon, since it indicates that the growth-generating impact of FDI is not constant, but depends much on the type of investment as it was elaborated briefly in the previous section based on Casi-Resmini (2012). The data of Győr-Moson-Sopron county is of particular interest. The automotive cluster around the Győr factory of Audi attracted much investment during the 2000s. Yet, the impact on GDP growth remained more limited.

In the case of the other fast-growing county in the second half of the 2000s, Bács-Kiskun seemingly contributed no FDI, since amounts and shares of FDI did not increase significantly. This in fact is most surprising since starting in 2008 Mercedes launched large-scale production in the county's main city Kecskemét. When checking for the reason of not finding the imprint of the Mercedes investment in the FDI stock I found that the amount of registered capital was rather low.[9] Some other new investment projects in counties that did not belong to the "hard core" investment belt of the 1990s (Budapest and the North-Western part of Hungary) also affected FDI stock figures in the second half of the 2000s, mainly in Szabolcs-Szatmár and Hajdu-Bihar counties in the east.

Thus, we may conclude that spatial concentration of FDI has been and remained very high in Hungary throughout the 1990s and 2000s exceeding the concentration level of GDP production. However, in the second half of the 2000s some major new projects in non-traditional investment locations, as well as the withdrawal of

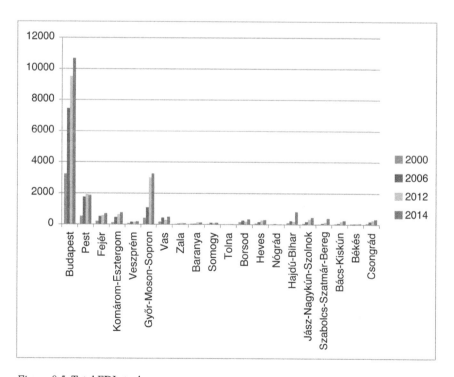

Figure 8.5 Total FDI stock

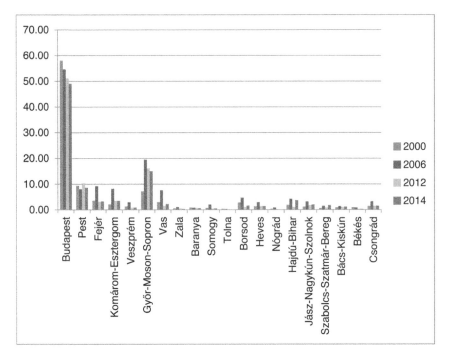

Figure 8.6 Share in FDI stock (%)

some investors in Budapest-based national services companies (banks, insurance companies, electricity suppliers)[10] altered the picture. The level of concentration decreased, though no fundamental change occurred in the spatial structure of FDI stock distribution or the production of GDP. The reason of the change can be seen in Figure 8.7: differences in growth rates of FDI. 2006–12 growth rates of FDI declined in some counties with high-level FDI penetration (Pest, Fejér, Komárom-Esztergom) and Budapest, but continued to grow at high speed in Győr-Moson-Sopron county (with also high FDI penetration) and some lower-level FDI penetration counties. Thus, there was some catching up in two to three "backward" counties, and the outstanding importance of Győr-Moson-Sopron county (with Audi Hungary) continued to rise, while other former FDI centres lost some weight.

Relationship of regional growth and FDI

The co-evolution of FDI and GDP growth could be visually expressed on the previous charts. If we investigate correlation between the two datasets we can also verify the existence of the relationship (though not so much the direction of the relationship). Antalóczy and Sass (2005) found a strong and increasing relationship between FDI stock and total GDP as well as per capita FDI and per capita GDP

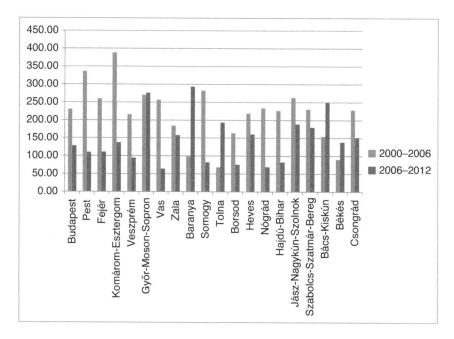

Figure 8.7 Growth rate of FDI stock (%)

measures (with, for example, 0.8631 Rsquare for the later measure in 2001). They found a weaker but still rather strong correlation between per capita FDI stock and regional GDP growth indices.

Our calculations are shown in the coming charts. As is seen, the strongest correlation was found in the total amounts of investment and GDP. The per capita values' correlation is also high, especially for 2000, but it has declined to the year 2014. The chart also shows the reason: two outliers in the high end, one being Budapest, the other Győr-Moson-Sopron county. The county surpassed Budapest in per capita GDP level. However, the per capita GDP did not increase proportionally and remained below the trend line. This indicates high capital intensity of production which is in accordance with our previous observation on the different impact of various types of FDI (e.g. in manufacturing and in services). But the other outlier, Budapest, also shows a changed pattern: it moved in the opposite direction above the trend line indicating lower/decreasing FDI level with GDP production remaining on the same scale. This can be explained by the withdrawal of services investments that reduced capital reported for Budapest without changing the amounts of output (companies' activity was partly nationalized partly taken over by Hungarian firms). Nevertheless, due to these changes relationship between per capita FDI and per capita GDP weakened considerably.

Last but not least perhaps the most important relationship of FDI stock and GDP growth rates are compared. Antalóczy and Sass (2005) reported above average

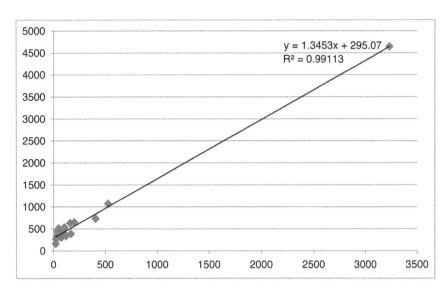

Figure 8.8a Total GDP and total FDI stock, 2000

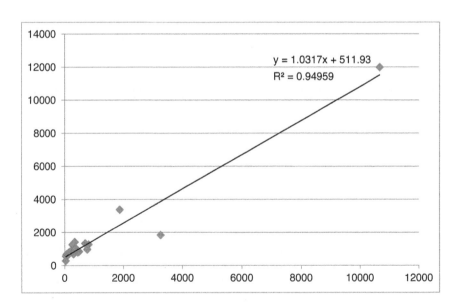

Figure 8.8b Total GDP and total FDI stock, 2014

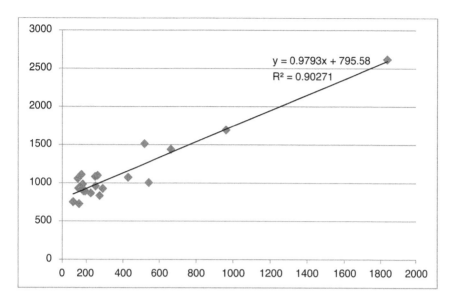

Figure 8.8c Per capita GDP and per capita FDI stock, 2000

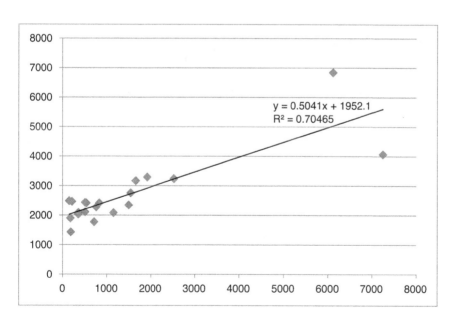

Figure 8.8d Per capita GDP and per capita FDI stock, 2014

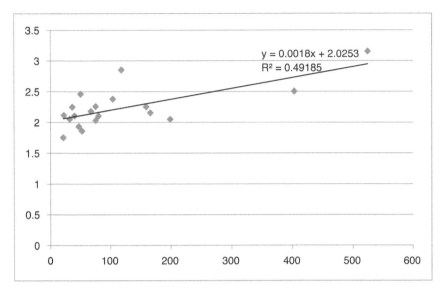

Figure 8.8e FDI stock in year 2000 and GDP growth rates of counties without Budapest, 2000–2014

correlation between the two variables with a better fit for the dataset without Budapest. Calculations for the total dataset that included Budapest were not successful. Regardless of the growth periods and the years of the FDI stock observation all calculations reported the lack of correlation. Calculation results for the whole period using FDI stock data of the initial year 2000 for data without Budapest is depicted on the last chart. As is seen there is an average level correlation, which is lower than what calculations for the 1990–2002 period showed (Rsquare 0.725). This strong decline of the relationship is the consequence of those changes in the spatial composition of FDI stock that I described above. Two main reasons stand out. The first is the changing composition of FDI stock financing that makes FDI statistics less reliable than during the 1990s. Instead of capital stock real shares in production, employment and investments should be used. The other reason is the largely different qualities of manufacturing and services investments which is reflected in their growth-enhancing effects, but also in some methodological problems due to differences of places of registration and actual activity.

Concluding remarks

Foreign direct investments and the activity of multinational business largely contributed to major structural changes in the Hungarian economy after 1990. Completely new industries have been established in this process equipped with the most up-to-date technologies (electronics, automotive); meanwhile more branches like mining, much of metallurgy and the textile industry have disappeared. The creative part of structural change was mainly driven by FDI, and the destructive process was coupled to the lack of it (except for some regulated markets, where activity was abandoned by foreign affiliates of multinational firms, for example due to changes in European policies, like in the case of the Hungarian sugar industry). Hence, both processes were bound mainly to new investments or to the lack of these. In this chapter an attempt was made to check the spatial consequence of these changes by figuring out the relationships of FDI and regional economic growth.

Economic growth may depend on several factors, although the fundament is always created by the establishment of adequate production capacities, that is investments. The relationship is, however, not necessarily direct. Many papers have dealt with indirect growth-enhancing effects of FDIs (spillover effects) with mixed results. I have concentrated on the primary effects, since simple comparison of the spatial structure of FDI in Hungary and the level of development and economic strength of the various regions showed strong correlation. This was also proved by Antalóczy and Sass (2005) who found strong correlation not only between measures of FDI stock and the size of economic activity, but also economic growth. This later aspect was especially important since this could be interpreted as empirical evidence on the role of multinational affiliates in creating and increasing spatial differences in Hungary.

My empirical survey of the period 2000–2014 showed a much weaker correlation between FDI stock and regional economic growth. The analysis of the statistical data showed that the very strong concentration of investments in the traditional (historic) growth centres of the country (Budapest and the north-west) decreased somewhat. While during the 1990s investment in the eastern and southern part of the country was rather sporadic, during the 2000s some important investments took place here. At the same time, the rate of growth of investments in Budapest declined (although the share of the capital city in new investments remained rather high). The city of Győr in the north-west has always been an important hotspot and this role was also strengthened during this decade. Nevertheless, the basic spatial features (e.g. the level of concentration) of FDI changed only very little due to the previously accumulated capital stock in the traditional investment target areas. Yet, the statistical measure of correlation between FDI stock and regional economic growth weakened considerably.

Notes

1 The longer context provides more information on what he exactly meant: "The mysteries of trade become no mystery; but are as it were in the air. Good work is rightly appreciated, invention and improvements in machinery, in processes and general organization of business have their merits promptly discussed: if one man starts a new idea, it is taken up by others and combined with suggestions of their own; and thus it becomes the source of further new ideas" (ibid.).
2 Increasing returns on scale are on the base line of endogenous growth theories and the new economic geography.

3 Main guidelines of the privatization process were set in rather clear political and social consensus and the bulk of the process was carried out rather quickly during the 1990s. Criticisms of the privatization process were intensifying mainly during the 2000s when the process was already over. The (rather few) unsuccessful FDI-bound privatization transactions were criticized, but no evidence could be provided if other policies could have delivered more advantageous results. In fact, criticisms were put forward mainly due to political reasons: a new political (and related business) elite wanted to create social capital using this argument (Szanyi, 2016).

4 The IFTZ was considered extraterritorial for purposes of duties, foreign exchange and other legislation including not only goods but also means of production. For details see Antalóczy et al. (2011).

5 For example, Audi Hungary was referred several times in company reports as the most productive unit of the concern.

6 The large and for long periods increasing gap in capitalization, technological sophistication and productivity between Hungarian- and foreign-owned business sectors throughout the transition process and thereafter have been highlighted many times through empirical research (e.g. Szanyi, 1996; Major, 1999; Laki, 2002; Laki and Szalai, 2015).

7 There are multiple problems with the usage of capital stock. The most frequently used data of subscribed capital can express mainly the distribution of ownership rights, but cannot provide reliable estimation of size or economic importance, since it disregards increases of capital stock financed from reinvested profits. This is reflected in the term of own capital. Nevertheless, even own capital cannot reflect capacity increases financed by credits (mostly intra-firm). Another problem comes from the spatial differences of headquarters and the actual location of activities. In the case of Hungary this problem comes up mostly in cases of the multiple premises of companies. Detailed data (production, employment) is reported locally, bound to factory premise; however, capital stock is not separated spatially.

8 From then restrictive economic policies were pursued by Hungarian governments in order to restore budget balance.

9 There has also been another important bias of the FDI database in Hungary: the lack of differentiation between registered capital and own capital. As it was shown in the Introduction, starting with the second half of the 1990s an ever growing part of the increase of FDI stock was financed either from reinvested profits or intra-company loans. These forms of finance do not change registered capital, and hence FDI stock, if calculation is based on registered capital.

10 For details of the renationalization activity of the Hungarian government after 2010 see Szanyi (2016).

References

Antalóczy, K. and Sass, M. (2005) A külföldi működőtőke-befektetések regionális elhelyezkedése és gazdasági hatásai Magyarországon ("Regional location and economic impacts of foreign direct investments in Hungary"), *Közgazdasági Szemle*, 52(5): 494–520.

Antalóczy, K., Sass, M. and Szanyi, M. (2011) "Policies for attracting foreign direct investment and enhancing its spillovers to indigenous firms: the case of Hungary". In E. Rugraff and M.W. Hansen (eds) *Multinational Corporations and Local Firms in Emerging Economies.* Amsterdam University Press, pp. 181–210.

Casi, L. and Resmini, L. (2010) "Evidence on the determinants of foreign direct investment: the case of EU regions", *Eastern Journal of European Studies*, 1(2): 93–118.

Casi, L. and Resmini, L. (2012) *Foreign Direct Investment and Growth: The Role of Regional Territorial Capital*. Unpublished manuscript.

Central Statistical Office (2015) *Statisztikai Tükör* 2015/101.

Fridmuc, J., Grozea-Helmenstein, D. and Wörgötter, A. (1999) "East–West Intra-Industry Trade Dynamics". *Weltwirtschaftliches Archiv*, 135(2): 332–346.

Görg, H. and Greenaway, D. (2004) "Much ado about nothing? Do domestic firms really benefit from foreign direct investment?", *World Bank Research Observer*, 19(2): 171–197.

Iwasaki, I., Csizmadia, P., Illésy, M., Makó, C. and Szanyi, M. (2012) "The nested variable model of fdi spillover effects: estimation using Hungarian panel data", *International Economic Journal*, 26(4): 673–709.

Iwasaki, I. and Tokunaga, M. (2014) "Macroeconomic impacts of FDI in transition economies: a meta-analysis", *World Development*, 61(9): 53–69.

Kalotay, K. and Sass, M. (2012) "Inward FDI in Hungary and its policy context". *Columbia FDI Profiles*. Vale Columbia Center on Sustainable International Investment. 18 October.

Krugman, P. (1991) *Geography and Trade*. MIT Press.

Krugman, P. (1998) "What's new about the new economic geography?", *Oxford Review of Economic Policy*, 14(2): 7–17.

Laki, M. (2002) A nagyvállalkozók tulajdonszerzési esélyeiről a szocializmus után ("About chances of obtaining property by entrepreneurs after socialism"), *Közgazdasági Szemle (Economic Review-monthly of the Hungarian Academy of Sciences)*, 49(1): 45–58.

Laki, M. and Szalai, J. (2015) *Ten Years After: Hungarian Grand Entrepreneurs in the European Union*. Institute of Economics, Hungarian Academy of Sciences.

Lengyel B., Iwasaki, I. and Szanyi, M. (2011) "Industrial concentration, regional employment and productivity growth: evidence from the late transition period of Hungary", *IWE Working Paper* No. 195. February.

Lengyel, B. and Szanyi, M. (2011) Agglomerációs előnyök és regionális növekedés felzárkózó régiókban – a Magyar átmenet esete ("Agglomeration advantages and regional growth in catching-up regions: the case of Hungarian transition"), *Közgazdasági Szemle*, 58(10): 858–876.

Major, I. (ed.) (1999) *Privatization and Economic Performance in Central and Eastern Europe*. Edward Elgar Publishing.

Marshall, A. (1890) *Principles of Economics*. Macmillan.

Nölke, A. and Vliegenthart, A. (2009) "Enlarging the varieties of capitalism: the emergence of dependent market economies in East Central Europe", *World Politics*, 61(4): 670–702.

OECD (2001) *OECD Territorial Outlook 2001*. OECD.

Sass, M. and Szalavetz, A. (2014) "Crisis-related changes in the specialization of advanced economies in global value chains", *Competition and Change*, 18: 54–69.

Szanyi, M. (1996) "Adaptive steps by Hungary's industries during the transition crisis", *Eastern European Economics*, 34(5): 59–77.

Szanyi, M. (2002) *Spillover Effects and Business Linkages of Foreign-Owned Firms in Hungary*. IWE Working Paper no. 126. May.

Szanyi, M. (2003) *An FDI-based development Model for Hungary – New Challenges?* IWE Working Paper no. 141. December.

Szanyi, M. (2008) *A versenyképesség javítása együttműködéssel: regionális klaszterek.* ("Improving competitiveness through cooperation: regional clusters"). Napvilág Publishing House.

Szanyi, M. (2016) "The reversal of the privatization logic in Central European transition economies". *Acta Oeconomica*, 66(1): 33–55.

Venables, A.J. (2002) "Geography and international inequalities: the impact of new technologies". In B. Pleskovic, N. Stern and D. McCarthy (eds) *Annual World Bank Conference on Development Economics* 2001/2002, pp. 147–169.

Villaverde, J. and Maza, A. (2015) "The determinants of inward foreign direct investment: Evidence from the European regions", *International Business Review*, 24: 209–223.

9 Financialization and inequalities

The uneven development of the housing market on the eastern periphery of Europe

Zsuzsanna Pósfai, Zoltán Gál and Erika Nagy

Introduction

When linking financialization and inequalities, the effects of this process on increasing social inequalities are often discussed (van der Zwan, 2014). Financialization is seen as a process that benefits wealth-generation, but pushes down on wage income, thus increasing the gap between social classes (Lapavitsas, 2015). There is also a transfer from "productive" capital to "non-productive" capital, which results in the restructuring of the corporate field (Aalbers, 2015b). However, the spatial dimension of financialization is seldom discussed. There is a growing body of literature in economic geography arguing that financialization is an inherently spatial process, and that economic geography has to come to the forefront of current debates on the transformation of capitalism, linking the latter to notions of space (Engelen 2012; Sokol 2013). For this, the notion of uneven development is often mobilized; adapting this term which was coined in the 1980s (Smith, 1984) to the context of financialization (French et al., 2011; Pike and Pollard, 2010). Sokol argues that financialization can be understood as the quest for a spatial fix (Harvey, 1982) – in this sense the term becomes central to making sense of the spatiality of contemporary capitalism (Sokol, 2013).

We insert ourselves in this line of thought and propose an argument about how financialization produces uneven spatial development on various scales on the European semi-periphery. We will analyse the production of spatial inequalities through the case of housing, which is one of the important forms of a spatial fix in financializing European economies (Aalbers, 2008, 2015a). The literature on financialization highlights how this process deepens social inequalities (increasing differences between wealth and wage income). Our argument is that the transfer of wealth does not only happen in terms of social class, but also in terms of spatial core and periphery, and that financialization also inherently carries a logic of uneven spatial development.

First, we will make a conceptual argument about how financialization is spatially articulated on various geographical scales, producing socio-spatial polarization. For this, we will mobilize the notion of dependent financialization. Then, we will empirically support this argument through the case of the Hungarian housing market – discussing the articulation of the dependent financialization of housing first on a European, then on a national and finally on a local scale.

Conceptually linking financialization, uneven development and housing

In the domain of economic geography, uneven development as a concept was developed in the 1970s and 1980s in an attempt to analyse how capitalism unfolds in space (Harvey, 1982; Smith, 1984). On the other hand, the body of literature on financialization expanded in the aftermath of the global financial crisis of 2007–2008, in an attempt to make sense of the financial meltdown that had occurred.[1] Recently, there has been a push from the part of economic geographers to be more present in debates on financialization and to put a bigger emphasis on the spatial aspects of contemporary capitalist processes (Engelen 2012; Sokol 2013). This new body of literature (much of which is coined under the "geographies of money and finance" literature) reaches back to ideas developed in the 1980s about the spatiality of capitalism – such as uneven development and the spatial fix[2] – and adapts them to the current political and economic context.

In our chapter we will largely build on this strand of thought that links the notions of uneven development and financialization; claiming that financialization is an inherently spatial process (Aalbers, 2015a).

We can identify three common approaches to understanding financialization in the literature: (1) as a new accumulation regime (see, e.g., Kripner, 2005); (2) as a shift in corporate behaviour to respond to an increasing importance of shareholder value (see, e.g., Aalbers, 2015b); and (3) as the financialization of everyday life (see, e.g., Martin, 2002). In our analysis we will predominantly build on literature that understands financialization as a new regime of accumulation, understanding it as a systemic transformation of global capitalism (Stockhammer, 2004). In this approach Arrighi (1994) sees financialization as the declining period preceding shifts in systemic cycles of accumulation; Brenner (2004) interprets it as a crisis of profitability in the productive sector (resulting in growing investment in the non-productive sector); Lapavistas also defines financialization as "the rapid growth of the sphere of circulation, while the sphere of production has continued to face problems of profitability and productivity" (2009b, p. 109). The new financialized regime of accumulation which is in place since the 1970s produces an exponentially growing supply of money waiting to be invested (Fernandez and Aalbers, 2016). As this globally available supply of surplus capital searches for profitable forms of investment, it is fixed in space and spatially translates the inequalities inherent to financialization. Taking this line of thought further, Sokol defines financialization as a quest of surplus capital for a spatial fix (Sokol, 2013) – flowing into new institutional and geographical areas.

One of the most important channels for this capital expansion is the credit–debt relation – which became one of the core elements of contemporary financialization (Sokol, 2013). Sokol argues that "credit and debt is at the epicentre of the crisis" (p. 505), and as a further specificity of this period, this debt was increasingly borne by households. Mortgages are by far the most important element of this household debt. This means that in the early 2000s housing finance supporting a dominantly homeownership- and credit-based housing regime became an important pillar of a financialized regime of accumulation.

The credit–debt relation is especially important in the process of financialization on the (semi)peripheries of the global economy – and in our case, specifically on the European peripheries[3] (Becker et al., 2015; Raviv, 2008; Sokol, 2013). Becker et al. claim that financialization can take two dominant forms: either that of fictitious capital (such as shares, securities – which we commonly encounter in Anglo-Saxon studies), or that of interest-bearing capital, that is credit. The latter is more typical of the European periphery (Becker et al., 2015). Our claim is that if we understand financialization as a regime of accumulation – that is, not just as a shift in corporate or household financial strategies, or as the increasing dominance of the financial sector – then it is *not coincidental that financialization is manifested in different ways in different places of the global economy*. We argue for the value of theorizing financialization from a CEE perspective, because it sheds light on this spatially differentiated articulation of a globally unfolding process.

This brings us to the notion of *dependent financialization*. This is a term we use to grasp that the differences in how financialization unfolds in different places (and the inequalities it produces) are not coincidental, but reflect systematic patterns of unevenness and dependency, linked to positions taken up in the global economy.

Dependencies and the semi-peripheral position of the Eastern periphery of the European Union are the consequences of relative scarcities in capital and technology. This scarcity results in a constant need to attract foreign capital – which is satisfied in various ways in different periods – through FDI, loans or international transfers (Gerőcs and Pinkasz, 2017, forthcoming). In Hungary there was a shift towards a dominance of bank capital (from the previously dominant channel of foreign direct investment) in the early 2000s. In this context, dependent financialization was characterized by external capital dependencies, external institutional control and fragile financialized interconnectedness (Gabor, 2012; Gál and Schmidt, 2017). These mechanisms came as the new institutional channels of dependent linkages transmitting unequal power relations between the core and periphery of the European economy. In this sense, *financialization can be understood as a central element of dependent economic integration* (Becker et al., 2015).

The financialization of the periphery is thus part and parcel of the financialization of the core: abundant capital produced by processes of financialization in the core finds its way to investment in the peripheries, leading to increasing public and private debt in these countries. This unevenness is constitutive to the process of financialization – and calls for more in-depth research, which would contribute to our understanding of Central and Eastern European (CEE) economic contexts and new financial capitalism alike.

Typically, financial investment coming from the core does not go into long-term financing of productive activity on the periphery. Rather, it often goes into state or household debt, which offers less risky and more profitable forms of investment – due to high interest rates and the possibility to offer short-term loans (Gabor, 2012). This financialization-based consumption model relying on short-term bank capital gradually replaced the FDI-based model in terms of external finance. Credit flows were reoriented towards households and had a limited role in corporate finance and economic development goals, the latter being central in the logic of investment towards these countries (Raviv, 2008). In credit-based household consumption, housing-related costs became more and more important – with many consumption loans actually also being used for housing acquisition or renovation (Dancsik et al., 2015).

The term of the "financialization of housing" has gained huge popularity since the financial crisis. It captures the idea that housing has increasingly become a form of financial investment, and also that housing markets have become increasingly important in maintaining the current financialized regime of accumulation. An increasing number of authors are arguing for a political economic understanding of contemporary housing regimes (see, e.g., Harvey, 2006; Madden and Marcuse, 2016) or even argue for centring housing in political economy more generally (Aalbers and Christophers, 2014). Linking financialization and housing is important for research in political economy and economic geography because it allows to conceptually ground macroeconomic processes in very concrete space. In our analysis the housing market is the empirical material which allows us to make claims about the spatial unevenness that financialization produces.

The financialization of housing can take many forms, and can happen (for example) through equity markets, through property acquisitions by financial actors, or through mortgages. The latter was the most common form of the financialization of housing on the European peripheries. In the years preceding the crisis the housing markets of Southern and Eastern European countries became important spatial fixes for European and global financial capital. This process was supported by public policies promoting the spread of a credit-based homeownership model. Owner occupancy achieved through private indebtedness became the dominant form of accessing housing in many places of the world – including all over Europe. This general tendency is, however, articulated in different ways in different contexts. In the following sections we will elaborate on how this process rolled out in the context of Hungary.

By focusing on how the latest cycle of financialization has increasingly channelled capital into real estate – and specifically into housing – we ground the notion in concrete space. Furthermore, by linking the notion to uneven development and by taking empirical material from CEE as our starting point, we reflect on how this region is embedded in broader processes of capitalist transformation. This will lead to a framework that allows us to understand the Hungarian housing finance system in the context of dependent integration in the European economic space.

Methodology and geographical scales

In the following section we will give a brief overview of both the conceptual and empirical basis for the methodological frame we employ.

While we admit that financialization unfolded as a highly uneven process dominated by powerful agents of financial capital operating on a global scale (French et al., 2011), we interpret housing financialization here as a multi-scalar process – shaped also by regulative frameworks and institutional practices linked to various scales as well as by locally embedded household strategies. Our approach rests basically on Neil Smith's concept that considers scale as the "product" of struggles of various social classes and groups. In this approach, scales manifest in spatial hierarchies and related (bounded) spaces that are subject to control exercised by social groups/agents through institutional settings and practices to reproduce existing power relations – under capitalism, to provide (or improve) the conditions for capital accumulation (Smith, 1992; Herod and Wright, 2002). Thus, the scalar organization of institutional structures is changing – new temporal fixes are introduced as a result of economic crises and political struggles (Brenner, 1998; French et al., 2011) – and have various forms emerging from diverse socio-cultural contexts (see, e.g., Brenner et al., 2010 on variegated neoliberalization).

By adopting this concept, we shift from the interpretations that consider scales as sets of bounded "containers" in the physical space. Rather, we take them as temporary assemblages of institutional frameworks and practices in which social (power) relations manifest. Thus, in the following, we use this concept of scale-production as an analytical framework to understand how globalized capital flows, national institutional contexts and locally embedded social relations interact and shape one another, producing an uneven landscape of housing markets – thus, changing not only profit rates but the conditions of everyday lives and social reproduction. We focus on three powerful scalar dimensions of the dependent financialization of the housing sector to understand the mechanisms of uneven development: (1) We discuss the integration of CEE into the European economic space as a key momentum of financialization – interrelated with state rescaling (shifting power to supranational institutions) that opened up CEE markets to financial capital and its multiscalar and spatially highly selective strategies. (2) We consider the national scale as a homogeneous regulative-institutional space (the privatization of the housing stock and the banks, liberalization of capital flows, etc.) that is differentiated not only by the spatial logic of financial capital, but also an arena of competing interests for financial resources. (3) Understanding local processes is also a key issue due to the spatial fixity of capital and the mutually constitutive nature of scales (Cox, 2001): dependent financialization materializes in local (dis)investments that reflect all social relations that are at work in the polarizing spaces of the housing market and also local socio-cultural contexts that affect housing-related strategies of households.

The toolkit we relied on within this methodological framework includes earlier results on the geography of financial institutions in Hungary (Gál, 2005; Gál-Burger, 2013) that "mapped" the uneven landscapes of the financial markets through institutional practices and relations. Moreover, to have an insight in local processes, we analysed fieldwork results from two peripheral places (both from Békés County, Hungary) based on (i) a series of semi-structured interviews (altogether 38, in 2005–2006 and 2013–2015) conducted with various agents of the local housing market (banks, professional and owner-developers, local state), and (ii) a survey concerning well-being/living conditions of households (200 units in Northeast Békés in 2015, with representative sampling by key demographic indicators) (Nagy et al., 2015). Combining the empirical results with the quantitative analysis of the data provided by the European Mortgage Federation (for the European scale) and the Hungarian National Bank (national scale), we move beyond studying macro-processes and have an insight into the (re)production of regional and local inequalities through housing market mechanisms.

Financialization of housing and uneven development on various scales

In the following sections we propose an analysis of how the financialization of housing produces uneven spatial development on various scales. We will trace the patterns of capital investment from the European through the national to the local; showing how these different scales are interlinked.

Dependent financialization as a vehicle of core–periphery relations on a European scale

The spatial implications of housing financialization on a European scale are vastly numerous and also very diverse in nature from unfinished holiday resorts on the Spanish coasts to displacement from inner-city German social housing units. We obviously cannot attempt to cover them in this chapter. Thus, we will focus on the element that we have identified as one of the most important in dependent patterns of housing financialization in Hungary (and in CEE more generally): that of mortgages and ensuing household indebtedness.

The functional interconnectedness of core and periphery becomes apparent if we consider some basic data on mortgage lending and household debt in various European countries. One of the main cases for this is Germany. Preceding the crisis, much of Germany's current account surplus went into bank lending on the European periphery, creating housing bubbles and debt-driven consumption booms (Sokol, 2013). After the crisis, the flow of credit came to an abrupt halt, leaving the semi-periphery with a massive debt burden and leading to a near-complete freeze of these housing markets (ibid.). As we will see, Hungary was quite an extreme case even among other Central and Eastern European countries, but the tendency of external capital-dependency on CEE housing markets can be generally drawn up (see Yesin, 2013; Schepp and Pitz, 2012).

As developed in the previous section, mortgage lending on the European peripheries became an important form of spatial fix for surplus capital from the core of the European economy in the period preceding the crisis, in the context of the accession of CEE countries to the European Union (with the implications of this process for market liberalization). Housing credit thus became a crucial vehicle of dependent financialization. In order to underpin this argument we will compare various characteristics of mortgage lending on a European scale.[4]

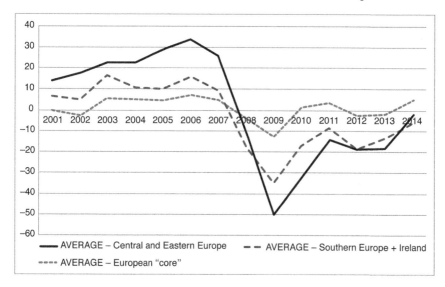

Figure 9.1 Real gross fixed investment in housing between 2001 and 2014 (annual percentage change)[5]

Source: EMF, 2015

Comparing the change in real gross investment in housing on a European scale, it becomes quite apparent that the peripheries of Europe went through much stronger fluctuations than core housing markets (EMF, 2015; see Figure 9.1). This is important because literature on the financialization of housing often only considers the stock of outstanding mortgages (which is not so high in CEE) – while the drastic changes in available capital on housing markets reflects the higher vulnerability of the periphery to crisis.

Furthermore, a significant part of mortgages disbursed in CEE were denominated in foreign currencies (most often in euros or Swiss francs; see Figure 9.2). This is a specific characteristic of bank lending in the region, and exposed households directly to the volatility of the global economy through a significant exchange rate risk.

Another element of vulnerability relates to the structure of issued loans. From the analysis of the European Mortgage Federation (EMF) it becomes apparent that in core countries the majority of mortgages were long term and with fixed interest rates, while peripheral countries mostly had short-term and flexible exchange-rate mortgage schemes (see EMF, 2015, p. 15). This is a crucial element in understanding the nature of dependent financialization of housing, and is also central to understanding why household indebtedness became such a problem on the European peripheries. Higher levels of interest rates – resulting in more expensive mortgages (see Figure 9.3) – are a systematic characteristic of the periphery, due to its constant need to attract foreign capital. Maintaining high interest rates is attractive for foreign investment, but at the same time leads to soaring imports, and – through the necessity to finance these imports – to a worsening of the current

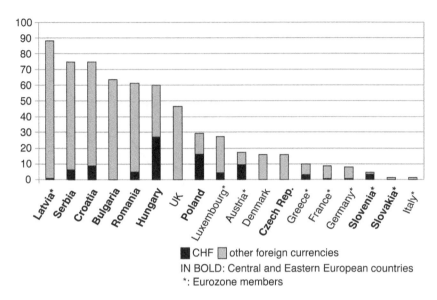

CHF ◼ other foreign currencies

IN BOLD: Central and Eastern European countries

*: Eurozone members

Figure 9.2 Share of foreign currency loans as a percentage of total loans to the non-banking sector in Europe, 2012

Source: Author's compilation based on data from Raiffeisen International and from the Swiss National Bank's CHF Lending Monitor

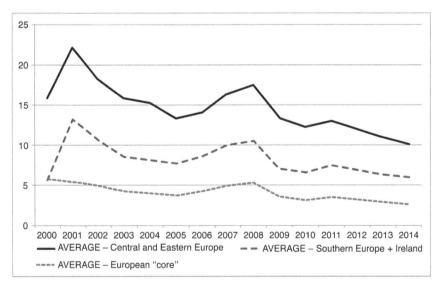

Figure 9.3 Representative interest rates on new residential loans (annual average based on monthly figures, per cent)[6]

Source: EMF, 2015

account and escalating foreign debt (Faria, 2007: 98, cited in Becker et al., 2015). (In Hungary interest rates were very high even compared to other CEE countries due to the high refinancing rate of a large public debt.)

A further concern of CEE vulnerability lies in the high share of foreign liabilities vis-à-vis local savings in mortgage lending. The share of foreign liabilities provided by foreign parent banks in the total volume of liabilities in Hungary grew from 8 per cent in 2005 to 25 per cent in 2008, contributing to the growing current account deficit. Combined with the very high proportion of foreign bank ownership in the region this meant that banks investing in CEE subsidiaries made a significant (if not dominant) part of their profits here.[7] Investing in Central and Southern European housing markets was a very lucrative venture, and a way of overcoming falling rates of profitability in Western Europe – especially since the dominantly ownership-based housing market structures of these countries meant that there was a high demand for (or lack of alternative to) individual mortgages (since the means of securing one's housing in a long-term stable way are very limited beyond the option of homeownership). This lending practice led to an extraction of capital from the periphery to the core on a European scale.

Currently, household lending on the European peripheries is coming to a period of revival – but this often just means inventing new forms of a financialized housing regime, producing new inequalities.

Household indebtedness is one of the main consequences of pre-crisis excessive mortgage lending. This is a very important phenomenon on a European scale – according to the EMF "one in four European households currently has a mortgage" and "the total value of these outstanding mortgages is equal to roughly half of the GDP of the EU" (EMF, 2015, p. 4) – but whether or not these outstanding mortgages start defaulting or lead to household bankruptcy shows patterns of unevenness.

The proportion of nonperforming mortgages increased Europe-wide in the years following the crisis. However, the countries with the highest rates of non-performing mortgages (above 25 per cent) were exclusively countries of the Southern and Eastern periphery (Bulgaria, Croatia, Romania, Hungary, Cyprus and Greece) (ibid.). Apart from the more "predatory" nature of mortgages issued in these places, the indebtedness of peripheral households also reflects certain characteristics of more general household finances. Credit-fuelled consumption and the household sector's foreign currency borrowing was a direct consequence of dependent financialization in an environment characterized by low-incomes and low savings levels (Gabor, 2010). This resulted in households acquiring loans with higher loan to income and loan to value ratios – which produce much higher risks of a spiralling indebtedness as a consequence of incidental non-payment. Certain authors even argue that due to practices of foreign-exchange (FX) mortgage lending CEE can be considered to be Europe's subprime mortgage market (Smith and Swain, 2010).

Altogether, our claim is that the financialized housing regime that was built up all over Europe from the 1980s/1990s onwards resulted in increasing polarization between the cores and peripheries of Europe in the aftermath of the financial crisis of 2007–08, when housing-related investment was re-centred to the core of the European economy (mostly on the German and British housing markets). Since all European housing systems are increasingly prioritizing the development of homeownership through increased access to household credit; patterns of mortgage lending gave us a glimpse of the patterns of uneven development related to housing finance. Dependent financialization of the Eastern peripheries of the EU entails not only a growing dependence on external banking resources but is also accompanied by asymmetric power relations (translated by external creditor control over the region) (Gál, 2014).

A financialized housing regime on the national scale

We saw in the previous section that the credit boom of the early 2000s was not something specific to Hungary, but was a consequence of globally abundant capital being channelled into profitable housing markets.

For our national scale analysis of the consequences of a financialized housing regime on spatial inequalities, we will continue to put the issue of mortgages centre-stage (which we have identified as the main element of housing financialization in Hungary). Our argument is that the value extraction from the peripheries to the cores through channels of housing finance is also happening on a national scale. Furthermore, the model of dependent housing finance developed in the years preceding the crisis has led to deepening spatial inequalities within the country. We will analyse these processes through the spatial patterns of the mortgage market and of financial institutions active in housing finance mechanisms.

A system of dependent housing financialization and the mortgage crisis

As we claimed in previous sections, in the period of financialization there is a general shift of lending to households instead of to firms. Household lending (and thus household debt) accelerated globally, especially in the early 2000s (on household debt in the USA see Lapavitsas 2009a; Stockhammer, 2012). This was the case in Hungary too, where household lending as a share of total domestic lending climbed from approximately 10 per cent in 1999 to over 30 per cent in 2005 (Raviv, 2008). In the CEE as a whole, the annual year-on-year growth rate of mortgage lending has exceeded 40 per cent since 2000 (Unicredit, 2007, cited in Raviv, 2008). At the same time, less profitable lending to non-financial corporations stagnated or slightly declined (Gál 2014). As a result, the indebtedness of Hungarian households was close to 70 per cent of their personal disposable income in 2011 (ibid.).

There were important implications of the fact that pre-crisis housing financialization happened primarily through household indebtedness – and within this, mostly through mortgage lending. The rapid growth in domestic credit was financed by foreign-owned banks engaged increasingly in carry trade, disbursing mortgages denominated in foreign currencies (mainly in Swiss francs). Despite the immediate benefits of these products – lower interest rates, longer maturities – FX loans carry a significant exchange-rate risk (since the Hungarian currency was not pegged to the euro after 2008). When speaking of dependent financialization, it is not necessarily the volume of outstanding debt that is the most important factor (overall debt to gross domestic product ratios or even debt to disposable income ratios are still significantly lower in CEE countries than in the core of the European economy – see EMF, 2015). The key element is the vulnerable nature of a dependent model of housing financialization, which can be grasped from various aspects.

Data provided by the Hungarian National Bank shows that in the run-up to the crisis mortgages were disbursed with higher and higher loan-to-value ratios, to ever broader segments of society (with lending criteria becoming more relaxed) (Dancsik et al., 2015). Broadening the scope of access to credit was a political project fostered by the political elite aiming to improve the perceived living conditions of lower middle classes through a model of consumption based on indebtedness (Scheiring, 2016). This process is also described in the literature as privatized Keynesianism (see Crouch 2009). While large swathes of the population thus accumulated debt, state redistribution favoured an ever smaller and better-off social group. After the crisis hit Hungary in 2008, and the Hungarian Forint depreciated, FX mortgage debtors' monthly instalments increased by 75 per cent on average between 2009 and 2013[8] (Bohle, 2013; Schepp and Pitz, 2012). As a consequence, the number of non-performing mortgages rapidly increased, and a political and economic "mortgage crisis" developed, with many households falling into a debt spiral.

A number of governmental measures were introduced in the years following 2010 in order to tackle this mortgage crisis (for an overview see Hegedüs-Somogyi, 2016). As a result, there are currently practically no more mortgages denominated in foreign currencies in Hungary, but a significant part of the population nevertheless still carries an unmanageable debt burden (partially due to the fact that most governmental measures targeted the debt management of the middle classes only). An analysis published last year by the Hungarian National Bank (Dancsik et al., 2015) states that non-performing mortgages still account for one fourth of the total mortgage portfolio, the majority of which are FX mortgages, and that "for over 80 per cent of customers, the total debt amount (outstanding principal and arrears) exceeds the advanced loan amount" (ibid., p. 6). This means that many households now owe more money than when they took out their mortgage. Another very important indicator is that the total outstanding debt currently accounts for 140 per cent of the pledged collateral – that is, a high share of debtors are in negative equity – partially because of increasing values of debt (due to changes in exchange rates and interest rates) and partially because of declining house prices (especially in disadvantaged regions). This means that even if debtors were to sell their property, they would not be able to conclude their debt – which in turn leads to social and geographical immobility.

Altogether the highly vulnerable, dependent housing finance regime which was built up before the crisis substantially increased social inequalities. Those who could profit from the period of the "credit rush" could significantly increase their wealth with the leverage of relatively cheap credit. Meanwhile, those who were initially in a more vulnerable position (because they had to take mortgages at a very high loan-to-value for lack of own capital, or because their livelihoods were destabilized by the crisis, which affected lower-status jobs more – see Kolosi et al., 2014) fell into a debt spiral that will continue to weigh on large segments of the Hungarian society for years to come.

What does this process mean for spatial inequalities? According to the already mentioned MNB study, 70 per cent of non-performing mortgages are in smaller cities and settlements, in regions with quite immobile housing markets and dropping house prices (Dancsik et al., 2015). If we combine this with the previously mentioned issue of negative equity, it is quite clear that in the aftermath of the credit boom an uneven geography of "subprime" lending unfolds (for an application of the term to CEE see Smith and Swain, 2010), where debtors struggling to repay their mortgages are trapped in economically disadvantaged areas (in Hungary there is a strong correlation between settlement size and socio-economic status – on this issue see, for example, Gerse and Szilágyi, 2015; GfK Hungary 2014).

If we compare data on the number of transactions in villages in the years following the crisis and data on the activity of the National Asset Manager (NET) – a state-owned company buying up properties of defaulting mortgage debtors – we can assume that rural housing markets were "active" (had some transactions to register) in the post-crisis years only if the NET acquired properties in the region. This, however, would be a question to investigate more in-depth.

Lending practices of financial institutions and spatial inequalities

As previously argued, mortgages were important in how dependent financial-ization unfolded in Hungary. Mortgages essentially represent a credit–debt relation, which can be seen as an extraction of value from the debtor to the creditor (Sokol, 2013). This extraction of value can be understood both in a social and in a geographical sense. As Sokol argues, financial institutions are key actors in making this process possible, and thus actively reproduce inequalities (ibid.). The study of the geography of financial institutions allows us to grasp the precise mechanisms of this value extraction.

Following the liberalization of the banking sector, which accelerated from the end of the 1990s, the massive influx of foreign banks into the country led to an extensive growth of the banking network. Foreign banks investing in the Hungarian banking system established the headquarters of their subsidiaries in the capital city, Budapest, and built up their nationwide branch network by expanding gradually outwards into the provincial areas (Gál, 2005), effectively creating a "dual banking system" (as in most CEE countries). We can speak of the dual nature and fragmentation of the banking sector both in organizational and geo-graphical respects.[9] The sector is characterized by the concentration of large, predominantly foreign-owned commercial banks on the one hand, and small domestic providers of financial services (e.g. cooperative banks) on the other hand. A dual banking system (Gál, 2005) is characterized by the dominance of the former group, with the market weight of domestically owned banks remaining insignificant. In line with arguments in the literature, commercial banks in Hungary used a "cherry picking" strategy during their initial expansion in the 1990s, selecting the best larger corporate clients (often the international companies also freshly entering these markets) with the lowest risks, and consequently proposing fewer loans to small and medium-sized enterprises (SMEs). From the early 2000s, these banks (still following the same logic of risk-avoidance) became leading actors of the shift in crediting activity towards households.[10] Between 2008 and 2014 household loans exceeded the volume of corporate loans for the first time, reflecting the importance of the consumer credit boom in contemporary financialization.

The credit boom of the early 2000s further amplified the institutional segmentation and inequalities within the banking system. The main cause of polarization is the strongly centralized hierarchical control of the branch network and the lack of locally founded banks, since only cooperative banks have their headquarters in the countryside. Two-thirds of savings cooperatives branches are located in settlements that have fewer than 5,000 inhabitants, while only 4 per cent of commercial banks is present in the same settlement category (Gál, 2012). This reflects the fact that the expansion of commercial banks was not primarily driven by regional preferences on a subnational scale, but instead they followed the urban hierarchy of the Hungarian settlement structure. The emerging dual structure of financial services, which has also become manifest in spatial terms, is consonant with the centralization and concentration accompanied by capital outflows from the peripheries within the country.

The magnitude of capital outflows is indicated by the fact that 82 per cent of the deposits collected by commercial branch networks in 2008 was lent in the national financial centre, Budapest – despite the fact that only 50 per cent of deposits was collected in Budapest (Gál, 2011). This uneven capital outflow, in line with Myrdal's (1957) capital drainage and Dow's (1999) liquidity preference theories, proved that savings collected in peripheral regions by commercial banks flowed towards core regions, contributing to the further strengthening of the financial centre.

One could imagine that cooperative banks could counterbalance this process by collecting deposits and giving out credits locally, in geographically more peripheral areas. However, Gál and Burger (2013) found that the loan-to-deposit ratio of cooperative banks is only around 50 per cent (the same ratio for commercial banks was 168 per cent in 2008). These banks, which were present in less developed areas, were rather small institutions preferring to invest their liabilities in the more stable, paradoxically more profitable and less risky interbank or government bond markets instead of lending to the local community. Practically, this means that cooperative banks channelled their resources directly to the financial core and therefore contributed to further strengthening the financial centre, as well as to the persistence of the credit gap between the core and the periphery. The results also reveal that, similar to the main actors of financialization and unlike their Western counterparts, cooperative banks operating in an unfavourable

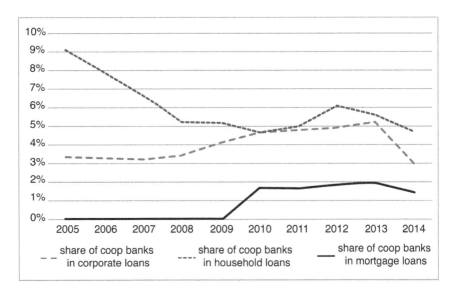

Figure 9.4 Share of cooperative banks in lending activity between 2005 and 2014

Source: Author's compilation based on data from the Hungarian National Bank

economic environment are also responsible for the capital flight from their respective regions.

Cooperative banks registered significant losses in their market weight in the years preceding the crisis (see Figure 9.4). This was a consequence of the fact that – unlike commercial banks – they were unable to tap into the credit boom of the early 2000s oriented towards household consumption. The main reason for this was that in the absence of a foreign parent bank or efficient network integration, the relatively undercapitalized cooperative banks were unable to obtain external funding from international wholesale markets for FX lending (which thus remained negligible in their loan portfolio).

Thus, in spite of the fact that the majority of cooperative banks is located in smaller settlements, the phenomenon of financial exclusion develops (Chakravarty, 2006), since commercial banks, which provide most credit to households, are predominantly located in large urban centres. In CEE dual banking systems both forms of financial exclusion, namely the spatial and social exclusions, have appeared (Alessandrini–Presbitero–Zazzaro, 2009; Dymski 2005, 2009). The former means that the access to services in certain disadvantaged areas (rural peripheries, small settlements, deprived urban neighbourhoods) is limited, the latter applies when certain social groups are excluded from the banking services provision.

The pre-crisis expansion of banking networks alleviated territorial differences in access to financial services. However, the better access can also be seen as a pattern of exploitative inclusion (Sokol, 2013) in the case of housing-related credit – for the reasons described in the previous section. Today, however, the organizational centralization and post-crisis rationalization of banking networks (i.e. the closing down of certain branches) results in new patterns of financial exclusion[11] and capital drainage from the peripheries, as well as poor access to banking services at some territorial and settlement levels; increasing territorial inequalities once again.

Housing financialization goes local: stuck markets, social immobility and cross-scalar dependencies

The uneven spread of mortgage lending and the freezing of the credit market from 2008 contributed to socio-spatial polarization at the sub-national scale. On the one hand through depreciating house prices in peripheral spaces, and on the other hand through various mechanisms of dependencies and marginalization rooted in the "frozen" housing markets and in the immobility of local societies. In the following section we will give an analysis of housing markets in the South Békés and Northeast Békés LAU-I regions (Békés County, Southeast Hungary) to reveal the cross-scalar, housing financialization-related mechanisms[12] that reproduce uneven spatial development. The region entered the period of European modernity as a periphery (in the sense of Wallerstein, 2004) dominated economically by foreign and Budapest-centred financial capital in the mid-nineteenth century (Beluszky, 2001; Gál, 2010). In the socialist period, the local agricultural sector was subject to (further) capital extraction and later became the scene of dependent industrialization (1960s/1970s) orchestrated by state corporations headquartered in Budapest and major industrial centres (Barta et al., 2003). After the post-socialist transition, the region entered a long-lasting structural crisis and (again) a peripheral trajectory within the spatial division of labour resulting in the depreciation of local assets including labour and all forms of spatially fixed capital. As a consequence, new local dependencies emerged due to the dependent (vulnerable) position of local small and medium-sized enterprises in global production networks (Barta, Nagy, 2004), and the unfolding dominance of the state as an economic agent – as an employer (public services, national public works programmes) and as a developer/financer (from urban rehabilitation programmes to the common agricultural policy) (Nagy et al., 2015).

In the region, housing market processes have been driven by the historically systematically low levels of capital accumulation and low incomes due to the peripheral position of the county's labour market and as a consequence, the limited pool of investment opportunities providing safe and rapid return. In the past two decades international developers and investors limited their activities to the Budapest region and dynamic county towns with more than 100,000 residents. As a result peripheral and more uncertain local markets such as Békés County were left to local developers who had a deep and thorough knowledge of more peripheral markets. Such local developers are either (i) SMEs acting as professional developers or (ii) households constructing housing for themselves.

Both major groups grew strongly dependent on bank financing and state policies that made housing development processes highly selective and volatile in the boom period.

(i) In Békés County the group of professional developers (in Smith's term, 1996) included five locally dominant (medium-size) enterprises and 15–20 (fluctuating group of) individual entrepreneurs up until the crisis. The first group's strategy was focused on condominium developments in the three largest towns. Due to their dominant role on the county's property market, to the credit boom, and to the safe return of the proposed projects (which were at central locations with mixed use, targeting well-off social groups) they easily acquired bank loans in the 2000–2007 period. However, as the state withdrew from the housing market and the market growth was spurred increasingly by the entry of "small-income, vulnerable groups of consumers having no savings and calculable future"[13] relying on foreign currency-based bank loans, major local developers reduced their housing investments substantially from 2005. Meanwhile, small individual businesses gained a growing share on the housing market by developing detached family housing across the county. For these constructions the entrepreneurs acquired capital from the banks and also from the prospective owners (who themselves also relied on bank loans), sharing the risks. The outcome of such schemes were highly uncertain and often ended in deep indebtedness for the households involved, since small developers mostly did not operate guarantee systems for refunding in case of project failure. Thus, the spatially selective strategies of professional developers and the rise of small businesses exploiting the credit boom – along with the limited transparency of the local market – have thrown less well-off households in peripheral spaces into risk and, later, into a debt spiral.

(ii) For lack of professional developers and external capital flows, households had a decisive role in housing construction in rural places (in this role we can call them "owner-investors"). Investments for new construction and (more frequently) for house extension projects relied dominantly on obtaining credit from banks (mostly from nationally present commercial banks, taking loans denominated in foreign currencies). Owner-investors' borrowing activity was stimulated by the abundance of bank loans, by increasing income levels in the early 2000s, as well as by the state-subsidized mortgage scheme introduced in this period. Households benefiting from this scheme were concentrated in the towns of central Békés where houses had sufficient exchange value. In rural places of peripheral areas (South and Northeast Békés) where households had limited (or no) access to mortgage loans, only renovation/renewal schemes of existing housing were prevalent. Commercial banks' lending policies were highly selective even in the boom period. Their redlining practices on the market of mortgages[14] shifted household demand towards income-based consumption loans denominated in foreign currency. The latter had more permissive underwriting criteria, but higher interest rates. This meant that households living in geographically disadvantaged areas could only access more expensive credit and were thus more prone to default following the crisis. Households with regular incomes could also borrow from local savings banks that provided loans only on HUF-basis at higher interest rates (+1.5 per cent) – but on flexible terms that rested on a deep knowledge of local markets and trust. Nevertheless, those who were employed in public works programmes or lived on social benefits were excluded from all loan schemes. Moreover, local banks scarcely offered mortgage loans in peripheral spaces where "houses have no value at all".[15] Thus, rural residents only had access to the relatively expensive, income-based HUF loans through the local savings banks – which led to credit defaults in many cases (e.g. 30 per annum in South Békés in the last six years). The stricter regulations on borrowing and the normative, centralized lending policy introduced in the post-crisis years further limited many businesses' and households' access to credit through cooperative banks, particularly in rural spaces.

The peripherality of Békés County in capital flows and housing developments was reflected in terms of scale (volume), the temporality, and the spatiality of housing developments in the boom and the crisis period. The upsurge was belated (taking off in 2001/2002), and new housing constructions were strongly fluctuating[16] – following the changes in housing policies and the introduction on of FX-based bank loans. The growth period exhausted rapidly (by 2008/2009), and produced only 4.3 per cent of the total housing stock of the county (167,257 units), which is a figure far below the national average. Since the beginning of the crisis, housing construction has been stagnating at an extremely low level: since 2010, 925 new units have been completed and there are no signs of relaunch.

The peripherality of the county is also reflected by the mechanisms of households entering a debt spiral induced by poverty and by difficulties of financing basic needs. Taking on credit in these cases was thus not a leverage for the accumulation of wealth, but a means of survival. Such poverty-based indebtedness was much less prevalent in the economic core of the country. Our survey in northeast Békés (2014) suggested that 42 per cent (twice more than the national average) of the interviewed residents are struggling with paying utility bills regularly and 17 per cent of them are already in debt – which means they are in danger of losing their property, which in turn means losing their housing with no viable alternative. Furthermore, 40 per cent have no savings and 30 per cent are exploited through usury – the illegal mechanisms of exploitative inclusion for those who are excluded from the formal credit market that further intensify personal dependencies.

Another key element of peripheralization through housing financialization was a pattern of "freezing" housing markets in the aftermath of the crisis, especially in the rural spaces in the south and the northeast of the county. Here, the depreciation of spatially fixed capital (that is, dropping house prices of a housing stock built dominantly in the pre-war period and in the 1960s/1970s) and the lack of local labour possibilities made the majority of residents entrapped in places that lack long-term employment opportunities face the shrinkage of local services and suffer from environmental problems of the emerging rural slums (decaying and empty houses, abandoned gardens, etc.). However, housing property emerged as a pillar of household survival strategies by attaching specific use values to it (a place of residence) such as (a) having the right to social benefits and being employed in public works programmes, spaces to produce food for self-supply and (b) providing "securities" to usury. Certainly, such strategies reproduced the immobility of the households (30–80 per cent in the discussed rural places) and their dependence on agricultural land owners and the local state as employers; on local agents of usury and on local networks of the economy (labelled, and thus marginalized, as "informal") to fulfil basic needs. Such systems of dependency and marginality were (are being) reinforced by the shrinking state support to those who are in need, as well as by housing policies that led to evictions in cities and to the migration of urban poor.[17] Affordable house prices in geographically marginal areas have led to a change in urban-rural relations, transferring poverty and related conflicts (crime, drugs, prostitution) to rural peripheries and contributing to the rise of rural ghettos (see also Váradi, 2015; Virág, 2010).

The key agents of marginalized local societies have grown even more powerful since the crisis. As agricultural land was the only fixed capital asset that had a rapidly increasing exchange value (tripled between 2008 and 2014), the owners (who regained their land from socialist cooperatives) and their heirs sold smaller tracts to live on it or finance their family's mobility. This led to a rapid concentration and a strong external control in the sector. This resulted in a rather classical situation of accumulation by dispossession (Harvey, 2003) and contributed to these rural communities' peripheral position within the national (and global) labour market. Meanwhile, the local state was taking a central role in the realms of everyday life, such as employment (through workfare programs), managing households' everyday life (through finance/debt management, child care, etc.), satisfying basic needs (providing food, access to water/public wells, subsidies to heating) and recycling the decaying housing stock. The latter occurs through the practice of transferring the ownership of dilapidated houses to the municipality that clears the area and re-uses it for agricultural production (mostly for growing vegetables), employing public workers in workfare programmes. This contributes to autarchy as a municipal strategy that aims at "feeding everyone in the village" – and makes the whole system dependent on national governmental labour policy.

As a consequence, self-contained worlds of poverty are emerging within peripheral spaces in which housing has a central role – anchoring poor, non-mobile residents – and everyday lives are governed by local relationships and dependencies on a small group of powerful agents. This helps keeping social problems within local spaces – and marginalizing them by employing specific policies that fail to target the whole complex of rural ghettoization. Meanwhile, in more dynamic spaces of the county, dependent positions are being reproduced through housing market mechanisms and the growing external control over locally fixed assets – confining the overwhelming majority of the residents to the peripheral/ low-paid/uncertain pool (Harvey, 1989) of the labour market.

Conclusion

We have argued that patterns of uneven development are inherent to processes of financialization, and that in addition to the more often described contribution of financialization to social inequalities, financialization also produces spatial inequalities through the mechanisms of homogenization and differentiation (Smith, 1996). We demonstrated this process through the example of the Hungarian housing market on various scales. We have seen that the financialized housing regime that unfolded in Hungary in the years preceding the crisis led to capital transfers from the periphery to the core both on an international (European) and on a national scale.

The financialization of the Hungarian housing market took place within an institutional context that was embedded and adjusted to an increasingly homogeneous institutional/regulative context within Europe (a precondition of capital flows and equalization of profit rates); however, within this context, business strategies and practices of financial institutions rested upon exploiting the differences (interest rates, returns in various forms of investments, etc.), in which core–periphery relations had embodied. Financialized housing regimes in CEE were the manifestations of such capital accumulation strategies and channelled the resources of the periphery into the core and meanwhile pushed (the majority of) risks and shocks stemming from the financial system's logic to peripheral economies/ spaces. This contributed to the production of increasing inequalities and reinforced existing structures of dependencies on various spatial scales (European core/periphery; metropolitan/non-metropolitan; urban/rural; global/local) and dimensions (within local societies and institutional hierarchies).

The mechanisms of dependent financialization of the housing markets contributed to the social polarization processes within CEE peripheral economies and societies as well. The financialization of housing took varied forms in these peripheral spaces from the dispossession of homes (in some cases manifesting in evictions from homes serving as collateral for credit) through the depreciation of fixed assets in peripheral spaces (slowing down capital accumulation), up to the sale of land to cover household needs. Such processes are leading to the loss of local control over local resources, and contribute to the erosion of household assets accumulated under socialism (homeownership) and during the period of transition (during restitution of agricultural land). Thus, peripheral spaces developed as scenes of accumulation through dispossession (Harvey, 2009) and, as a consequence, gave rise to various dependencies linking local societies to global capital flows and national market processes.

The way the recent financial crisis unfolded in CEE has to be understood in a *longue durée* perspective; as a consequence of the dependent integration of the region into the world economy. Indebtedness and financial vulnerability have been important elements of this dependent integration since the 1970s. The regime of dependent (housing) financialization that was built up in the early 2000s (on the basis of housing finance policies developed since the 1980s) explains the way in which the recent crisis rolled out.

Notes

1 Although periods of financialization have systematically occurred in previous cycles of accumulation (Arrighi, 1994), the term was not necessarily used as such, and definitely not with such frequency.

2 According to David Harvey's definition a spatial fix represents the necessity to find new material forms and geographical spaces for the investment of surplus capital in order to overcome periods of crisis (Harvey, 1982). This surplus capital is often channelled into real estate and infrastructure. Harvey also describes how historically important circuits of "fictitious capital" have been invested "in mortgages, public debt, urban and national infrastructures and the like" (Harvey, 2014: 240).

3 The "European periphery" is understood here as the countries on the periphery of the European economic space; broadly speaking the countries of Southern and Eastern Europe. This is not meant to be a static categorization, but rather a heuristic device that helps us grasp relations of dependency. It is also in this way that we refer to the category of "semi-periphery" introduced by Arrighi (1990). He identifies the semi-periphery as an "intermediate position in the core–periphery structure of the capitalist world-economy" (Arrighi, 1990: 11). In his categorization Southern and Eastern European countries belong to the global semi-periphery (distinguishing them from the peripheries of the non-industrialized global South) – this is what we refer to here as the "European periphery".

4 For this, we rely on statistical data provided by the European Mortgage Federation. Unless stated otherwise, all data analysis in the following section is based on this database.

5 For this graph we have grouped the countries with available data in the following way: "core": Austria, Belgium, Denmark, Finland, France, Germany, Italy, Luxembourg, Netherlands, Sweden, United Kingdom; "Southern Europe and Ireland": Cyprus, Greece, Ireland, Malta, Portugal, Spain; "Central and Eastern Europe": Bulgaria, Croatia, Czech Republic, Estonia, Hungary, Latvia, Lithuania, Poland, Romania, Slovakia, Slovenia. We base this categorization primarily on Arrighi's notion of the semi-periphery (Arrighi, 1990 – see footnote in section 2), modified by the type of housing regime these countries have (Fernandez-Aalbers, 2016).

6 For this graph we have grouped the countries in the same way as in the case of Figure 9.1, with Croatia figuring additionally in the CEE group.

7 For example, 42 per cent of the Austrian banking system's total profits are earned by CEE operations in 2007. In the case of its largest players (Erste and Raiffeissen Bank) pre-tax profit generated in CEE exceeded 64 per cent and 78 per cent respectively on 30 June 2008.

8 Beside the changes in currency exchange rates, this drastic increase also occurred because the majority of mortgages had variable interest rates.

9 The term "dual economy" can stand for characteristics caused by *organizational and structural differences among economic actors (large and small enterprises)*. In Hungary's case, these are embodied in differences between foreign-owned large enterprises, on the one hand, and Hungarian SMEs, on the other. One can also speak, however, of a *dual regional economy*. This term points to a developmental gap between dynamic centre(s) and peripheries.

10 The investigations of Berger and Udell (1995) confirmed that larger banks were less interested in higher-risk lending to small businesses, as shown by Berger et al. (2001) on the example of Argentina. With the exception of OTP and FHB Banks, the parent banks of market leader banks were foreign owned in 2010. A necessary precondition of their shift to household lending was the legal regulation of mortgage loans and of collateral.

11 Kovács (2014) examined the different indicators of territorial exclusion in Hungary characterised by the lack of bank branches, and he found a strong correlation between

the size of the settlement and the number of bank account holders as the most essential indicator of the access to financial services. Social exclusion is also justified by the positive relationship between household incomes and access to basic financial services.

12 We refer here to Cox's (2001) and Massey's (2008) concepts on scale and place that emphasis their mutually constitutive nature.

13 A quotation from a major local developer, interviewed in 2005.

14 Our local interviews revealed this spatial practice, even though it has never been declared officially by banks.

15 Quoted from an interview with a local saving bank's executive (South Békés); he referred to all non-urban places in Northeast and South Békés.

16 E.g. the number of projects completed by professional developers (for the term's definition, see Smith, 1996) tripled from 2002 to 2003 (as a consequence of the introduction of a state-subsidized mortgage programme). This number halved by 2006 (affected by the fiscal austerity scheme), and was then followed by a two-year upsurge (stimulated by the spread of FX loans).

17 In South Békés, houses are advertised by the owners/heirs of late local residents for 1 HUF on the Internet to get released from the related duties controlled by the local municipalities, which involved an inward migration from Budapest.

References

Aalbers, M.B. (2008) "The financialization of home and the mortgage market crisis", *Competition & Change*, 12: 148–166.

Aalbers, M.B. (2015a) "The potential for financialization", *Dialogues in Human Geography*, 5(2): 214–219.

Aalbers, M.B. (2015b) "Corporate financialization", in D. Richardson, N. Castree, M.F. Goodchild, A. Kobayashi, W. Liu and R.A. Marston (eds) *The International Encyclopedia of Geography: People, the Earth, Environment, and Technology*. Oxford: Wiley.

Aalbers, M.B. and Christophers B. (2014) "Centring housing in political economy", *Housing, Theory and Society*, 31(4): 373–394.

Alessandrini, P., Presbitero, A.F. and Zazzaro, A. (2009) "Banks, distances and firms' financing constraints", *Review of Finance*, 13(2): 261–307.

Arrighi, G. (1990) "The developmentalist illusion: a reconceptualization of the semi-periphery", in W.G. Martin (ed.) *Semiperipheral States in the World-Economy*. Westport, CT: Greenwood Press, pp. 11–42.

Arrighi, G. (1994) *The Long Twentieth Century: Money, Power and the Origins of Our Times*. London: Verso.

Barta, Gy. (1990) Centrum–periféria folyamatok a magyar gazdaság területi fejlődésében? [Core–periphery relations in the spatial organization of the Hungarian economy?]. In J. Tóth (ed.) Tér – idő – társadalom: Huszonegy tanulmány Enyedi Györgynek. Pécs: MTA Regionális Kutatások Központja, 170–190.

Barta, Gy, Bernek, Á. and Nagy, G. (2003) A külföldi működőtőke-befektetések jelenlegi tendenciái és területi elmozdulásának esélyei Magyarországon [The Current Tendencies and the Possibilities of Regional Moving of Foreign Direct Investments in Hungary]. *Tér és Társadalom*, 17(4): 173–190.

Becker, J., Jager, J. and Weissenbacher, R. (2015) "Uneven and dependent development in Europe – the crisis and its implications". In J. Jager and E. Springler (eds) *Assymmetric Crisis in Europe and Possible Futures*. Abingdon: Routledge.

Beluszky, P. (2001) A Nagyalföld történeti földrajza [The historical geography of the Great Plain, Hungary]. Pécs: Dialóg Campus.

Bohle, D. (2013) "Post-socialist housing meets transnational finance: foreign banks, mortgage lending, and the privatization of welfare in Hungary and Estonia", *Review of International Political Economy*, 21(4): 913–948.

Brenner, N. (1998) "Between fixity and motion: accumulation, territorial organization and the historical geography of spatial scales", *Environment and Planning D*, 16(4): 459–481.

Brenner, N., Peck, J. and Theodore, N. (2010) "Variegated neoliberalization: geographies, modalities, pathways", *Global Networks*, 10(2): 182–222.

Brenner, R. (2004) "New boom or new bubble? The trajectory of the US economy", *New Left* Review, 25 (Jan–Feb): 57–100.

Chakravarty, S.P. (2006) "Regional variation in banking services and social exclusion", *Regional Studies*, 40: 415–428.

Cox, K. R. (2001) "Territoriality, politics and the "urban"", *Political Geography*, 20(6), 745–762.

Crouch, C (2009) "Privatised Keynesianism: an unacknowledged policy regime", *The British Journal of Politics and International Relations*, 11: 382–399.

Dancsik B. et al. (2015) "Comprehensive analysis of the nonperforming household mortgage portfolio using micro-level data", *MNB Occasional Papers Special Issue*.

Dow, S.C. (1999) "International liquidity preference and endogenous credit". In J. Deprez and J.T. Harvey (eds) *Foundations of International Economics – Post-Keynesian Perspectives*. New York Routledge.

Dymski G. (2005) "Banking strategy and financial exclusion: tracing the pathways of globalization", *Revista de Economia*, 31: 1–29.

Dymski, G. (2009) "The global financial customer and the spatiality of exclusion after the end of geography", *Cambridge Journal of Regions, Economy and* Society, 2: 267–85.

Engelen, E. (2012) "Crisis in space: ruminations on the unevenness of financialization and its geographical implications". In T.J. Barnes, J. Peck and E. Sheppard (eds) *The Wiley-Blackwell Companion to Economic Geography*. Oxford: Blackwell, 242–257.

European Mortgage Federation (2015) Hypostat 2015, A review of Europe's mortgage and housing markets.

Ferencz, Z. (2015) A kutatás módszertani szempontjai. [The methodology of the research project]. In V. Szirmai (ed.) *A társadalmi egyenlőtlenségektől a társadalmi jól-lét felé*. Székesfehérvár: Kodolányi János Főiskola, 433–445.

Fernandez, R. and Aalbers, M.B. (2016) "Financialization and housing: between globalization and varieties of capitalism". *Competition and Change*, 20(2): 71–88.

French, S., Leyshon, A. and Wainwright, T. (2011) "Financializing space, spacing financialization", *Progress in Human Geography*, 35: 798–819.

Gabor, D. (2010) "(De)Financialization and crisis in Eastern Europe", *Competition and Change*, 14(3–4): 248–70.

Gabor, D. (2012) "The road to financialization in Central and Eastern Europe: revisiting the early policies and politics of stabilizing transition", *Review of Political Economy*, 24(2): 227–249.

Gál, Z. (2005) "The development and the polarised spatial structure of the Hungarian banking system in a transforming economy". In G. Barta, É. Szörényiné, I. Kukorelli and J. Timár (eds) *Hungarian Spaces and Places: Patterns of Transition*. Pécs: Centre for Regional Studies of the Hungarian Academy of Sciences, pp. 197–219.

Gál, Z. (2010) *Pénzügyi piacok a globális térben*. Budapest: Akadémiai kiadó.

Gál, Z. (2011) "Bankhálózat". In K. Kocsis and F. Schweitzer (eds) *Magyarország térképekben*. Budapest: MTA Földrajztudományi Kutatóintézet, pp. 203–209.

Gál, Z. (2012) "A hazai takarékszövetkezeti szektor szerepe a vidék finanszírozásában", *Területi Statisztika*, 15(52): 437–460.

Gál, Z. (2014) "Role of financial sector FDI in regional imbalances in Central and Eastern Europe", in A. Gostyńska and P. Tokarski (eds) *Eurozone enlargement: challenges for the V4 countries*. Warsaw: The Polish Institute of International Affairs, pp. 19–30.

Gál, Z. and Burger, Cs. (2013) A vidék bankjai? A magyar takarékszövetkezeti szektor hitelezési aktivitása [Limits to local embeddedness: lending activity of the Hungarian cooperative banking sectors], *Közgazdasági Szemle* 60(4): 373–401

Gál, Z. and Schmidt, A. (2017) "Geoeconomics in Central and Eastern Europe: implications on FDI". In Mark Munoz (ed.) *Advances in Geoeconomics*, Abingdon: Routledge, pp. 76–93.

Gerőcs, T. and Pinkasz, A. (2017, forthcoming) "Debt-ridden development on Europe's Eastern Periphery". In M. Boatcă, A. Komlosy and H. Nolte (eds) *Political Economy of the World-System Annuals: Global Inequalities in World-Systems Perspective*. Boulder, CO: Paradigm.

Gerse, J. and Szilágyi, D. (2015) Magyarország településhálózata 2: Városok-falvak. Budapest: Központi Statisztikai Hivatal.

Gfk Hungary (2014) Purchasing power in Hungary. Country report and database. Gfk GeoMarketing GmbH, Bruchsal, Germany.

Harvey, D. (1982) *The Limits to Capital*. London: Verso.

Harvey, D. (1989) *The Condition of Postmodernity: An Inquiry into the Origins of Cultural Change*. Oxford: Blackwell.

Harvey, D. (2003) *The New Imperialism: Accumulation Through Dispossession*. Oxford: Oxford University Press.

Harvey, D. (2006) "Neo-liberalism as creative destruction", *Geografiska Annaler*, 88 B (2): 145–158.

Harvey, D. (2014) *Seventeen Contradictions and the End of Capitalism*. New York: Oxford University Press.

Hegedüs, J. and Somogyi, E. (2016) "Moving from an authoritarian state system to an authoritarian market system: housing finance milestones in Hungary between 1979 and 2014". In J. Lunde and C. Whitehead (eds) *Milestones in European Housing Finance*. Chichester: Wiley-Blackwell, pp. 201–218.

Herod, A. and Wright, M. W. (2002) "Placing scale: an introduction". In A. Herod and M.W. Wright (eds) *Geographies of Power: Placing Scale*. London: Blackwell, pp. 1–15.

Kolosi, T. and Tóth I. Gy. (eds) (2014) Társadalmi Riport 2014. Budapest: TÁRKI.

Kovács, S. Zs. (2014) Elérhetőség és kirekesztés Magyarországon a pénzügyi szolgáltatások aspektusából. [Availability and exclusion from aspect of Hungarian financial services], *Területfejlesztés és Innováció [Spatial Development and Innovation]*, 8(3): 28–35.

Krippner, G. R. (2005) "The financialization of the American economy", *Socio-Economic Review*, 3: 173–208.

Lapavitsas, C. (2009a) "Financialised capitalism: crisis and financial expropriation", *Historical Materialism*, 17: 114–148.

Lapavitsas, C. (2009b) "Financialisation embroils developing countries", *Papeles de Europa*, 19: 108–139.

Lapavitsas, C. (2015) "Theorizing financialization", *Work, Employment and Society*, 25(4): 611–626.

Madden, D. and Marcuse, P. (2016) *In Defense of Housing: The Politics of Crisis*. London: Verso.

Martin, R. (2002) *Financialization of Daily Life*, Philadelphia, NJ: Temple University Press.

Massey, D. (2008) *For Space*. London: SAGE.

Myrdal, G. (1957) *Rich Land and Poor.* New York: Harper & Row.

Nagy, E., Timár, J., Nagy, G. and Velkey, G. (2015) "The everyday practices of the reproduction of peripherality and marginality in Hungary". In T. Lang, S. Henn, K, Ehrlich and W. Sgibnev (eds) *Understanding Geographies of Polarization and Peripheralization.* London: Palgrave Macmillan, 135–155.

Pike, A. and Pollard, J. (2010) "Economic geographies of financialization", *Economic Geography*, 86: 29–51.

Raviv, O. (2008) "Chasing the dragon east: exploring the frontiers of Western European finance", *Contemporary Politics*, 14(3): 297–314.

Scheiring, G. (2016) A nemzeti burzsoázia diszkrét bája – A demokrácia hanyatlásának politikai gazdaságtana [The discrete charm of the national bourgeoisie – the political economy of the decline of democracy]. In A. Antal and Gy. Földes (eds) *Holtpont: Társadalomkritikai tanulmányok Magyarország elmúlt 25 évéről* [*Deadlock. Critical Social Science Studies about the Past 25 Years of Hungary*]. Napvilág Kiadó.

Schepp, Z. and Pitz, M. (2012) Lakossági devizahitelezés Magyarországon: problémafelmérés és a frankhitelek banki árazásának empirikus vizsgálata. *Műhelytanulmányok 2012/3.* Pécsi Tudományegyetem Közgazdaságtudományi Kar Közgazdasági és Regionális Tudományok Intézete.

Smith, A. and Swain, A. (2010) "The global economic crisis, Eastern Europe, and the Former Soviet Union: models of development and the contradictions of internationalization", *Eurasian Geography and Economics*, 51: 1–34.

Smith, N. (1984) *Uneven Development: Nature, Capital, and the Production of Space.* Athens, GA: University of Georgia Press,

Smith, N. (1992) "Geography, difference and the politics of scale". In J. Doherty, E. Graham and M. Malek (eds) *Postmodernism and the Social Sciences.* London: Macmillan, 57–79.

Smith, N. (1996) *The New Urban Frontier: Gentrification and the Revanchist City.* London: Routledge.

Sokol, M. (2013) "Towards a 'newer' economic geography? Injecting finance and financialisation into economic geographies", *Cambridge Journal of Regions, Economy and Society*, 6: 501–515.

Stockhammer, E. (2004) "Financialisation and the slowdown of accumulation", *Cambridge Journal of Economics*, 28(5): 719–741.

Stockhammer, E. (2012) "Financialization, income distribution and the crisis", *Investigación Económica*, 71: 39–70.

Szivós, P., Bernát, A. and Kőszeghy, L. (2011) *Managing Household Debt – Hungarian Country Report.* Budapest: TÁRKI.

van der Zwan, N. (2014) "Making sense of financialization", *Socioeconomic Review,* 12(1): 99–129.

Váradi, M. (2015) Szegénység, projektek, közpolitikák. [Poverty, projects, public policy]. *Tér és Társadalom*, 29(1): 69–96.

Virág, T. (2010) *Kirekesztve: Falusi gettók az ország peremén* [Excluded: rural ghettoes on the margin]. Budapest: Akadémiai Kiadó.

Wallerstein, I. (2004) *World System Analysis: An Introduction.* Durham, NC: Duke University Press.

Yeşin, P. (2013) "Foreign currency loans and systemic risk in Europe", *Federal Reserve Bank of St Louis Review*, 95(3): 219–235.

Part III

Sustainable development issues

10 The triple crisis

How can Europe foster growth, well-being and sustainability?[1]

Miriam Rehm, Sven Hergovich and Georg Feigl

Introduction

Even before the start of the financial and economic crisis in 2007, a feeling emerged that something had gone wrong in the economy, despite relatively high growth rates and declining unemployment. At least in Europe, economic growth seemed decoupled from subjective well-being, while there were rising concerns about its ecological consequences.

The discussion gained prominence in 2008 with the 'Commission on the Measurement of Economic Performance and Social Progress' (Stiglitz et al., 2009), better known as the Stiglitz–Sen–Fitoussi Commission (SSFC). Although a lot of similar initiatives had been started in the past 40 years, this Commission sparked off a new broad debate. It became widely known in the European political sphere under the headline of 'Beyond GDP' (European Commission, 2009).

In 2012, the Commission should have presented a report on the implementation of 'indicators that do what people really want them to do, namely measure progress in delivering social, economic and environmental goals in a sustainable manner' (ibid.: 11). These could have laid the foundation for the future economic and social policy

The deep economic crisis since 2008 should have made it obvious that the current economic strategy failed to deliver sustainable progress for everybody in Europe, and thus fuelled the initiative. Furthermore, the crisis also demonstrated painfully that a lack of growth and especially a shrinking gross domestic product (GDP) can have disastrous negative effects on subjective well-being, especially through rising unemployment and poverty, and the concomitant pessimism and misery. However, what happened was a fragmentation of the different initiatives: 'Beyond GDP' more or less ceased to be an issue, and even the related Europe 2020 strategy has seen major setbacks, as the policy was entirely focused on short-term crisis measures. This is a lost chance for more coherent economic governance in Europe.

The lack of growth since 2008 leads directly to a crucial point in the Beyond GDP debate (BGD). GDP is not a goal in itself, but it can be a means to achieve progress. The nature of this progress is difficult to define a priori as it is the result of a deeply political process. Philosophy has nonetheless attempted to give some answers – the well-known capabilities approach of Amartya Sen (2009) and Martha Nussbaum (2000), for instance, focuses on the ability to reach happiness rather than the actual achievement of desired ends. Robert and Edward Skidelsky (2012), economist and philosopher, in contrast develop a set of basic goods that are elements of a 'good life', reviving a debate that dates back at least to Aristotle.

Some strands of this debate seem relevant for the discussion here. First, economic activity can either be funnelled into a higher standard of living, or into increasing leisure. Both 'lead us out of the tunnel of economic necessity into daylight' as Keynes stated it ardently in 1930 (Keynes, 1963: 7). Second, we have to look at the distribution of these possibilities, which are determined mainly by income and wealth. Third, as gross national product (GNP) 'measures everything [. . .] except that which makes life worthwhile', as Senator Robert F. Kennedy put it in 1968 (see Tayler, 2012), it is important to incorporate various other aspects that influence the quality of life and that are not directly measured by the level of economic activity. These include (non-exhaustively) health, social inclusion, individuality, a broadly defined security, leisure, harmony with nature and religious principles, and high-quality public services. The SSFC largely skirts around the philosophical pitfalls by asking which statistical information is missing for better, evidence-based policies. This contribution follows their pragmatic approach while acknowledging that the determination of the set and ranking of additional indicators is a fundamentally political question that cannot be decided by experts.

The first part of this contribution places the BGD in the context of current European economic policy and governance. We argue that these two hardly fit together and that the latter has to be changed if the former is to be taken seriously. The second part attempts to shed some light on the main dimensions of the triple crisis in economic performance, social progress and their potential (ecological) limits, and relates these crises to the attempts to find a better way of measuring progress. The third part outlines the historical background of the BGD, which had its first peak in the 1970s. In particular, we ask why GDP became an ever more important indicator while the alternatives are hardly known today, and what can be learned for the current debate from discussions that took place over 40 years back. Finally we propose employment, distribution and socio-ecological transition as the three pillars of a project to increase welfare, which we find necessary to move beyond a focus on GDP.

The BGD in the context of European economic policy

In August 2009, when the first positive quarterly growth rates after the deepest economic crisis in Europe in decades occurred, the European Commission set out a roadmap 'to better measure progress in a changing world' (European Commission, 2009: 4).

The first change was a reformulation of the initiative of 2007, which was the first sign of a significant change of direction. No longer was the goal to go 'beyond GDP', but to focus on 'GDP and beyond'. The thesis set out in the communication was that GDP 'is a powerful and widely accepted indicator for monitoring short to medium term fluctuations in economic activity, notably in the current recession' which 'is still the best single measure of how the market economy is performing' (ibid.: 10). It stated implicitly that additional indicators are only needed in the long run to measure economic and social progress, as if this were a luxury after the main mission of growth has been accomplished.

However, the Commission got one of the main points right when it noted that 'EU policies will be judged on whether they are successful in delivering these goals and improving the well-being of Europeans' (ibid.). By 2012, five key actions should have been undertaken in this direction:

- Complementing GDP with highly aggregated environmental and social indicators.
- Near real-time information for decision-making.
- More accurate reporting on distribution and inequalities.
- Developing a European Sustainable Development Scoreboard.
- Extending National Accounts to environmental and social issues.

Up to now, there is hardly any sign that the Commission has put this agenda forward politically, although there was significant progress on the technical level via EUROSTAT, the European Statistical System (see the second section of this chapter). The only Commission activity outside EUROSTAT in 2012 on the joint website www.beyond-gdp.eu is the website's fifth anniversary. The European Council does not fare much better. It only recalls the need to use 'indicators that complement GDP' as one of 35 conclusions in the context of Rio+20 (see www.beyond-gdp.eu/news.html).

We suggest two main reasons for the observed shortcomings. One is the quite ambitious nature of the project. For example, there is a huge gap in the area of reliable distribution indicators at European Union level, which is not easy to fill within three years without noteworthy new resources. Especially in times of crisis with tighter government finances this is a difficult task. But first of all, the current lack of ambition is caused by ideology. At least as early as the Greek financial crisis, starting in 2010, Europe witnessed a rapid shift in crisis management from coordinated economic stimulus management and tackling the roots of the crisis to an exit strategy based on macroeconomic surveillance (see Degryse and Pochet, 2012) of national economic policies, with a focus on some kind of macroeconomic trinity consisting of austerity, structural reforms and competitiveness. This ideological tightening leaves no space for an equal treatment of social indicators. It is clear that slashing social spending, a reduction of social security to gain flexibility and real wage cuts to improve cost competitiveness will lead to negative results in well-being indicators.

The Europe 2020 strategy faces similar problems. Its headline targets such as higher employment, better educational outcomes and less social exclusion – which can be read as a specific, less ambitious and too narrow version of 'indicators that measure progress in delivering social, economic and environmental goals' – also came into contradiction with austerity measures.

It is therefore not surprising that social actors challenging current European economic policy are also those trying to push the BGD (and to a smaller extent the Europe 2020 strategy) further. In 2012, parts of the trade-union movement started a number of initiatives. The IG-Metal conference 'Changing Course – For a Good Life' stressed that 'financial market-driven capitalism is a mistake and what is needed is changing the course towards a good life, which includes preventing the exploitation of nature and the destruction of social systems' (IG Metal, 2012). The connection between social and ecological aims is also accentuated by the discussions on the nature of progress, started by the Upper-Austrian Chamber of Labour. They highlight that from an employees' perspective, environmental problems cannot be solved by the market, in the same way as questions of wage policy or income distribution cannot be solved by the market. In addition, the European Federation of Public Service Unions (EPSU) and the European Trade Union Institute (ETUI) organised a Beyond GDP conference in March 2012 and a conference 'From (un)economic growth to future well-being' in October 2012. These activities show that the trade-union movement recognises that the BGD is of high and growing relevance, and that a socio-ecological transition with a concomitant set of alternative statistical indicators of well-being are necessary for real progress and an improvement in well-being without the exploitation of the environment.

However, despite this positive picture it should be borne in mind that the actions taken by the trade unions so far fall short of their rather ambitious discourse (see Galgóczi and Pochet, 2012). A shift from 'the social partnership model that developed in Europe after World War II [which] was based on the resource-intensive industry and consumption paradigm' to a strategy of a 'just transition' (ibid.: 252f.) is an ongoing process, which in practice is not yet free of contradictions.

Meanwhile, the emerging new European economic governance stressed the need for a statistical work programme focused on the development and enforcement of a new Macroeconomic Scoreboard and more detailed statistics on public finances. This was the new political priority where 'more comprehensive information to support policy decisions' (European Statistical System, 2011: 11) should be provided, and not aims such as social progress or environmental issues.

A direct link between the indicators programme and the new macroeconomic surveillance approach can be found in the bilateral work of the economic advisory councils in Germany and France (Conseil d'Analyse Économique and Sachverständigenrat, 2010). Their follow-up report to the SSFC, published at the end of 2010, contained a set of various indicators with an overwhelming focus on economic sustainability in the third pillar. Some of them have a clear connection to European guidelines, such as the rate of R&D-expenditure to GDP, the cyclically adjusted public deficit or the credit-to-GPD-ratio (ibid.: 27).

This shift is quite ambiguous. On the one hand, it became clear that macroeconomic stabilisation cannot be entrusted to market forces, and thus has to be a topic for economic policy intervention – and therefore supported by some indicators. On the other hand, it could open a back door for a new merely GDP growth-focused economic strategy that covers up environmental conflicts by watering down the sustainability concept.

Such a concept of an indicator-based economic policy, focused on macro-economic stability and using central surveillance mechanisms, was further developed in the 'Six-pack' and the 'Euro-Plus-Pact'. The new so-called macro-economic imbalance procedure, in particular, with the set of indicators, the 'Scoreboard' (see European Commission, 2012) might be interpreted as some kind of 'GDP and beyond', as it implicitly sets out additional indicators to measure good/stability-oriented economic policies.

However, this development has the potential to narrow the broader guidelines for economic policy stated in the Treaty on the Functioning of the European Union (TFEU), where the 'well-being of its peoples' is the basic aim, followed by some kind of a 'magic polygon' of economic policy (Rothschild, 2005) with the 'corners' being balanced growth, price stability, full employment, social progress, quality of the environment and scientific and technological advance. The 'Europe 2020' strategy also has a broader focus than the macroeconomic scoreboard.

The BGD can only become a success if the new indicators are directly linked to the economic agenda through broad long-term goals. Dullien and van Treeck (2012) propose – in the context of Germany – a reformulation of the magic poly-gon through legislation, highlighting 'social sustainability', 'material prosperity and economic sustainability', 'ecological sustainability' and 'sustainability of public activity and finances', all of which should be treated equally and further specified by a set of indicators. This should be the basis on which economic policy is evaluated. For that purpose, they propose an 'annual prosperity report', which should clearly point to development in these fields, lay out the basic trade-offs between the goals and suggest what should be done to establish a balanced policy mix. In the European context, such a report could replace the annual growth report and become a basic tool to broaden the economic debate in the European Semester.

An important precondition for such a report would be timely data, comparable time series and at least rough projections for the near future. For example, the European Quality of Life Survey (Eurofound, 2012) aims at measuring the overall objective of the TFEU and contains a lot of pertinent information. It also shows that a publication interval of four years is a major barrier for policy relevance. At the same time, quarterly reports would probably not add a lot of information, since the broad determinants of well-being and happiness are known (see, for example, Layard, 2005) and rather stable. On the other hand, some of the available indicators, for example in the case of unemployment, are published in a more timely manner and with higher accuracy than GDP. The importance of data quality should thus not be overestimated.

The main dimensions of reformed statistical indicators

As mentioned, Europe witnessed some positive developments regarding statistical indicators. In the last years a consensus emerged on better measurements of progress, at least on a relatively general level. The SSFC laid the basis with its 12 reform recommendations. This ground-breaking work was referred to in the more detailed work of the 'Sponsoring Group on Measuring Progress, Well-being and Sustainable Development' launched by the European Statistical System Committee, the joint report of the French and German economic expert councils and the OECD's 'Better life' initiative (see European Statistical System, 2011). They identified three areas that should be at the centre of such indicators: economic performance, societal well-being and the sustainability of these, with a special focus on the environment. This section is structured along these lines, since these are also the areas in which Europe is facing a crisis.

This is certainly a new quality of treatment, as the SSFC provided a coherent and integrated approach with a scientific foundation that enjoyed significant political back-up, and which led to coordinated efforts by major international organisations. Although economists play a leading role, the approach is inter-disciplinary, with an at least implicit grounding in happiness research (see Layard, 2005). The main findings of this research area are that after reaching a certain level, further increases in aggregate production and income have only a minor effect on subjective well-being. It is instead determined more by the distribution of financial resources, unemployment, job quality, leisure and other non-economic factors such as health or social inclusion. This evidence is corroborated by a recent survey by the OECD (2008), which concludes that there are large and robust negative effects of unemployment on well-being, after age, education and even household income are controlled for.

The SSFC integrated environmental sustainability into the thinking about progress. Their focus is limited to avoiding irreversible damage, which they postulate as a guideline for an ecological transformation of the economy. However, it is not always clear how this can be applied in practice. For example, from this point of view, finance can be considered as one of the 'sustainable' economic sectors on account of its being a service sector. This, however, is subject to a few reservations that should be mentioned here. First, the financial sector can endanger macroeconomic stability and is thus not necessarily sustainable in this particular economic sense. Furthermore, while the ecological effects of boom and bust cycles are not clear and would merit further research, there is no reason to believe that financial markets will be successful in incorporating long-term ecological risks into business and government policy valuations, since they fail at appro-priately pricing even medium-term economic risks. Finally, rather than being an end in itself or even a means to an end, finance is a 'means to a means', since it serves the purposes of investment and economic growth, which themselves are means to the end of a good life or a good society. The regulatory framework of the economy should therefore be formulated to take this subordinate status of the financial sector into account. An inversion of the importance of finance through the back door of 'sustainability' is counter-productive to this debate. A more strin-gent formulation of the sustainability goal might thus improve the framework within which the BGD is conducted.

The following subsections put the BGD debate in context within the economic, social and environmental crisis in Europe. These are areas which would need to be addressed by policy-making at European level, but the positive response so far remains limited to the area of technical indicators.

Economic performance

Welfare as measured by standard indicators has fallen in Europe. While worries regarding a double dip in the United States have so far proven unfounded, the European economy experienced its second year of recession in 2012 after the shared recession experience in the US and in Europe in 2008–2009. The European slump deepened throughout the year 2012, and it is both the EU and the eurozone area that have seen negative growth rates for two consecutive quarters in the aggregate. Europe is thus undoubtedly in an economic downturn.

From a viewpoint not centred on GDP, this does not, a priori, give rise to worry. It is quite possible for low output levels to go together with fairly high living standards and vice versa, as the differences in the ranking of per capita GDP and the human development index for, among others, Cuba and India demonstrate. However, this does not necessarily extend to falling output, i.e. negative growth rates. Standard indicators of economic hardship, such as poverty and unemployment rates, have risen sharply in the eurozone with the crisis. Much-cited disastrous record unemployment rates above 25 per cent and youth unemployment rates reaching around 60 per cent in Spain and Greece provide an indication of the extent of the negative effects of falling output on the quality of life. The bleak picture is described in detail by the European Commission's report (EC 2012) on employment and social developments.

The negative effects of unemployment on both health and happiness have been known for decades, as the research by Jahoda et al. (1975 [1933]) in their seminal study of Austrian unemployed demonstrates. Economic crises thus have the potential of worsening alternative welfare indicators. Some reports' evidence from the European crisis countries and in particular from Greece suggests that health-service quality and coverage have declined, and that suicide rates have increased.

Beyond their aggregate impact, one reason for this substantially negative effect of economic crises on the quality of life is their differential impact on income groups; in particular, low-income groups may be less capable of cushioning negative income shocks and preventing slides into poverty – defined by Eurostat as the inability to afford basic necessities for a good life. Since inequality also leads to negative effects with respect to health outcomes, especially regarding psychological illnesses, lower educational outcomes, higher prevalence of gender discrimination and higher crime and incarceration rates (Wilkinson and Pickett, 2009), the particularly negative effects of the crisis on low-income groups is likely to impact the quality of life for society as a whole. In this context, broader measures for economic well-being, which focus more on consumption than on production and income, are required. Furthermore, better measures for wealth and consumption and of the distribution of income, wealth and consumption will make a discerning investigation of differential policy impacts possible. The steps taken by Eurostat (2011) towards providing these indicators are ambitious and very useful, even though the measurement of household assets beyond housing are likely to be available only in the medium term. Similarly, those capturing distribution will likely take some time due to the difficulties in harmonising the EU Statistics on Income and Living Conditions (SILC data) across countries.

Transfers and public services in European welfare states are designed, among other things, to insure against these losses in welfare resulting from economic crises. As a consequence, so-called structural reforms that reduce the redistributive effects of the public sector in the midst of an economic slump can have a negative effect on social indicators. This insight lies at the root of John Maynard Keynes's request not to focus on growth reduction in times of economic turmoil, but rather to rekindle growth in the short run. Viewed from a quality of life perspective, it is therefore crucial to address the cyclical nature of the current economic downturn.

The attempt to resolve the severe imbalance of aggregate demand within the eurozone one-sidedly leads to a generalised inadequacy of aggregate demand, which is exacerbated by debt overhang in some countries. Unless the import deficit countries like Austria or Germany begin to address their weakness, the downward spiral of deficit cuts and reduced economic growth in the eurozone and the EU is likely to continue unabated. The repeated downward revisions of economic growth projections by the European Commission are a warning indication of the pressures on quality of life in Europe in the near future.

In this light, the governments in Europe should institute growth packages to stimulate demand in the short run. These should be formulated bearing in mind the long-term environmental effects of economic growth, and could therefore include increases in government expenditures to finance employment-intensive projects with a small ecological footprint, such as government services in health, education, research and care, as well as investments in renewable energy.

While the overwhelming recent evidence on fiscal multipliers (Romer and Romer, 2010; Blanchard and Leigh, 2013) shows that especially in economic crises the financing of such measures need not be a primary concern, eurozone countries have to contend with their self-imposed austerity. Given these constraints, countries with fiscal leeway under the existing framework should balance their import deficits by expanding government demand.

However, given the current macroeconomic policy setting in the eurozone, one promising route to stabilising growth and the quality of life in Europe are Haavelmo-neutral government reforms. Named after Norwegian Nobel Prize-winning economist Trygve Magnus Haavelmo, the theorem states that extending public expenditure while at the same time increasing taxation has an expansionary effect. The effect will be even stronger if the policy includes redistribution from groups with high saving propensities to those with high consumption propensities, as this can foster growth while maintaining a balanced budget. Since inequality, along with macroeconomic imbalances and unregulated financial markets, was one of the main causes of the financial and economic crisis, its reduction will have important stabilising effects on economic development.

Quality of life

Over the past 130 years, average work hours have fallen between one half and a third in continental Europe, and by about a quarter in Anglo-Saxon countries. For instance, weekly hours in Germany decreased from about 68 to 39 hours per week from 1870 to 1929. However, most of that fall took place at an accelerating pace until 1929, when European weekly hours reached between 46 in Germany and 49 hours in Switzerland (Huberman and Minns, 2007: 548). Subsequent reductions in work time have been comparatively small, leading us to an average of about 37 hours per week in 2000.

These averages undoubtedly miss out on important differences between and within countries, including national determinants such as gender, age, job type and sector, but also internationally religion and culture, and, crucially, the strength and strategy of trade unions. Nonetheless, a secular trend of an overall fall in work hours, which is marked by a decelerating reduction since the 1930s, can be clearly distinguished across all countries.

In contrast, labour productivity increased by about 2 per cent per year, reasonably in line with Keynes's predictions in his essay on the 'economic possibilities of our grandchildren'. However, the continued rise in productivity resulted in higher production and incomes, not a levelling off of production and extended leisure time. In addition, income inequality increased after a period of low inequality following World War II, not just between labour incomes but especially between labour and capital income. The gains from increased productivity thus did not accrue to the working population on average in the form of either decreases in work time at constant pay, or remuneration rising in line with labour productivity gains.

The slowdown in the reduction of working time is what lies behind the failure of the 'economic possibilities of our grandchildren' to materialise, namely, for three-hour work days to produce the means for a comfortable life for the entire population. As a consequence, despite the remarkable productivity growth, these gains did not provide the material basis for a fulfilling and leisurely paced, yet productive work life and ample opportunities for other welfare-enhancing activities for the vast majority of the population. These other elements of a good life beyond leisure feature heavily in more philosophy-based characterisations of a good society. Social ties, health, security in a broad sense, individuality, democratic participation and the natural environment are considered to play a part in a good quality of life. SSFC address these concerns by recommending indicators that capture the quality of life. Eurostat proposes to base itself on a set of indicators – that are, crucially, to be published individually, and not aggregated into a single index – on the data from the EU-SILC project. While the harmonisation of the country-wise developed and collected indicators is a formidable task, the thrust of the SILC data is well aligned with the measurement of quality of life, including the differential access by various socio-economic groups. The indicators proposed by Eurostat are by-and-large outcome-based, and can be expected to give a comprehensive and comparable picture of the quality of life

202 Miriam Rehm, Sven Hergovich and Georg Feigl

in Europe, even though additional indicators like involuntary unemployment and underemployment provide useful information.

The vision of a good society underlying both Keynes's essay and the SSFC recommendations contrasts starkly with the situation in Europe today, where mass unemployment co-exists with a rising toll of (mainly psychological) health problems from overwork. Unemployment in many countries in Europe, and in particular in the eurozone, is reaching levels that are threatening social cohesion. Unemployment rates of around 11 per cent in Europe blight lives, depress aggregate demand and polarise societies. High youth unemployment rates have a devastating effect on the job market prospects of an entire generation of recent graduates.

It is therefore crucial to distinguish between falls in average work hours due to lay-offs, short work hours and involuntary part-time work, and across-the-board reductions of work time following policy changes in the standard working week and legal work time limits.

Sustainability

One goal of Eurostat is to further develop the data-collection system concerning the environmental goods and services sector. The focus on the 'green sector' is problematic if social criteria, such as the quality of work, and economic factors, such as the net effect on the number of jobs from the change towards more eco-friendly products, are not included in the analysis. Most importantly within the environmental logic, estimating the ecological benefit of the environmental goods and service sector is difficult, because this effect depends on the basis scenario to which the ecological gain is compared. For instance, a boom in the environmental goods and service sector could be caused by more waste that requires cleaning up. Similarly, the sale of an eco-friendly car may be more eco-friendly than that of a conventional car, but it is less eco-friendly than an increase in public transport. Both the waste treatment and the eco-friendly car would result in a growing environmental goods and services sector. The environmental goods and services sector thus shares the problems of GDP of which it forms a part, in that its size is not an indication of its environmental quality. The green economy should therefore be evaluated by results. It might thus be useful to concentrate on sustainability indicators that measure the outcome of an activity, such as for example greenhouse gas emissions, and not the activity itself, such as recycling.

Some people argue that our economic system is based on depleting natural and environmental resources and that this system could reach its limits. However, it is important to bear in mind that there are certain biophysical limits beyond which the ecological system approaches the risk of a 'tipping point'. This contribution takes an anthropocentric view, so we concentrate here on environmental problems that may threaten so-called 'life support systems', and sustainability indicators that signal whether the economic system is located within or beyond the 'safe operating space of humanity'. Research initiated by the Stockholm Environment Institute identified nine such 'life support systems' that exhibit limiting boundaries. These are climate change, the rate of terrestrial and marine biodiversity loss, interference with the nitrogen and phosphorus cycles, stratospheric ozone depletion, ocean acidification, global freshwater use, the change in land use, chemical pollution and atmospheric aerosol loading (Rockström et al., 2009).

In three of the nine life support systems, the economic system is in the danger zone. These are the interference with the nitrogen cycle, the rate of biodiversity loss and climate change (Rockström et al., 2009). The latter receives the most attention in environmental issues, which is in part due to its feedback effects on other environmental problems. For instance, 15–40 per cent of all species on earth are considered at risk of extinction because of climate change (Stern, 2007). Because of this key function, and because of its impact on human life, we concentrate here on climate change.

The main indicator for evaluating the effects of policy measures that aim at tackling climate change are greenhouse gas emissions. These are measured in tons of CO_2 equivalents, and the available evidence shows clearly that greenhouse gas emissions are increasing.

While some countries in the northern hemisphere could potentially benefit from moderate climate change that brings about slightly higher temperature, the consequences of the current pace of climate change are negative, especially for low-income regions and the poorest. Climate change increases damage from extreme weather events, it leads to declining agricultural yields and rising sea levels (Stern, 2007).

Addressing climate change would have beneficial side effects. First, economic effects in the medium to long run include reduced cost from climate damages. According to some calculations, expenditures on tackling climate change would cost just 1 per cent of GDP, while unhampered climate change could lead to costs of at least 5 per cent of GDP (Stern, 2007).[2] Second, tackling climate change ameliorates social imbalances. While the high-income groups and countries disproportionately cause climate change, the negative consequences of climate change affect the poor more severely.

New, greener technologies can play a pivotal role in reducing emissions, mostly through the realisation of efficiency gains. However, the rebound effect counteracts this benefit of technological change, since efficiency gains can cause more energy or natural resources to be used. If prices are lower due to improved technology, then this can lead to higher consumption. In the aggregate, some or all of the reduction in resource use per unit produced may be thus offset. The price effect can also work through the paradoxical effect of a successful reduction in energy consumption. The lower resource demand resulting from improved technology can lead to falling energy prices, which then induce higher energy consumption.

As a consequence, most countries have not managed absolute decoupling of GDP growth from material and resource use. While the EU's decreases in greenhouse gas emissions could be seen as an example for absolute decoupling, it is important to recognise that this decrease was essentially due to the devastating deindustrialisation in Eastern Europe and, more recently, a by-product of the dramatic economic crisis. However, there are some positive examples. The United Kingdom and Germany were able to reduce greenhouse gas emissions in growing economies. This effect holds even when the de-industrialization in the former German Democratic Republic is taken into account.

It should also be noted that for emissions, their global level is the relevant factor. Shifting emissions between countries, for instance by relocating production, does not improve the overall situation with respect to climate change.

For the purpose of this chapter, the relevant question is which economic policy measures could support a socio-environmental change, which includes tackling climate change. In this context, the social consequences of policy solutions are crucial not just because quality of life encompasses social goals, but because of social justice and pragmatic policy considerations. As mentioned, the rich are disproportionately responsible for causing climate change, while the poor are affected disproportionately. From a realpolitik point of view, governments disregarding social issues are unlikely to have sufficient clout to take strong measures to address climate change.

On this basis, some economists and many environmentalists argue that no growth or even de-growth strategies can help overcome environmental problems (see Jackson, 2009). The reason is that greenhouse gases are primarily determined by population, the level of per capita GDP and the greenhouse gas intensity of GDP, that is technology. Because population growth is not easy to influence quickly and while respecting human rights, and reductions in the greenhouse gas intensity have not taken place fast enough at least historically, zero or negative growth seems to them to be the only feasible way to reduce emissions.

However, such a strategy has substantial disadvantages. De-growth endangers social security systems, it exacerbates conflicts in distribution and it increases unemployment. Falling income can even exacerbate local environmental problems.

The relationship between greenhouse gases and growth also depends on the nature of growth. On average, it seems plausible that growth in the secondary sector is more greenhouse gas intensive than growth in the tertiary sector.

Even proponents propose de-growth only as a solution for rich countries. As a consequence, many countries including China, the world's largest greenhouse gas emitter, would not be affected by this solution.

Considering the political and social hurdles, a political consensus for de-growth seems very unrealistic. Finally, from a political economy point of view the argument is logically inconsistent. Because politicians have been demonstrably unable to take measures against climate change, they are requested to take even stronger measures against growth.

The BGD in the 1970s and thereafter – lessons learned?

As the current BGD is quite similar to critiques of GDP as a measure of progress in the 1970s, this section asks how this time could be different, and what factors can be identified as supportive to the establishment of new indicators for the measurement of economic performance and social progress. These historical aspects have received limited attention in the current debate, although such an analysis could be a good starting point.

In the 1970s, the critique of GDP had two main dimensions. On the one hand, there was a discussion on the ecological limits to growth, mainly triggered by the eponymous study on behalf of the Club of Rome (Meadows et al., 1972). On the other hand, there was a discussion about social/welfare statistics as a complement to the system of national accounts, mostly driven by international organisations.

Illustrating the first aspect of these critiques, Gunnar Myrdal (1973: 208) put it bluntly by concluding that 'The concept of GNP and the whole structure of theoretical approaches built up with the GNP as a central axis, will have to be dethroned'. However, he was realistic about the difficulties of such a project, because 'the psychology and ideology of unrestrained economic growth has meanwhile retained its hold over peoples' minds' (ibid.: 219). Necessary as it might have been from an ecological point of view, a planned slowdown of economic growth or even de-growth did not seem likely (Chaloupek and Feigl, 2012).

The second strand of the BGD in the 1970s, concerning social indicators, did not fare much better in terms of changing economic debate, even though it received more attention. The basic idea was to create a broader set of relevant indicators, which should then be the main focus in evaluating the progress of societies. GDP or another indicator from the system of national accounts could be part of the set, but would not receive more relevance than for example employment, health or education. In the economic policy debate, the 'magic polygon' (Rothschild, 2005) can be seen as a first attempt to include not only economic growth, but also full employment, price stability, income distribution and a balanced foreign sector into the analysis. However, this formulation did not lead to the definition of concrete indicators. It did make clear, though, that a balanced economic policy mix cannot focus on one single indicator or even a composite index, as there are trade-offs between the policy goals.

A more specific project was first launched in the context of the United Nations even earlier, when the international foundations for the system of national accounts – and therefore GDP and GNP – were established in the 1940s and 1950s. Costanza et al. (2009: 5) mention the Bretton Woods conference as a starting point, where the political goal was to foster 'economic progress everywhere' to prevent war and destruction. At that point, GNP became the key indicator. However, before the final report was published in 1953, the UN Economic and Social Council appointed an international expert group to elaborate 'the most satisfactory methods of defining and measuring standards of living and changes therein in the various countries' (United Nations 1954: 176). They proposed a set of indicators as 'levels of living must be approached in terms of a series of components (health, nutrition, education, etc.) and their statistical indicators, rather than in terms of any unitary monetary index, such as per capita national income' (ibid.).

However, the implementation of the social indicators was sluggish due to a lack of political support, technical problems and poor coordination between the UN organisations, while the system of national accounts became the central reference point for economics. In 1970 the OECD launched a social indicator project on their own (see Beirat für Wirtschafts- und Sozialfragen, 1976) with similarly mixed results. The successor report, 'Society at a Glance', was published two decades later in 2001 and did not gather widespread public attention either.

The only example of a successfully established new indicator is the UNDP's Human Development Index (HDI), which is now part of every country profile. Amartya Sen was one of HDI's 'parents'. As he also played an important role in the current efforts to go beyond GDP, there might be reason to hope that the current debate will lead to tangible outcomes. The HDI is theoretically based on Sen's capability approach and thus includes education, life expectancy and GDP per capita as a measure of the potential for 'the conversion of income into the fulfilment of human needs' (UNDP, 1990: 13). This strategy of going beyond GDP without abandoning it entirely might have been one of the ingredients for the HDI's relative success.

However, in sum the proposals for alternative indicators did not achieve the same statistical quality, nor did they receive similar attention, as GDP. On the con- trary, GDP itself has become ever more important. Today even minor changes in projected economic growth are covered extensively by the media and discussed in politics. The reasons for the limited importance of alternative indicators may lie in developments in the economy and in society more generally. After the second oil-price shock, the golden age of full employment drew to an end, with a major shift of policy away from redistribution and growth of the real economy towards financialisation and liberalisation. Andrew Sharpe, Director of the Canadian 'Centre for the Study of Living Standards', characterises the era as one of 'tighter government finances; a more conservative ideology adopted by a number of govern- ments; and a perceived lack of usefulness of social indicators in policy making' (Sharpe, 1999: 7). He relates this to alternative indicators by noting that 'this latter factor in turn may have been due to the overly simplistic view of how knowledge influences policy that had been put forward by the social indicators movement'.

With the ensuing slowdown of economic growth and a tightening of public finances, the attention has since been no longer focused on the problem of 'too much' but 'too little' economic growth. This slowdown was not a harbinger of the ultimate limits to growth, as demonstrated by the next decade, which saw a long upswing with yearly growth rates around 2.5 per cent of GDP.

A report in the context of the UN Statistical Commission comes to a similar conclusion, but furthermore highlights the role of societal structures, group interest and decision making (Becker et al., 2000: 404): 'Society expends resources on the collection of official statistics because of the perceived need by the society for the data in public policy decision-making. Most of the central discussions, in market economies at least, have been economic ones. In many cases social discussions have taken a back seat to economic ones.' Therefore, more and better information is no guarantee for better policies. The major barrier is rather the lack of homogenous interests and the resulting conflicts over welfare decisions.

In the early debate in Austria, Herbert Ostleitner concluded that it is unlikely that social indicators will take the place of GDP in a capitalistic society. That is because the latter is related to private capital accumulation, which can be seen as the central systemic variable of capitalism (Ostleitner, 1975: 15). Following Polanyi (1977), this begs the question of how the economic system can be re-embedded into society; that is, how the logic of enforced growth can be fenced in so that societal goals achieved through democratically legitimated decisions can be moved to the foreground. This includes the question of how ecological boundaries can be respected, since societies are ultimately embedded in nature.

This section provided a brief brush over the historical debate on alternative indicators of societal progress. A more thorough evaluation of past initiatives would be helpful to inform the current BGD, but the general thrust is clear: notwithstanding the HDI, the debate in the 1970s failed to sustainably shift the focus of policy makers from GDP to well-being and the environment. Against this background and the conclusion from the first section that the current debate in Europe is threatened with a similar fate despite the economic, social and environmental crises, the next section focuses on policy suggestions, from a progressive vantage point that can possibly lead to improvement in all three of these areas.

Employment, distribution and ecological transformation as the way beyond GDP?

If there was political will to shift the focus from GDP and macroeconomic surveillance to topics that are more directly linked to well-being, such as a more balanced policy mix, it would not be that hard to find appropriate indicators measuring progress. Furthermore, there are some areas of economic policy where stronger engagement can reinforce other economic goals, with only minor conflicts with other aims. These potential areas of increasing well-being without harming other goals should be the central focus point of economic policy. We think that there are basically three areas: good and sufficient employment, a more equal distribution of income, working time and wealth, and stronger investment in the ecological transformation of the economy so that environmental degradation will be constrained.

If the European governance and policy framework were thus focused more on combating unemployment, fostering a fair distribution of income, wealth and working hours and encouraging an ecological transformation of the economy, it would feed more naturally into an agenda of progress and well-being. De-growth, on the other hand, cannot be a viable common solution for environmental, social and financial problems. As a consequence, we propose a reduction in working hours as one central measure of a socio-ecological transition. Furthermore, we argue that redistribution is a precondition to a reduction in working hours and that both have favourable environmental effects.

Theory tells us that productivity gains can be channelled into an increase in production and consumption, or into a reduction of working hours. An important caveat to an environmentally and socially effective reduction in working time is that it is usually found to raise productivity (Foley and Michl, 1999; Rezai et al., 2013). However, these gains are not sufficient to offset the decrease in work hours entirely. Another caveat concerns the affordability of work time reductions, especially for low-income groups. Here it is important to remember that these measures are the result of a political process. As a consequence, their costs have to be shared between employers and employees, so that the outcome will have to lie somewhere between the two extremes of a full pay cut and a continued payment of wages in their entirety. Under a socially responsible solution, the reduction in work time per person can decrease unemployment rates, it has the potential of improving the gendered imbalance in market work and unpaid care work, and it can improve health through a better work–life balance and therefore increase well-being. Decreasing working hours also means less greenhouse gases. Moreover, more time for leisure is also an incentive for an environment-friendly lifestyle, because people are able to switch from energy intensive but time-saving consumption styles to more time intensive consumption styles, such as walking instead of driving a car. Both effects are established in the empirical literature (Hayden and Shandra, 2009; Knight et al., 2012; Rosnick and Weisbrot, 2006). A crucial obstacle to an effective reduction in working time and an ecological transition of consumption and lifestyle patterns is the 'rat race', in which the members of high-income societies are caught despite the latter being able to afford a high standard of living for everybody. Known among economists as the 'relative income hypothesis' (Bowles and Park, 2005; Stiglitz, 2008), it describes the situation in societies with entrenched inequality, where top earners try to increase income gaps by working more and harder, while the poor and the middle class try to reduce the gap to the top by also working more and harder. This behaviour is a zero sum game. If everybody works more, nobody gains in relative status, and everyone including the environment is worse off. Inequality is therefore not only a social and financial problem, but because it prevents a reduction in working hours, it is also an environmental problem (see Sturn and van Treeck, 2010). Redistribution, as part of a changed economic policy framework that improves the quality of life, is thus the central element in the strategy proposed here.

Redistribution helps the environment beyond its effect on working hours. Eco-friendly behaviour can be explained as a form of altruism, because it is unclear how much of its positive effects will accrue to the individual undertaking it. At the same time, more egalitarian societies engender altruism, because they are experienced as fairer, which increases the likelihood of non-self-serving behaviour. This is the reason why people in more egalitarian societies recycle more waste, the acceptance of environmental friendly measures is higher and greenhouse gas emissions tend to be lower (Wilkinson and Pickett, 2010).

Redistribution also has positive effects on a number of social indicators. Inequality leads to negative effects on health outcomes, in particular with respect to psychological illnesses. More unequal societies tend to have lower educational outcomes, they have worse gender discrimination and they also exhibit higher crime and incarceration rates (Wilkinson and Pickett, 2009). In the context of the ongoing crisis in Europe, redistribution, especially of working time, would be a crucial step in coping with the effects of the ongoing crisis and changing the economic policy framework to one that is more conducive towards a better quality of life. High and increasing inequality was one of the key contributors to the build-up of imbalances in the eurozone (Fitoussi and Stiglitz, 2009; Horn et al., 2009). Redistribution fosters stable economic growth due to adequate aggregate demand, and the shrinking of volatile speculative capital which results from the high saving rates of high-income groups.

Finally, this socio-environmental transition needs to be supported by investments in environmentally friendly technologies. Investments in, for instance, renewable energy, public transport and thermal insulation would not only help reduce greenhouse gas emissions but also improve current accounts. Whereas the net employment effects of a transition to renewable energy are small, yet positive, investment in public transport systems and thermal insulation can help reduce unemployment substantially.

Conclusions

This contribution has aimed at giving an overview of the current Beyond GDP debate. Although its start in Europe was promising, it was brought up short by the ideological shift in the wake of the financial crisis towards a narrow macro-economic trinity consisting of austerity, structural reforms and competitiveness. This effectively closed off the opportunity to shift the economic policy focus in the EU to well-being and social progress within environmental boundaries.

This development shows remarkable parallels to a similar debate in the 1970s. At that time, neoliberal forces gained momentum in an economic crisis that pushed the development of alternative indicators out of the focus of economic policy makers. Yet, there is hope that the debate will be kept on the agenda this time by the fact that the debate today is much more evidence-based, and by the growing literature on the shortcomings of GDP as a measure of well-being and societal progress. The advances in European statistics in developing alternative indicators of economic, social and environmental well-being nourish this view. However, it is far from clear whether more statistical indicators by themselves will necessarily lead to tangible policy outcomes of continued progress along social and environmental lines. This contribution thus proposed central measures to improve the quality of life, including a reduction in work time, redistribution and investments in socio-ecological transformation.

The success of the project depends on continuing political pressure from environmental groups, as well as from the European labour movement and others, to change the economic policy mix. Their critique needs to be combined with a new social-ecological project with common goals, which in turn will have to be measured. Conferences like that organised by IG Metall in 2012 on 'Change for a good life' (IG Metall, 2012), with the aim of combining good working conditions, ecological transformation and democracy, prove that important players are conscious of the need to establish such alliances.

Notes

1 The original version of this chapter was published as: Georg Feigl, Sven Hergovich and Miriam Rehm (2013), 'Beyond GDP: can we re-focus the debate?' In D. Natali and B. Vanhercke, *Social Developments in the European Union 2012*, Brussels: European Trade Union Institute and European Social Observatory, pp. 63–89. Permission for republication from ETUI is gratefully acknowledged. Any opinions expressed are the authors'.

2 It should be noted that these results hinge on the discount rate, and that the one used in the Stern Review is extremely low (0.1 per cent). A higher discount rate affects the size of the results, but leaves them qualitatively unchanged.

References

Becker, B., Habermann, H. and Melnick, D. (2000), 'Measuring social phenomena 1954 to 1997 – Progress?', in *Handbook of National Accounting – Studies in Methods*, Series F 75, United Nations, New York, pp. 401–407.

Beirat für Wirtschafts- und Sozialfragen (1976), *Qualitative Aspekte der wirtschaftlichen und gesellschaftlichen Entwicklung (Wohlfahrtsindikatoren)*, Beirat, Wien.

Blanchard, O. and Leigh, D. (2013), 'Growth Forecast Errors and Fiscal Mulitipliers', International Monetary Fund Working Paper, 13/1, 1–43.

Bowles, S. and Park, Y. (2005), 'Emulation, Inequality, and work hours: was Thorsten Veblen right?', *The Economic Journal*, 115: 397–412.

Chaloupek, G. and Feigl, G. (2012), 'Die Wachstumskontroverse vor vierzig Jahren und heute', *Wirtschaft und Gesellschaft*, 38(4): 771–800.

Conseil d'Analyse Économique and Sachverständigenrat (2010), *Monitoring economic performance, quality of life and sustainability* (www.sachverstaendigenrat-wirtschaft. de/fileadmin/dateiablage/Expertisen/2010/ex10_en.pdf).

Costanza, R., Hart, M., Posner, St. and Talberth, J. (2009), *Beyond GDP: The Need for New Measures of Progress*, Pardee Papers No. 4, Boston.

Degryse, Ch. and Pochet, Ph. (2012), 'Worrying trends in the new European governance', in D. Natali and B. Vanhercke (eds), *Social Developments in the European Union 2011*, ETUI and OSE, Brussels, pp. 81–108.

Dullien, S. and van Treeck, T. (2012), *Ziele und Zielkonflikte der Wirtschaftspolitik und Ansätze für Indikatoren und Politikberatung* (www.boeckler.de/pdf/p_imk_pb_5_2012. pdf).

Eurofound (2012), *Third European Quality of Life Survey – Quality of life in Europe: Impacts of the Crisis*, Publications Office of the European Union, Luxembourg.

European Commission (2009), *GDP and Beyond – Measuring Progress in a Changing World*, COM (2009) 433 final, Brussels.

European Commission (2012), Employment and Social Developments in Europe 2012. DG Employment, Social Affairs and Inclusion, Brussels.

European Commission (2012), *MIP Platform* (http://ec.europa.eu/economy_finance/ indicators/economic_reforms/eip/).

European Statistical System (2011), *Report of the Sponsorship Group on Measuring Progress, Well-Being and Sustainable Development* (http://epp.eurostat.ec.europa.eu/ portal/page/portal/pgp_ess/0_DOCS/estat/SpG_Final_report_Progress_wellbeing_and_ sustainable_deve.pdf).

Fitoussi, J.-P. and Stiglitz, J. (2009), The Ways Out of the Crisis and the Building of a More Cohesive World, OFCE Document de travail 17.

Foley, D. and Michl, T. (1999), *Growth and Distribution*, Harvard University Press, Cambridge, MA.

Hayden, A. and Shandra, J. (2009), 'Hours of work and the ecological footprint of nations: an exploratory analysis', *Local Environment: The International Journal of Justice and Sustainability*, 14(6): 575–600.

Galgóczi, B. and Pochet, Ph. (2012), 'How trade unions cope with the challenge of the green transformation in Europe?', in J. De Munck, C. Didry, I. Ferreras and A. Jobert (eds), *Renewing Democratic Deliberation in Europe*, P.I.E. Peter Lang, Brussels, pp. 239–254.

Heller, W. (1973), 'Coming to terms with growth and environment', in S.H. Schurr (ed.), *Energy, Economic Growth and the Environment*, Taylor & Francis, Baltimore.

Horn, G., Dröge, K., Sturn, S., van Treeck, T. and Zwiener, R. (2009), Von der Finanzkrise zur Weltwirtschaftskrise (III): Die Rolle der Ungleichheit, IMK Report 41, pp. 1–24.

Huberman, M. and Minns, C. (2007), 'The times they are not changin': days and hours of work in Old and New Worlds, 1870–2000', *Explorations in Economic History*, 44: 538–567.

IG Metall (2012), Kurswechsel für ein gutes Leben. Conference, Berlin, 5–7 December. www.igmetall-kurswechselkongress.de.

Jackson, T. (2009), *Prosperity without Growth – Economics for a Finite Planet*, Earthscan, London.

Jahoda, M., Lazarsfeld, P. F. and Zeisel, H. (1975 [1933]), Die Arbeitslosen von Marienthal. Ein soziographischer Versuch über die Wirkungen langandauernder Arbeitslosigkeit. Suhrkamp, Frankfurt a.M.

Keynes, John Maynard (1963), *Economic Possibilities for our Grandchildren* (www.econ.yale.edu/smith/econ116a/keynes1.pdf).

Knight, K., Rosa, E. and Schor, J. (2012), 'Sustainability: the role of work hours', *Working Paper*, No. 304, Political Economy Research Institute, University of Massachusetts, Amherst.

Layard, R. (2005), *Happiness: Lessons from a New Science*, Penguin, London.

Meadows, D. H., Meadows, D. L., Randers, J. and Behrens, W. W. (1972), *The Limits to Growth*, Universe Books, New York.

Morgenstern, O. (1972), 'Descriptive, predictive and normative theory', *Kyklos*, 25(4): 699–714.

Myrdal, G. (1973), *Against the Stream, Critical Essays on Economics*, Pantheon Books, New York.

Nussbaum, Martha (2000), *Women and Human Development: The Capabilities Approach.* Cambridge University Press, Cambridge.

OECD (2008), *Employment Outlook.* Paris, Organisation for Economic Co-operation and Development.

Ostleitner, H. (1975), *Wachstum und gesellschaftliche Stabilität*, in: Wirtschaft und Gesellschaft, No. 1, AK Wien, Wien, pp. 15–32.

Polanyi, K. (1977), *The Great Transformation.* Europaverlag, Zürich.

Rezai, A., Taylor, L. and Mechler, R. (2013), 'Ecological macroeconomics: an application to climate change', *Ecological Economics*, 85: 69–76.

Rockström, J., Steffen, W., Noone, K., Persson, A., Chapin, F., Lambin, E., Lenton, T., Scheffer, M., Folke, C., Schellnhuber, H., Nykvist, B., de Wit, C., Hughes, T., van der Leeuw, S., Rodhe, H., Sörlin, S., Snyder, P., Costanza, R., Svedin, U., Falkenmark, M., Karlberg, L., Corell, R., Fabry, V., Hansen, J., Walker, B., Liverman, D., Richardson, K., Crutzen, P. and Foley, J. (2009), 'A safe operating space for humanity', *Nature*, 461: 472–475.

Romer, C. and Romer, D. (2010), 'The macroeconomic effects of tax changes: estimates based on a new measure of fiscal shocks', *American Economic Review*, 100: 763–801.

Rosnick, D. and Weisbrot, M. (2006), *Are Shorter Work Hours Good for the Environment? A Comparison of U.S. and European Energy Consumption*. Center for Economic and Policy Research, Washington.

Rothschild, K. (2005), 'Some primitive robust tests of some primitive generalizations', *Post-Autistic Economics Review,* No. 35, pp. 2–10 (www.paecon.net/PAEReview/issue 35/Rothschild35.htm).

Sen, A. (2009), *The Idea of Justice*. Allen Lane, London.

Sharpe, A. (1999), *A Survey of Indicators of Economic and Social Well-being*. Centre for the Study of Living Standards, Ottawa.

Skidelsky, R. and Skidelsky, E. (2012), *How Much Is Enough? Money and the Good Life*. Other Press, New York.

Stern, N. (eds.) (2007), *The Economics of Climate Change: The Stern Review*. Cambridge University Press, New York.

Stiglitz, J. (2008), 'Towards a general theory of consumerism: reflections on Keynes' economic possibilities for our grandchildren', in P. Lorenzo and P. Gustavo (eds), *Revisiting Keynes: Economic Possibilities for our Grandchildren*, MIT Press, Cambridge, MA, pp. 41–85.

Stiglitz, J., Sen, A. and Fitoussi, J.-P. (2009), *Report by the Commission on the Measurement of Economic Performance and Social Progress* (www.stiglitz-sen-fitoussi.fr).

Sturn, S. and van Treeck, T. (2010), Wachstumszwang durch Ungleichheit und Ungleichheit als Wachstumsbremse, in: SPW, 2, S.15–20.

Tayler, T. (2012), *Robert Kennedy on Shortcomings of GDP in 1968* (http://conversable economist.blogspot.co.at/2012/01/robert-kennedy-on-shortcomings-of-gdp.html).

UNDP (1990), *Human Development Report*. UN, New York.

United Nations (1954), *Yearbook of the United Nations*. UN, New York.

Wilkinson, R. and Pickett, K. (2009), *The Spirit Level*. Allen Lane, London.

Wilkinson, R. and Pickett, K. (2010), 'The impact of income inequalities on sustainable development in London'. A report for the London Sustainable Development Commission on behalf of the Equality Trust.

11 The challenge of hydropower as a sustainable development alternative

Benefits and controversial effects in the case of the Brazilian Amazon

Nicola Caravaggio, Valeria Costantini,
Martina Iorio, Salvatore Monni and
Elena Paglialunga

Introduction

Global environmental challenges require collective actions to mitigate the negative effects associated to climate change due to exploitation of natural resources, abatement of polluting emissions but also water scarcity, deforestation and risks of biodiversity losses. In this context, climate change potential damages and sustainability targets are key issues to be addressed also by the emerging economies. Indeed, as the ongoing international negotiations suggest, these economies have the greatest pollutant potential and simultaneously the highest likelihood to shift from a dirty to a clean development paradigm.

In this context, renewable energies are increasingly considered on the global scale as first best solutions to combine development achievements while preserving the ecosystem services. The electricity sector, in particular, is characterized by the pressing need for expansion so that in the Brazilian context the Amazonian water resource represents a competitive alternative to fossil fuels despite the structural problems it entails. The North of the country, whose hydro potential is well below the actual installed capacity, is going to be transformed into a key energy frontier as proposed by the *Ministero de Minas e Energia* (MME)[1] (ANEEL, 2008; EPE, 2015a, 2015b).

Accordingly, the Brazilian Amazon is a peculiar case to reflect on both potential benefits and controversial issues arising when a large deployment of hydropower as a renewable energy source is planned. Thus, the aim of this chapter is to contribute in the analysis and inform policy makers on all the potential benefits and costs related to hydropower exploitation. In this regard, a cost–benefit analysis (henceforth CBA) approach is proposed as analytical framework, as it represents a suitable methodology that allows a "from the cradle to the grave" analysis. In the next section, an overview of the Brazilian's energy system is presented, with a particular focus on hydroelectric. The third section introduces the trade-off between development and sustainability in the specific case of water exploitation – for hydroelectric purpose – in the Brazilian Amazon Region, further focusing on the State of Pará and the two hydroelectric power plants of Tucuruí and Belo Monte. In the fourth section the CBA of the two projects (Tucuruí and Belo Monte) are presented, while the fifth section concludes.

The Brazilian sustainable energy strategy

Energy security is an important indicator of the growth of a country and access to electricity plays a major role in terms of economic development. Accordingly, the possibility of benefiting from modern and efficient forms of energy is important for improving the living conditions of populations (Goldemberg and Johansson, 2002). Brazilian energy demand has grown remarkably during the last decade, from 344,284 GWh in 2005 to 473,393 GWh in 2014 (an increase of 50 per cent) coupled with an increase of 23 per cent in total gross domestic product (GDP) and 32 per cent in GDP per capita (from R$7.346,733 to R$9.084,146). The demand of electricity also has grown continuously during the last decades (2004–2014) at an average rate of 4 per cent. As Figure 11.1 shows, with electricity consumption and GDP per capita both increasing, access to energy and electricity has a crucial role in economic development, in particular for emerging economies (EPE, 2015a).

In 2014 the Brazilian energy's system was characterized by a supply mix where the main role was covered by oil and its derivatives (38.2 per cent), followed by sugar cane (16.8 per cent), hydropower (13.5 per cent) and natural gas (11.3 per cent) (EPE, 2015a). Although Brazil is not completely energy independent, it has one of the cleanest energy matrixes worldwide with about 40 per cent produced from renewable energy sources (39.4 in 2014), as the comparison with the rest of

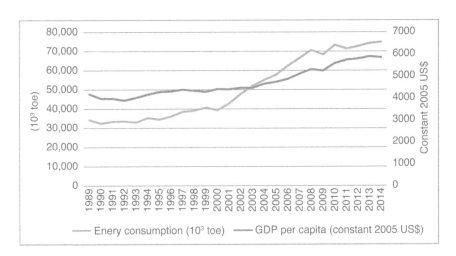

Figure 11.1 Electricity consumption and GDP per capita, 1989–2014

Source: EPE (2015a)

the world (13.5 per cent in 2013) or OECD countries (9.17 per cent in 2014) stresses (OECD, 2016). However, the Brazilian energy matrix was even cleaner before: from 1990 (cf. after the end of dictatorship and the launch of the *Plano Real*) the share of not renewable energy increased to 61 per cent in 2001. In the following years, the trend diverted and the share of renewable energies increased until 2009, when the divergence restarted (EPE, 2015a).

Focusing on the electricity sector, in the 1990s hydropower accounted for around 90 per cent of the installed capacity. This value dropped to 74 per cent in 2008, compensated by the increase of other sources, such as natural gas, biomass and wind (EPE, 2015a). In December 2014, the Brazilian electricity supply – 132,878 MW – was composed as shown in Figure 11.2 where the share of hydroelectricity amounted to 62 per cent (EPE, 2015b). Moreover, the inconsistency of energy supplies due to the hydrological conditions (as the droughts occurred in 2001–2002), led to the necessity of partially resorting to thermoelectric and nuclear power (Kelman, 2001; Bagher, 2015).

In order to decrease the electric sector dependence from the water source, investments in bio fuels, biomasses and natural gas have increased, especially in 2011–13. Hence, according to the *Plano Decenal de Expansão de Energia 2024*,[2] by 2024, a reduction in petroleum consumption (from 43.1 per cent of 2014 to 40.3 per cent in the relative share) and an increase in the use of biodiesel (7 per cent in the share), ethanol (4.8 per cent), natural gas (3.5 per cent) and electricity (4.1 per cent) are expected. However, the share of hydroelectric will decrease,

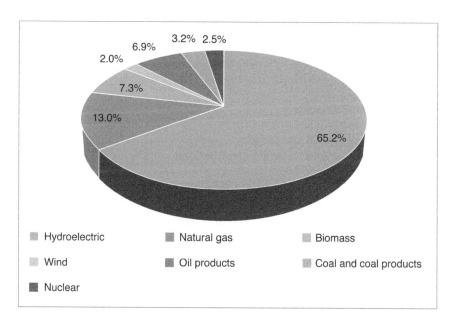

Figure 11.2 Brazilian electricity supply (installed capacity, December 2014)

Source: EPE (2015b)

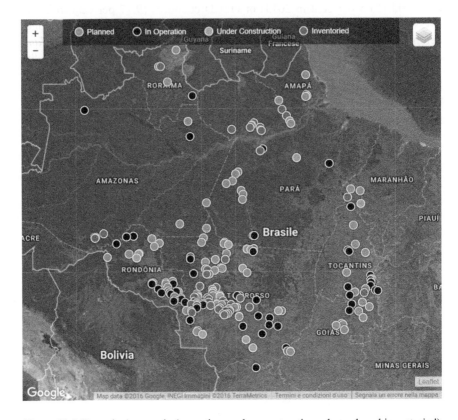

Figure 11.3 Dams in Amazonia (operative, under construction, planned, and inventoried)

Source: Fundación Proteger et al. (2016)

giving more space to other sources (EPE, 2014). Water will continue to play a major role, even though the domestic supply of energy from water sources (hydroelectric) is expected to drop to 56.7 per cent in 2024 (EPE, 2015b; Corrêa da Silva et al., 2016).

In the Amazon Region,[3] the total number of existing and planned dams is 137,100 in operation and 137 planned in the whole Amazon Basin, whereas for the Brazilian *Amazônia Legal*[4] (Figure 11.3) only there are 74 dams in operation and 94 planned (Tundisi et al., 2014).

Therefore, in the *Programa de Aceleração do Crescimento 2*,[5] 48 projects of hydroelectric station are planned (Figure 11.4), 12 of which are completed and operating (with a total capacity of 4.988 MW), eight projects are under construction (19.129 MW), four are in the contract and 24 in the preparatory phase[6] (PAC2, 2014). Focusing on the Pará State, there are two major hydroelectric complexes: Tucuruí and Belo Monte.[7] Alongside these, there are the smaller plant of Curuá-Uma and eight more stations designed.

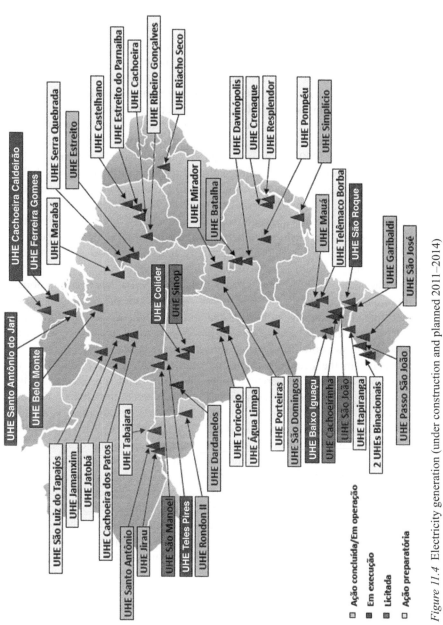

Figure 11.4 Electricity generation (under construction and planned 2011–2014)

Source: PAC2 (2016)

A further issue to consider is the geographical division of Brazil in five areas (South, Southeast, Central-West, Northeast and North) with entirely different characteristics resulting in asymmetrical energy designs and access among cities, industries and population. Indeed, the size of the areas not fully served by electricity is directly connected to their geographical location and the related physical and economic difficulties to extend the power grid. Even if more than 95 per cent of the population has access to electricity, in the richer and more developed southern states the access can be over 99 per cent, while in the poorer regions – especially in the North Region – the supply of electric energy is even below 50 per cent (PNUD et al., 2013). Figure 11.5 shows the relation between GDP per capita and electricity access among Brazilian Municipalities in 2010. Moreover, in 2003 a plan to expand the national electric grid called *Luz Para Todos*[8] was launched with the aim of reaching millions of households without electricity access: in 2015 more than 15.5 million inhabitants benefited from this project, which has been extended to 2018 (Portal Brasil, 2015). Nevertheless, more efforts are required. In fact, not surprisingly, comparing the evolution and regional divergence between the Human Development Index in Brazil (Figure 11.6) to the pattern of electricity access, these two aspects appear strictly related.

Notwithstanding, the *Sistema Elétrico Brasileiro* (SEB)[9] has been the object of important changes since the mid-1990s with the aim of introducing more competition: a regulatory authority *Agência Nacional de Energia Elétrica* (ANEEL)[10] and the *Operador Nacional do Sistema Elétrico* (ONS)[11] has been introduced. Furthermore, the *Sistema Interligado Nacional* (SIN)[12] is the main infrastructure in the Brazilian electricity market, with about 101,000 km of networks managed by 64 operators under the control and coordination of the ONS. Smaller and isolated systems, mainly concentrated in the Amazon Region, are also linked to the SIN in the North and its future development is strictly related to the hydroelectric expansion (GSE, 2014; ONS, 2016). Also in this case, considerable disparities occur between the North and the South of Brazil. The *Subsistema Norte*[13] is expected to record the greatest growth in electricity demand from 2014 to 2024 (5.7 per cent), while the other subsystems show lower average annual growth: Northeast 4.4 per cent, Southeast/CO 3,6 per cent, South 3.5 per cent (EPE, 2015b).[14] In this respect, the main governmental strategy is to promote the development of large hydroelectric power plants (LHPs) in the Northern Region due the great availability of water while leaving projects of small hydro-electric power plants (SHPs) spreading out in the South, Southeast and Midwest (Ferreira et al., 2016). This expansion will be obviously followed by a simultaneous expansion of the SIN which is expected to increase its share from 14 per cent in the beginning of 2015 to 23 per cent in 2024, an expansion of approximately 27 GW of capacity (EPE, 2015b). Even if the share of hydropower in the electricity production is expected to decline compared with other renewable sources, the *Amazônia Legal* will face the greatest hydroelectric sector expansion of the whole state in order to satisfy the increased demand of electricity.

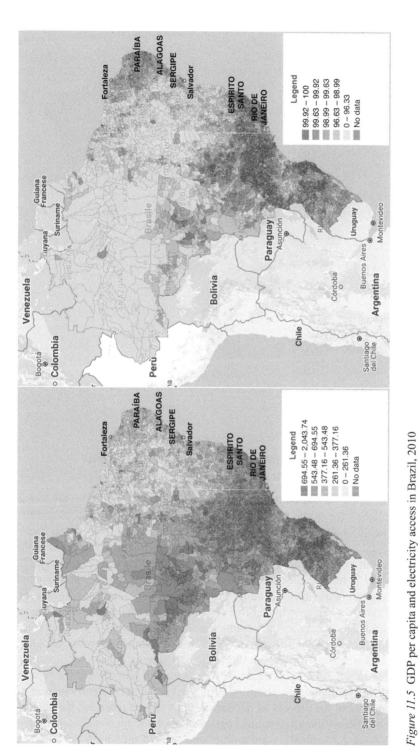

Figure 11.5 GDP per capita and electricity access in Brazil, 2010

Source: PNUD et al. (2013)

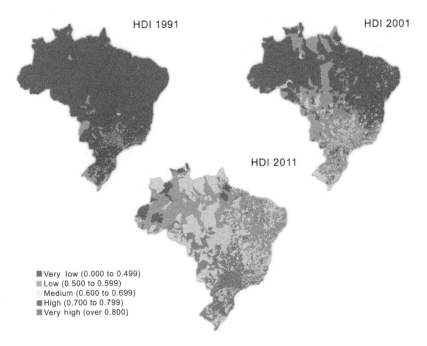

HDI 1991

HDI 2001

HDI 2011

■ Very low (0.000 to 0.499)
■ Low (0.500 to 0.599)
  Medium (0.600 to 0.699)
■ High (0.700 to 0.799)
■ Very high (over 0.800)

Figure 11.6 Human Development Index evolution in Brazil, 1991–2010

Source: PNUD et al. (2013)

Conflicts between environmental sustainability and social development in hydroelectric generation

In recent decades, debate on the environmental impact caused by hydroelectric generation has come to the fore. Meanwhile, Brazil's environmental policy has become institutionalized and greater importance has been ascribed to the socio-environmental aspects in the planning of energy projects even with regards to the construction of hydroelectric power plants (Manyari and De Carvalho Jr., 2007). In fact, water is both a not-excludable and a not-rivalry (global) public good and its exploitation obviously entails externalities and sub-optimal equilibrium. While the exploiter can gain by the free use of water (more quantity of energy at a cheaper price), local communities could bear the not-paid costs (e.g. higher price of energy or environmental damages) for a lower water availability (Bakker, 2007). In this scenario, the state should operate to eliminate this kind of market failure by improving the cooperation between actors or enforcing a framework of property rights. Either the definition of property right or the participation of local community in the process of decision making should represent the leading role of the state in avoiding sub optimal equilibriums due to market failures in case of public goods. Accordingly, communities may spur institutions to a better and broader communication, aimed at avoiding bad phenomena like the so-called "tragedy of the commons", when a single actor exploits natural resources leaving the externality costs as an undesired burden to others (Kaul et al., 1999).

Furthermore, looking at the expanding hydroelectricity sector, it is not realistic to expect that the Amazon will remain uncontaminated forever. A population of approximately 20 million people lives there and most of Brazil's remaining hydroelectric potential is located in that region (Da Silva Soito and Vasconcelos Freitas, 2011). The trade-off between environmental protection and economic development is particularly severe for emerging countries, and the Brazilian case is a clear representation of it. Besides being prized for its fabulous biodiversity, the Amazon is the world's biggest river basin with a huge hydroelectric potential and, as for any other public goods, the uneven distribution of benefits and costs affects the energy strategy and the development of the region (Bakker, 2007). The unavoidable forthcoming exploitation of water in the Amazon Region will lead to an enormous beneficial effect for the region but could also have great negative impacts. In fact, while hydro is a carbon free source, the negative impacts on biodiversity, deforestation, water quality and supply and social inequality, especially for indigenous populations, should be necessarily considered within an effective sustainable-oriented development plan, in line with the new Sustainable Development Goals. In particular, plans of constructing several more reservoirs in the Amazonia Legal will also introduce a large-scale change in the hydrological cycle, in ecosystem services and in the connectivity between terrestrial and aquatic ecosystems.

Despite the costs of producing electricity from hydro sources being minimal, the costs of construction are very high and the payback period is very long. The initial construction phase of a plant is expensive. Building the dam and preparing the reservoir can also be very costly, both at the initial stage and during the entire plant's operational period (Barros et al., 2011; Fearnside and Pueyo, 2012). A further concern is related to the number and the size of new dams that can be installed in the Amazon Region. This is a strategic decision not only for Brazil but also for all the countries sharing this basin and should be planned with a long-term approach to energy strategy. In this context emerged the idea that a reduction in the scale of the hydro technology should be able to reduce or even eliminate the impact generated by large-scale plants, preserving the advantages of a potentially endless and clean resource like water (Ferreira et al., 2016). These are all key issues to the maintenance of evolutionary and biodiversity processes that can have profound consequences for the South American continent, and, given the Amazon contribution in term of environmental services, for the entire planet.

Table 11.1 summarizes the main steps that are required from Brazilian legislation in order to start the realization of a hydroelectric project.

The case of Pará

The construction of the Tucuruí plant in the Araguaia-Tocantins started in 1975, while a second phase of construction occurred between 1998 and 2002.[15] In 2006,

Table 11.1 Required steps for the realization of a hydroelectric power plant

Description	Output and role
Step 1	**EIA*/RIMA****

Step 1

After the promulgation of the Federal Constitution in 1988, the decisions on the construction of dams and the flooding land are now taken jointly by society, government institutions and especially with the affected population, who are now present in the decision-making process (Da Costa, 2014).

The first step of this legislative process is the *Licença Prévia* (Preliminary License), granted by the *Instituto Brasileiro do Meio Ambiente e dos Recursos Naturais Renováveis* (IBAMA – National Institute of Environment and Renewable Natural Resources), after review and approval of EIA/RIMA and the organization of some public hearings.

The projects have to be presented by the municipalities: once the construction site has been defined, the next step is the realization of technical and socio-economic assessment. Thus, specific offices conduct the feasibility study and eventually adjust the magnitude of the project. However, the risk of collusion and conflict of interest between officers and projects' owners is elevated.

The enterprise usually covers 90 per cent of the entire financing, leaving to the municipality a minimum quote of participation fixed at the 10 per cent (usually municipalities do not overtake this threshold). This is useful for promoting a joint responsibility, but there is the risk of leaving behind some extremely poor rural municipalities, which are unable of even collecting the 10 per cent of the investment.

EIA*/RIMA**

Aimed at assessing the environmental impacts arising from the installation of an enterprise and establish programmes for monitoring and mitigating these impacts. The EIA is responsible for the material collection, analysis, literature, as well as study of the likely environmental consequences that may be caused. It aims to analyse the impacts caused by the work, proposing conditions for its implementation and what procedure should be adopted for its construction. The difference between these two documents is that only the RIMA has public access, while the EIA contains more sensitive information. Thus, the text of the RIMA should be more accessible to the public, and instructed by maps, charts, graphs and many other techniques necessary to a clear understanding of the environmental consequences of the project (EEMI, 2013).

In this regard, some authors suggest to use different tools to evaluate the socio-environmental impact of those projects, for example the Strategic Environmental Assessment (Westin et al., 2014).

Step 2

The second step is the *Licença de Instalação* (Installation License), granted by IBAMA, which can be granted by stages before the construction of the plant. Once it is established which project is going to be realized, the recipient enterprise should select an operating enterprise (Da Costa, 2014; Santos et al., 2012).

Public bidding

The commitment may go from the simple support of some singular projects to the complete implementation of other ones, due to the not-fixed grade of technical, financial and administrative involvement of the former enterprise (Da Costa, 2014; Santos et al., 2012).

Description	Output and role
Step 3 The third and final step is the *Licença de Operação* (Operating License), granted by IBAMA, which authorizes the reservoir fill and the start of generation (Santos et al., 2012). Despite preliminary surveys, it is almost impossible to ensure a total absence of impacts, and the law 7990/1989 regulate the financial compensations due to the exploitation of water resource used to produce energy power (Da Costa, 2014).	**Transfers and compensations** The transfers and compensations to be paid by the enterprise should amount to about 6 per cent of the value of the produced energy and every Brazilian states, concessionaires, Federal District and municipalities affected by the physical siting of the plant or surrounding flooded areas are all eligible to receive specific compensations according to the impact they are exposed to. Upstream compensations are commonly recognized as mandatory, while there is a debate about the relevance of the downstream impacts (Fearnside, 1999).

Notes: * *Estudo de Impacto Ambiental* (Environmental Impact Evaluation); ** *Relatòrio de Impacto do Meio Ambiente* (Environmental Impact Report)

it achieved a total plant power generation of 8.370 MW with a total flooded area of 3,007 km². The owner of the project was and still is the public-private company Eletronorte,[16] a subsidiary of Eletrobrás (Eletronorte, 2016). This power plant was a pioneering work for the Amazon which was completely lacking in any kind of infrastructure. The Tucuruí has shown since the early stages a variety of controversial effects in the gap between the potential and expected benefits for Brazil as a whole and its actual impacts. It is a critical example and constitutes a relevant case study when the aim is to realize new hydroelectric projects in a fairer way in the *Amazônia Legal* (Fearnside, 2001). Conversely, the Belo Monte plant, on the Xingu River, is a modern project (almost completed) and located near the city of Altamira. Although the original project dates back to 1975, it has been revisited several times since the 2011 approval. This hydro plant – composed by two mayor dams – has a total reservoir[17] of 516 km² with an installed capacity of 11.233 MW which makes it the fourth biggest hydroelectric plant worldwide[18] (Eletrobrás, 2009; Norte Energia, 2016). The final Belo Monte project, held by another public-private company called Norte Energia S.A., has been followed by a huge amount of debates and protests[19] since its inception as with the previous plant as in both of the cases, several types of risks associated to large-scale dams occurred. Accordingly, three units of analysis are going to be presented in order to recognize disadvantages and advantages.

Ecology

From an ecological perspective both deforestation and artificial flooding are noteworthy. On the one hand, prior deforestation is needed in order to build the reservoir and it also increases due to people resettlement and the construction of new infrastructures, such as roads.[20] On the other hand, artificial flooding results in scarce water quality, arousing aquatic ecosystem losses. The reservoir of Tucuruí had an unfortunate pattern with an actual flooded area greatly exceeding the estimates by the viability study. The reservoir water quality is now one of the major problems and no fish ladders were built (Fearnside, 2000; La Rovere and Mendes, 2000). Referring to the Belo Monte case, the drastic reduction of the natural environment in the Volta Grande, with its great fish wealth, puts the existence of a huge number of species in jeopardy, leading to species disappearance and extinction (Mederios, 2009; Molina, 2009; Cunha and Ferreira, 2011). Differently from the Tucuruí experience, with Belo Monte several environmental compensation actions[21] have been planned. For example, the project realized some fish ladders with the aim of helping fish to return upstream despite the presence of dams (Norte Energia, 2016). However, recent facts about some falsified data[22] substantially validate the doubts and threats posed by Pinto (2012) and Fearnside (2001, 2006) regarding the realization of this major project.

Greenhouse gas emissions

Although authorities worldwide promote hydropower as a "clean" source of energy in contrast to fossil fuels, there is an increasing awareness that hydroelectric reservoirs are not carbon neutral and there has been an ongoing scientific debate on their role in the global carbon emissions cycle (e.g. Teodoru et al., 2010; Barros et al., 2011; Raadal et al., 2011; Steinhurst et al., 2012). In fact, hydroelectric plants emit GHGs through different processes: from above-water decay, reservoir surface, turbines, spillway and, indirectly, from the loss of sources and carbon sinks in living forest (Fearnside, 2000, 2016). Tucuruí produces a sixth of the greenhouse gas emissions from all over Brazil, with a global warming impact greater than that of fossil fuels burned by the city of São Paulo in 1990 (Fearnside, 2001). At the same time, although Belo Monte was presented as an emission-free project (Eltrobrás, 2009; Norte Energia, 2016), high risks of GHG emissions have been highlighted (De Sousa Júnior and Reid, 2010; Fearnside, 2016). In fact, hydroelectric power generation produces large pulses of CO_2 and CH_4[23] emissions in the first years after filling the reservoir, followed by lower emissions sustained indefinitely (Commerford, 2011; Steinhurst et al., 2012). In some extreme cases, particularly in tropical areas, GHG emissions per megawatt of electricity produced from water could be as high as those from fossil-fuel power plants (Barros et al., 2011). Moreover, considering the ageing process in the hydroelectric generation, emissions tend to decline exponentially in the initial stages and at slower rates in the following years, more rapidly in a cold-water environment than in warm ones (Teodoru et al., 2010; Steinhurst et al., 2012). This provides a reminder of the potential amount of emissions from the dozen reservoirs planned for construction in the Amazon over the coming decades. Not surprisingly, evaluating such an impact in terms of carbon emission is not very simple and there is no consensus about the real impact and their contribution to the global carbon cycle.

Social impacts

It is undeniable that Brazil is moving towards a growing energy autonomy and an increasing access to electricity. In this sense, since consumption of electricity per capita may be considered a proxy of well-being, it should result in a great improvement of the quality of life (Giannini Pereira et al., 2010). Besides providing the local communities with a great number of subsidies, aimed to compensate the exploitation of hydric resources, hydroelectric projects in the Amazon Region also promoted local development throughout fostering urbanization and hence road networks and other infrastructures. However, this strategy also includes social costs related to displacement of indigenous communities and resettlement of citizens, the spread of malaria and other diseases, inadequate monetary compensations, big downstream effects, high financial costs with minimal employment impact and important huge economic distortions (Fearnside, 2001).

For example, before the plant, the city of Tucuruí was isolated and completely rural: nowadays it is an urbanized centre with about 80,000 citizens. However, the dam has evicted several indigenous people and the resettlement programme for residents in the submergence area created severe social problems due to gross errors in the topographic map of the area to be flooded (i.e. areas unexpectedly flooded and areas unexpectedly left above the water line). Several segments of the affected population were excluded from Eletronorte's estimates of the population to be displaced and, consequently, from the resettlement programmes. Eventually, Eletronorte limited its assistance to cash payments and the amounts of money evaporated quickly in the absence of proper skills (tribes' lack of experience with money) without granting an enduring well-being for tribes (Fearnside, 1999). Moreover, despite fishing being one of the main sustenance activities, after the closing of the dam the total amount of fish captured in the lower Tocantins collapsed by 60 per cent (Survival International, 2010). Hence, the great loss occurred to fishermen cannot be underestimated, since it must be considered as a barrier to development (La Rovere and Mendes, 2000). With regard to employment impact, few achievements can be outlined, even though almost two-thirds of the power generated by the Tucuruí Dam is supplied at heavily subsidized rates to the aluminium industry in Barcarena and São Luís. The number of jobs generated by the aluminium processing is minimal, considering the urban agglomeration in Barcarena and São Luís (Scherer et al., 2003). Thus, the Tucuruí project could have done more to improve the quality of life of those living in the area, a fact dramatized by huge tension lines passing over hut after hut, lit only by the flickering of kerosene lamps (Fearnside, 1999).

In the light of the Tucuruí experience, positive externalities on local development and urbanization are almost certain for Belo Monte. However, there are some unpredictable health and socio-environmental threats due to some wrong information contained into the Belo Monte EIA/RIMA document (Magalhães et al., 2009). Implications on downstream and upstream effects remain uncertain too, and losses in economic activities may occur after filling the reservoir because it is partly covered by pasture lands (Eletrobrás, 2009; Magalhães et al., 2009;

Molina, 2009). Thus, different actions aimed to safeguard both citizens and indigenous people (e.g. about displacement and losses in economic activities) have been carried out. The project is also promoting employment, even if this job creation could remain momentary, being related only to the initial phase of construction. Furthermore, as in the case of Tucuruí, although the inhabitants of the Pará State will benefit from the enhancement of the SIN (EPE, 2015b), only 3.22 per cent of the whole Belo Monte power production will remain in the State of Pará. Indeed, the major amount of energy produced will flow to the North East (Bahia, 13.85 per cent) and the South-East (Minas Gerais, 14.56 per cent and São Paulo, 29.22 per cent) (Norte Energia, 2014, 2015).

Eventually, the huge debate around the Belo Monte project refers also to a lack of individual participation of affected people during the decision-making process. In the case of Tucuruí, participation was not required because of the dictatorship, but with the Brazilian Constitution of 1989 stakeholder participation for the realization of major project became mandatory. Although the owner society of Belo Monte affirmed that public hearings have been performed with the participation of around 5,000 people, the present public debate underlines lack in that sense (Fearnside, 2009; Norte Energia, 2016).

Cost–benefit analysis

The CBA approach is proposed to assess the welfare change due to an investment decision as, in this case, the realization of a big hydro plant. The rationale of a CBA lies in the observation that investment decisions taken only on the basis of profit motivations and price mechanism could lead to socially undesirable outcome. On the contrary, if inputs and outputs (including intangible ones) and external effects of an investment project are evaluated at their social opportunity costs, the return calculated is a proper measure of the project's contribution to social welfare. The CBA is based on the valuation of all costs and all opportunity costs, defined as the potential gains from the best alternative, when a choice needs to be made between mutually exclusive alternatives (e.g. hydroelectric and thermoelectric plants). Moreover, in order to run a CBA, the monetization of all tangible and intangible effects is needed; therefore, a proper choice in term of reference period and a discount rate needs to be made. The main output of the analysis is represented by the economic net present value, as a measure of the profitability of the project.

The analysis we are proposing is a simplified CBA version compared with the European Commission guideline for the realization of investment projects' CBA, according to needs and data availability (Sartori et al., 2014). Different data are used, in accordance with the reviewed literature, including information driven by other authors in prior works and new data, traced also for chasing more qualitative intuitions. Several CBA studies carried out in the specific hydroelectric sector have been consulted and presented below. With regard to the specific case of Belo Monte, the main adopted reference is the CBA carried out by De Sousa Júnior and Reid (2010). Referring to Tucuruí, the main reference is the evaluation conducted by La Rovere and Mendes (2000) for the World Commission on Dams. Furthermore, the analysis carried out by Commerford (2011), focusing on the Chinese hydroelectric plant of the Three Gorges Dam, analysing it both in ecological and social keys, has been considered. In addition, Chutubtim (2001) has proposed an interesting guide for the realization of an extended CBA of dam projects in Thailand (Kwae Nai Dam). Finally, we also consulted the Environmental Impact Study of the Colombian hydroelectric power plant of Guaicaramo realized by INGETEC (2014) and the methodology guide for environmental assessment of hydroelectric power plants realized by EPE (2012).

The realization of a CBA obviously does not represent the panacea for any policy-making decision with reference to infrastructures. Although it represents a practical tool able to account not only for financial aspects, several limitations still remain, hard to overcome: from the correct choice of the discount rate (Stern, 2006) to various problematics related to the estimation of shadow prices for environmental goods, thus pollution evaluation (Pearce, 1976). Heinzerling and Ackerman carried out a critical review of the CBA methodology stressing how "the process of reducing life, health, and the natural world to monetary values is inherently flawed" (2002, p. 3). They also state how the CBA is unable to account for families' risks and how it does not take into account the fact that market decisions are different from political decision. Therefore, a policy maker must always keep in mind the limitations of this evaluation with the possibility of resorting to other evaluation techniques (e.g. Posner and Adler, 1999; Pearce et al., 2006).

A preliminary version of this CBA has been already proposed in Iorio and Caravaggio (2016), of which the model here proposed represents a revisited and enhanced version. Therefore, the main elements of our CBA are presented below.

Reference period: according to Sartori et al. (2014), the analysis's reference period for major energy projects varies from 15 to 25 years. In the case of Tucuruí, we considered 1984 as year zero, when the hydroelectric plant became fully operative. Furthermore, in order to consider also the second phase of Tucuruí, started in 1998, we extended the reference period to 2014 for a total of 35 years. In the Belo Monte case we started our reference period in 2011, the beginning of construction work, until 2036 for a total of 25 years.

Social discount rate (SDR): according to Stern (2006), this value has to be, in general, positive. In the case of Brazil, Lopez (2008) suggests a SDR between 5.1 per cent and 9.5 per cent and Sartori et al. (2014) suggest that a 5 per cent discount rate is the appropriate one for major projects within the cohesion countries. However, the SDR suggested by Chutubtim (2001) is 10 per cent while INGETEC (2014) and De Sousa Júnior and Reid (2010) chose 12 per cent. For this analysis, we chose an SDR of 5 per cent. In addition, we performed a sensitivity analysis by varying the discount rate.

Exchange rate: monetized costs and benefits are transformed from *reais* to US$ using World Bank (2016) data. We used a deflated exchange rate of 0.26 US$/R$ for Belo Monte[24] and 0.73 US$/R$ for Tucuruí.[25]

Economic net present value and benefit/cost ratio: the evaluation of both projects and their social profitability has been carried out through the economic net present value (henceforth ENPV), which represents the difference between discounted social benefits and costs:

$$ENPV = \sum_{t=0}^{n} \frac{B_t - C_t}{(1+i)^t} \tag{1}$$

Furthermore, also the benefit/cost ratio (henceforth B/C ratio) has been calculated as the ratio between discounted economic benefits and costs:

$$B/C \ Ratio = \frac{\sum_{t=0}^{n} \frac{B_t}{(1+i)^t}}{\sum_{t=0}^{n} \frac{C_t}{(1+i)^t}} \tag{2}$$

Where B_t and C_t represents the benefits and the costs at time t respectively, i is the SDR and n the number of years considered.

Variables

The variables used in our CBA are not too numerous but are well-defined, meaningful and capable of capturing relevant environmental and social aspects. In both plants cases, we tried to use the same variables, suiting the data availability in order to have two comparable models. It must be stressed that the economic monetization of these socio-economic variables is not able to represent exhaustively their real cost and benefit and for this reason some main issues have been kept out of the analysis.

Realization costs: the costs related to the construction of the Tucuruí plant are divided into two parts. The phase I costs are charged to the 1984–1998 time frame (US$9,238,744,445), while the costs for phase II are referred to the range from 1999 to 2013 (US$5,840,620,635). Operation and maintenance (henceforth O&M) costs are included in those realization costs (La Rovere and Mendes, 2000). The total investment for the Belo Monte hydroelectric complex amounted to R$25,885 billion (base date April 2010) (ANEEL, 2009; Norte Energia, 2016). However, since this value embodies also compensations actions, we considered only eligible costs, which are equal to US$5,711,455,247 (R$21,692 billion). O&M costs were considered separately (Cabral da Costa, 2014; Norte Energia, 2014, 2015). Furthermore, we considered the fee (US$9,294,411.31) received by the owner of Belo Monte in 2016 as a cost (IBAMA, 2016).

Reallocation of population: the reservoir flooding entailed in both cases the need to reallocate displaced families. In the Tucuruí case several errors have been made (Fearnside, 1999). However, an estimated total cost of resettlement amounted at US$ 84,194,000 in 1998, according to the World Commission on Dams (La Rovere and Mendes, 2000). Referring to Belo Monte, in order to quantify this variable, we used the Commerford (2011) formula. In this case the number of displaced families is equal to 5.186 with 3.7 individual each Eletrobrãs (2009). With regard to the Belo Monte case, in order to quantified this variable, we used the Commerford (2011) formula. We quantified the cost of displacement using the National Index Cost of Civil Infrastructure for the Pará State in January 2011 for a 50m^2 house (R\$21,451.5 per family), the historical cost of reallocation taking Tucuruí as proxy (R\$25,441.2 per family) and the per capita GDP (2011) of the two interested municipalities Altamira (R\$8,841.19) and Vitória do Xingu (R\$7,100.62). Therefore, we obtained an initial cost of US\$75,724,892.82 followed by a yearly cost of US\$11,694,681.63 (La Rovere and Mendes, 2000; IBGE, 2011, 2015).

Loss in economic activities: the reservoir's realization inevitably leads to a loss in some economic activities, for example cattle ranching, agriculture, mining, fishing, and river transport (Merona et al., 2010). In the case of Tucuruí we were able to consider only losses due to timber. In fact, the flooding resulted in submerging 2.5 million m^3 of timber with commercial possibilities (La Rovere and Mendes, 2000), with an average value of products deriving from forestry (as timber use of land) of about 0.42 R\$/m^3. The estimated economic loss resulted in US\$766,500 per year (SIDRA, 2014). With regard to Belo Monte, considering the flooded area, we calculated losses in chattel ranching (US\$142,714.94 per year) and agriculture (US\$394,170.67 per year) (Eletrobrás, 2009; IBGE, 2009; Da Silva Barbosa and Da Trindade Júnior, 2014).

GHG emissions and deforestation: we considered two different types of GHG emissions, the former regarding deforestation as uncaptured CO_2 emissions, the latter specific related to the plant. In both cases we used a cost of US\$25 per t of CO_2e (Commerford, 2011; Sartori et al., 2014). Satellite data (INPE, 2016) show a remarkable increase in deforestation around the area of Belo Monte[26] in the last years and the same can be observed around the Tucuruí dam. To evaluate this loss, we considered the flooded area of the two projects as proxy of "induced" deforestation and the estimated (uncaptured) emissions of CO_2 in the Amazon Region due to deforestation (48.766 t CO_2e/km) (Aguiar et al., 2009; INPE, 2014). With regard to specific hydroelectric GHG emissions, Commerford (2011) evaluate emissions considering only the flooded area. Conversely, Steinhurst et al. (2012) proposed a relation between electricity production and emissions considering other previous studies (e.g. Teodoru et al., 2010; Bastien et al., 2011). In both of the cases we focused on the second methodology. We considered high levels of emissions in the first years (1,308 CO_2e/MWh) followed by a remarkably reductions in later years, thus a stabilization (0.147 t CO_2e/MWh). For the Belo Monte project, we calculated hypothetical electricity production considering the Tucuruí data of its first phase (La Rovere and Mendes, 2000; Norte Energia, 2016).

Saved GHG emissions: aware of the fact that Eletrobrás (2009), De Castro et al. (2011) and Norte Energia (2016) do not consider GHG emissions related with hydroelectric, in contrast with other authors (e.g. Fearnside, 1995, 2000, 2001, 2006, 2016; De Sousa Júnior and Reid, 2010; Commerford, 2011), we decided to take into account a kind of "saved" GHG emissions due to hydroelectric. In order to achieve this evaluation, we considered GHG emission from the main Brazilian alternative source of electricity, natural gas (450 t CO_2e/KWh), multiplying it by the annual production of electricity of the two plants of Tucuruí and Belo Monte (La Rovere and Mendes, 2000).

Electricity generation: this is the variable chosen to represent the main source of well-being and development of such hydro projects. In order to quantify this variable, we considered the opportunity cost to generate electricity through hydroelectric power plants rather than natural gas. Therefore, we considered the tariff difference between hydroelectric (65.03 R\$/MWh) and natural gas (143 R\$/MWh) and we multiplied it for the annual electricity production (De Castro et al., 2011; Norte Energia, 2016).

Transfers and compensations: for the case of Tucuruí the amount of data regarding compensation action are fragmented. Aware of this, we computed a total amount of social and environmental compensations equal to US\$493,089,908.67. Moreover, since 1991 Brazilian law has required royalties to be paid, therefore we calculated those as benefits (US\$17,109,872/y since 1991, US\$47,546,687/y since 2002) (La Rovere and Mendes, 2000). Conversely, the total amount that Norte Energia will pay in terms of compensation is equal to US\$974,201,752.56 (R\$ 3.7 billion) and we considered it as a benefit because compensation actions should boot the social development of the surrounded area (Eletrobrás, 2009; Norte Energia, 2015, 2016). Regarding transfers there are two different types: use of public property and compensation for use of water resource. As regards the former, the annual transfers amount to US\$ 4,375,327.80. Differently, the latter amounts to US\$46,036,620.25 per year and refers to the total warrant of the power plant (in 2019) (Norte Energia, 2015, 2016).

Employment: regarding the creation of employment, we considered direct and indirect job creation. Although is reasonable to think that the great part of new employment is referring only to the construction phase, we assume a virtuous cycle of employment – not necessarily directly connected to the hydroelectric power plant – for the entire period considered. Tucuruí boosted the creation of jobs especially in the aluminium industry. We calculated the value of directed (108) and undirected (145) jobs creation multiplying the number of workers by the minimum wages of Eletronorte and the aluminium industry respectively (Scherer et al., 2003; Eletrobrás/Eletronorte, 2011). With regard to Belo Monte the number of directed (9,163) and undirected (23,000) jobs created for the State of Pará are multiplied for the minimum paid wage of Eletronorte in the first case and the minimum Brazilian wage in the second one (Eletrobrás/Eletronorte, 2011, 2016; Cabral Da Costa, 2014; Norte Energia, 2016).

Omitted benefits and costs: Due to a lack of data – especially in the Tucuruí case – and the difficulty, if not impossibility, to quantify and thus monetize some variables, omitted cost and benefit variables are listed below. The main excluded cost variables are the following: decommissioning, indigenous peoples affected, loss in biodiversity, loss in economic activities, loss in local infrastructure and landscape perception alteration, risk of loss due to dam failure, social and cultural impacts, water logging and salinity. With regard to benefit, the main excluded variables are the following: biodiversity benefits, irrigation water, opportunity in economic activities, municipality and industrial water supply, reduction of flood losses (La Rovere and Mendes, 2000; Chutubtim, 2001; De Sousa Júnior and Reid, 2010; EPE, 2012; INGETEC, 2014). Some of these listed variables could be taken into account with some specific case studies "on the ground". The case of Tucuruí could represent a benchmark for studying the economic impacts of dams (fisheries and economic activities in general) in the Amazon region. Furthermore, the participation of population must represent a key factor in this analysis following the willingness-to-pay approach in order to quantify some qualitative and environmental aspects (Pearce et al., 2006).

Results

In the case of Tucuruí (Table 11.2), the ENPV (1) is remarkably positive and equal to US$972,571,608,392.43 while the B/C Ratio (2) amount to 23.26. Differently from the negative result presented by De Sousa Júnior and Reid (2010), here also the project of Belo Monte (Table 11.3) seems to be profitable, with an ENPV of US$1,729,886,584.24 and a B/C Ratio of 1.66. This means that for each dollar paid for the project it generates potentially US$1.66 of benefits.[27]

Table 11.2 Tucuruí hydroelectric power plant CBA analysis

Characteristics		Quantification	Source
Work methodology	Exchange rate	0.73 US$/R$ (2011 deflated)	World Bank, 2016
	CO_2 t cost	US$25	Commerford, 2011; Sartori et al., 2014
	Social discount rate	5 per cent	Sartori et al., 2014
	Reference period	30 years	INGETEC, 2014; Sartori et al., 2014
Costs			
Realization costs	Building cost	US$8,510,135,905.99	Cabral Da Costa, 2014; Norte Energia, 2014
	Operation and maintenance	Included in building costs	ANEEL, 2009; Cabral Da Costa, 2014; Norte Energia, 2014
Reallocation of population		US$84,194,000	La Rovere and Mendes, 2000
GHG emissions	Plant-reservoir	Level emissions: 1.308 – 0.147 t CO_2 e/MWh	Teodoru et al., 2010; Bastien et al., 2011; Steinhurst et al., 2012
	Deforestation	140 km² (48.766 t CO_2e/km²)	La Rovere and Mendes, 2000; Aguiar et al., 2009; INPE, 2014
Loss in economic activities	Loss related to timber use of the land	US$766,500/y	La Rovere and Mendes, 2000; SIDRA, 2014

(continued)

Table 11.2 Tucuruí hydroelectric power plant CBA analysis *(continued)*

Characteristics		Quantification	Source
Benefits			
Transfers and compensations	Water usage	US$17,109,872/y (1991–1996) US$47,546,687/y (2002–2014)	La Rovere and Mendes, 2000
	Socio-environmental compensations	US$100,452,811.64	Eletrobrás/Eletronorte, 2011, 2013; EEMI, 2013; Eletronorte, 2016
Employment	Direct (eletronorte minimum wage)	108 (R$1,117.67)	La Rovere and Mendes, 2000; Eletrobrás/ Eletronorte, 2016
	Indirect (aluminium minimum wage)	65 (1984–2000, R$1,120.6) 145 (2001–2014, R$1,300)	Scherer et al., 2003
Lower GHG emissions (compared with natural gas)		450 t CO_2e/GWh	La Rovere and Mendes, 2000; Norte Energia, 2016
Electricity opportunity cost (compared with natural gas)		65.03 R$/MWh	La Rovere and Mendes, 2000; De Castro et al., 2011; Norte Energia, 2016
Results			
Total discounted costs		US$43,676,449,608.07	Chutubtim, 2001; De Sousa Júnior and Reid, 2010; INGETEC, 2014; Sartori et al., 2014
Total discounted benefits		US$1,016,248,058,000.50	
Economic net present value (ENPV)		US$972,571,608,392.43	
Benefit/cost ratio		23.26	
Economic Internal Rate of Return (ERR)		–	

Table 11.3 Belo Monte hydroelectric power plant CBA analysis

Characteristics		Quantification	Source
Work methodology	Exchange rate	0.26 US$ / R$ (2011 deflated)	World Bank, 2016
	CO_2 t cost	US$25	Commerford, 2011; Sartori et al., 2014
	Social discount rate	5 per cent	Sartori et al., 2014
	Reference period	25 years	INGETEC, 2014; Sartori et al., 2014
Costs			
Realization costs	Building cost	US$5,711,455,247.69 2016 fee: US$9,294,411.31	Cabral Da Costa, 2014; Norte Energia, 2014; IBAMA, 2016
	Operation and maintenance	US$169,767,619/y (average)	ANEEL, 2009; Cabral Da Costa, 2014; Norte Energia, 2014

Characteristics		Quantification	Source
Reallocation of population		5,186 households (3.7 persons per family)	La Rovere and Mendes, 2000; Eletrobrás, 2009; Commerford, 2011; IBGE, 2011, 2015
GHG emissions	Plant-reservoir	Level emissions: 1.308 – 0.147 t CO_2 e/MWh	La Rovere and Mendes, 2000 ; Teodoru et al., 2010; Bastien et al., 2011; Steinhurst et al., 2012; Norte Energia, 2015; 2016
	Deforestation	516 km² (48.766 t CO_2e/km²)	Aguiar et al., 2009; INPE, 2014
Loss in economic activities	Agriculture	US$394.170.66/y	Eletrobrás, 2009; IBGE, 2009; Da Silva Barbosa and Da Trindade Júnior, 2014
	Pasture	US$142,714.94/y	Eletrobrás, 2009; IBGE, 2009; Da Silva Barbosa and Da Trindade Júnior, 2014
Benefits			
Transfers and Compensations	Water usage	US$46,036,620.25/y	Norte Energia, 2014, 2015
	Public good usage	US$4,375,327.80/y	Norte Energia, 2014, 2015
	Socio-environmental compensations	US$974,201,752.55	Eletrobrás, 2009; Norte Energia, 2015, 2016
Employment	Direct (eletronorte minimum wage)	9,163 (R$1,117.67)	Norte Energia, 2014, 2015; Cabral Da Costa, 2014; Eletrobrás/ Eletronorte, 2016
	Indirect (Brazilian minimum wage, 2011)	23,000 (R$545)	Norte Energia, 2014, 2015; Eletrobrás/ Eletronorte, 2011; Cabral Da Costa, 2014
Lower GHG emissions (compared with natural gas)		450 t CO_2e/GWh	La Rovere and Mendes, 2000; Norte Energia, 2016
Electricity opportunity cost (compared with natural gas)		65.03 R$/MWh	La Rovere and Mendes, 2000; De Castro et al., 2011; Norte Energia, 2016
Results			
Total discounted costs		US$10,318,536,860.51	Chutubtim, 2001; De Sousa Júnior and Reid, 2010; INGETEC, 2014; Sartori et al., 2014
Total discounted benefits		US$11,977,157,397.94	
Economic net present value (ENPV)		US$1,729,886,584.24	
Benefit/cost ratio		1.66	
Economic internal rate of return (ERR)		7.02 per cent	

We considered in both of the cases also the methodology of Commerford (2011) in order to evaluate the emission related to the reservoir. In this case the value of our costs is lower than the other. This is because with this different way emissions are accounted only in the first year and only related to the reservoir's size.

Furthermore, in order to test the robustness of our CBA we developed a sensitivity analysis by varying the SDR. In the case of Tucuruí, even reaching a SDR of 50 per cent the project remains considerably worthwhile, while the profitability of Belo Monte seems to be far more "fragile" and when the SDR overtakes the value of 7.02 per cent (Economic Internal Rate of Return) the ENPV becomes negative. In the case of Tucuruí, due to an extreme positive result, the project does not become unprofitable, event when the SDR reach the value of 100 per cent. We were expecting less optimistic results, especially for the Tucuruí case, which results remarkably profitable, despite SDR value. This could be due to the long reference period considered (where the benefits can overtake costs) and data constraints. As for Belo Monte, even if the result is positive, the profitability is negative with different SDR, highlighting how delicate and risky the project could be.

Conclusions

The main lessons that should have been learned from the Amazon experience with hydroelectric power are related to social-environmental costs and opportunity costs, beyond economic and financial figures. First of all, a holistic and systemic approach, integrating new technologies, economic attractiveness and social-environmental safeguards, should take into account the specific features of the basin, such as hydro cycle, climate conditions, geo-morphology, biodiversity and also local and regional economies. Interaction of eco-hydrology with engineering techniques could optimize hydroelectricity production and contribute to the conservation of the main processes in the Amazon Basin: gains and losses need to be considered, and a balance between energy production, economic development, and environmental conservation can be achieved with scientific data (Tundisi et al., 2014; Almeida Prado Jr. et al., 2016). Some cases strengthen the stand showed above so that in the tributaries of the Amazon new approaches of reservoir construction and ecosystem conservation are being introduced. For example, in the Tocantins river a sequence of five reservoirs was interrupted by a stretch of 200 km, free of dams in order to allow ecosystems recovery. In the Tapajós river initial feasibility studies are taking into account the strategy of construction with low retention time and less inundation area (such as in Belo Monte reservoir, Xingu river) and the "fish ladder" has been introduced (Tundisi et al., 2014). Small hydroelectric plants, instead of major projects, would represent a useful alternative, resulting in higher initial economic cost and lower environmental and social costs in the long run (Ferreira et al., 2016).

Secondly, it is useful to consider all costs within a framework, virtually represented by the question of to whom benefits accrue (of the entire hydropower project). However, it is always left without answer or, rather, the answer usually seems to be unclear. The matter of the individuation of real beneficiaries leads to a further lesson, related to the process of decision-making. In this kind of project, clearly concerning the public interests, the central government should be able to take public decisions free of opportunistic pressures by private companies, even if they are financing the project, even if they are the main investors (La Rovere and Mendes, 2000). Therefore, the publicity of information about projects of public interest has a pivotal role in public discussion, because it generates more awareness within the population and allows the people directly and indirectly affected to actively and consciously participate in public decisions and better succeed in influencing them (MAB, 2004). Social participation and public needs played a small role in the initial phase of the Tucuruí Dam, and the resulting impacts were seen by the population as the result of a deliberate action by the national government, and not due to a natural disaster. In addition, sensitivity to the role of the central government has its roots in the history of the Amazon Region, which has been for centuries exploited benefiting distant powers (Fearnside, 1999).[28]

Unfortunately, Brazil's impact assessment requirements for dams and other development projects are still vague with respect to the degree to which, for example, social impacts must be assessed and companies often took advantage of the vague language to interpret minimal inclusions of social aspects. Moreover, the government should guarantee the neutrality of the relationship between the companies that realize the hydropower project and the supervision body appointed to monitor the activities and generate clear and fair information (Fearnside, 1999).

In conclusion, new tools to improve the evaluation of costs are available and this is an important starting point to avoid the systematic underestimation of costs, often combined with overestimation of benefits (e.g. Tucuruí). Future challenges will imply better listening to the claims from indigenous, local people and international community and taking into account every quantifiable impact. Evaluating future development proposals can be greatly improved if lessons are learned from past experiences, but, beyond the overall costs and benefits, the individuation of real beneficiaries is a relevant aspect especially in emerging countries development. The history of the hydroelectric plant of Belo Monte, which is going to provide low-cost electricity and will become the third largest hydro plant in the world, is characterized by the same changes in direction as in the Tucuruí project. It will also flood a large portion of land, causing huge devastation to the rain forest and reducing the availability of fish on which many indigenous tribes depend, learning little from the past experience (Fearnside, 2001; Survival International, 2010). Nevertheless, while Tucuruí was conceived during a dictatorship period, Belo Monte is a great public work produced by democracy and still there is lack of transparency and corruption combined with the persistent underestimation of impacts (Pinto, 2012). The long history of Belo Monte shows how big projects should be adjusted according to inhabitants and indigenous necessity, reducing the flooded area and providing a huge amount of social and environmental compensations. However, the debate and the protests for the realization of this project (i.e. the recent fee imposed to the project's owner) still raise new puzzlement about the truly profitability of Belo Monte

(IBAMA, 2016). Noticeably, some lessons have been learned, but many others are still unlearned.

Acknowledgements

This chapter has been developed within the European join exchange programme of AguaSociAL (FP7-PEOPLE, Project ID: 612633).[29] The project involves European[30] and Brazilian[31] universities, focusing on water-related sciences and social innovation. Its aim is to strengthen research cooperation and knowledge along the Europe 2020 strategy of promoting social innovation for the most vulnerable populations, with a particular emphasis on the provision of innovative education and training.

We would like to thank all Brazilian researchers who have directly and indirectly had a role in the writing of this chapter. Furthermore, a special thanks goes to the coordinator of the project Salvatore Monni and to the project manager Elisa Natola.

Notes

1 Brazilian Ministry of Mining and Energy.
2 Ten-year Plan of Energy Expansion 2024.
3 The entire Amazon Region is composed of the following states: Brazil, Peru, Colombia, Venezuela, Ecuador, Bolivia, Guyana, Suriname and French Guiana.
4 This legislative area is composed of the states of Acre, Amapá, Amazonas, Pará, Rondônia, Roraima, and Tocantins, and part of the states of Mato Grosso and Maranhão.
5 Second Growth Acceleration Programme.
6 Beside these hydroelectric plants there are also eight small hydroelectric power plants (SMPs) (152 MW) already completed and five (100 MW) under construction. There are also 44 electric thermal plants (ETPs) UTEs (5.992 MW) and 62 wind plants (WPs) (1.729 MW) already completed and five UTEs ETP (2.110 MW) and 120 WP UEEs (3.035 MW) under construction (PAC2, 2014).
7 The project is about to be terminated (2019, expected) (Norte Energia, 2016).
8 Light for everyone.
9 Brazilian Electric System.
10 National Agency of Electric Energy.
11 National Electricity System Operator.
12 National Interconnected System.
13 The Subsystem North is one of the subdivision of the SIN and it covers part of the states of Amapá, Pará, Tocantins, Maranhão and Amazonas.
14 Notice that these values are lower compared with those of the previous programme (EPE, 2011).
15 A third phase of expansion is planned for the future (Eletronorte, 2016).
16 Centrais Elétricas do Norte do Brasil S.A.
17 The initial project expected a flooded area of 1.225 km².
18 After the Itaipú Dam, on the Parana River, between Brazil and Paraguay (jointly owned between these Countries); the Three Gorges Dam, on the Yangtze River and the Xiluodu Dam, on the Jinsha River, both in China.
19 It remains famous in the Brazilian memory, the image depicting a native woman leader Tuíra (Kayapó, one of the Brazilian indigenous groups) holding their machetes against the face of the then-engineer José Antonio Muniz Lope of Eletronorte. The episode, happened during the *I Encontro das Nações Indígenas do Xingu* (First Encounter of the

Indigenous Nations of the Xingu) also called "Altamira Gathering" in 1989 (Fearnside, 2006; Da Silva Barbosa and Da Trindade Júnior, 2014).

20 Note that Brazil still has to become a partner country of the UN-REDD programme (United Nations – Reducing Emission from Deforestation and Forest Degradation). The forthcoming participation of Brazil could help the country in facing deforestation due to the realization of hydroelectric power plants (UN-REDD, 2016).

21 Environmental Basic Projects.

22 The Norte Energia S.A. has been charged by IBAMA with a fine of R$ 35.3 million (about US$ 9.5 million) for falsified data and for the death of 16.5 tons of fish during the flooding process of the reservoir (IBAMA, 2016).

23 Methane is a gas with an impact on global warming 25 time higher than carbon dioxide (Fearnside, 2009; IPCC, 2014).

24 The value is obtained by comparing Brazilian GDP (current R$) in 2011 ($4.37 \cdot 10^{12}$) and Brazilian GDP (constant US$) in 2005 ($1.15 \cdot 10^{12}$).

25 The value is obtained by comparing Brazilian GDP (current R$) in 1998 ($7.38 \cdot 10^{11}$) and Brazilian GDP (constant US$) in 2005 ($1.01 \cdot 10^{12}$).

26 According to Eletrobrás (2009) the total deforested area covered by the Belo Monte's reservoir is equal to 241.72 km^2 and Norte Energia (2016) affirmed that the area would have been deforested before the flooding procedure. Not considering the "induced" deforestation due to a pull like Belo Monte, past Amazonian experience show how often the reservoir has been flooded without a previous deforestation action and how the maximum height declared has been overtake (Fearnside, 1995, 2001).

27 Obviously, especially in the case of Tucuruí, the positive output of the analysis results from the absence of data mainly associated in time with the dictatorship period. Moreover, it is worthy that in both of the cases we noticed the loss of data due to the incompleteness evaluation of social and environmental costs.

28 The exploiters were the Portuguese colonists first and then the *sulistas* (people from São Paulo, Rio de Janeiro, Brasilia and other locations of the "southern" Brazil).

29 European Commission, *AguaSociAL: Social Innovation in the Water Treatment Sector in the Amazon*. Marie Curie Action, Seventh Framework Programme, Community Research and Development Information Service (CORDIS). Official site: http://cordis.europa.eu/project/rcn/111055_en.html

30 Roma Tre University (faculty of economics), Universitat Autònoma de Barcelona, and Leeds Beckett University.

31 Universidade Federal do Pará (Belém) and Universidade do Estado do Amazonas (Manaus).

References

Aguiar, A.P., Ometto, J., Nobre, C., Câmara, G., Longo, K., Alvalá, R., Araújo, R., Soares, J.V., Valeriano, D., Almeida, C., Vieira, I. and Almeida, A. (2009), *Estimativa das Emissões de CO2 por Desmatamento na Amazônia Brasileira*, INPE. Available at: www.inpe.br/noticias/arquivos/pdf/Emissoes_CO2_2009.pdf.

Almeida Prado Jr., F., Athayde, S., Mossa, J., Bohlman, S., Leite, F. and Oliver-Smith, A. (2016), "How much is enough? An integrated examination of energy security, economic growth and climate change related to hydropower expansion in Brazil", *Renewable and Sustainable Energy Reviews*, 53: 1132–1136.

ANEEL (2008), *Atlas de Energia Elétrica do Brasil 3ª Edição*, Brasilia: ANEEL.

ANEEL (2009), *Leilão nº. 06/2009*, Processo nº. 48500.005668/2009-85. Available at: www2.aneel.gov.br/aplicacoes/editais_geracao/documentos_editais.cfm?IdPrograma Edital=82.

Bakker, K. (2007), "The 'Commons' Versus the 'Commodity': alter-globalization, anti-privatization and the human right to water in the Global South", *Antipode Volume*, 39(3): 430–455.

Barros, N., Cole, J.J., Tranvik, L.J., Prairie, Y.T., Bastviken, D., Huszar, V.L.M., Del Giorgio, P. and Roland, F. (2011), "Carbon emission from hydroelectric reservoirs linked to reservoir age and latitude", *Nature Geoscience*, 4: 593–596.

Bastien, J., Demarty, M. and Tremblay, A. (2011), "CO_2 and CH4 diffusive and degassing emissions from 2003 to 2009 at Eastmain 1 hydroelectric reservoir, Québec, Canada", *Inland Waters*, 1: 113–123.

Cabral Da Costa, M.N. (2014), *Financial Evaluation of Hydroelectric Power Plant. Belo Monte 11.233 MW*, Final paper, US: The George Washington University.

Chutubtim, P. (2001), *Guidelines for Conducting Extended Cost-benefit Analysis of Dam Projects in Thailand*, Chiang Mai, Thailand: Department of Economics, Chiang Mai University.

Commerford, M. (2011), *Hydroelectricity: The Negative Ecological and Social Impact and the Policy that Should Govern It*. Energy Economics and Policy, ETH (term paper), Available at: www.files.ethz.ch/cepe/top10/commerford.pdf.

Corrêa da Silva, R., de Marchi Neto, I. and Silva Seifert, S. (2016), "Electricity supply security and the future role of renewable energy sources in Brazil", *Renewable and Sustainable Energy Reviews*, 59: 328–341.

Couto, R.C. de S. and Silva, J.M. da. (2009), As questões de saúde no estudo de impacto ambiental do Aproveitamento Hidroelétrico Belo Monte, In *Painel de Especialistas: Análise Crítica do Estudo de Impacto Ambiental do Aproveitamento Hidrelétrico de Belo Monte, International Rivers*: 81–90.

Cunha, D. De A. and Ferreira, L.V. (2011), "Impacts of the Belo Monte hydroelectric dam construction on pioneer vegetation formations along the Xingu River, Pará State, Brazil", *Brazilian Journal of Botany*, 35(2): 159–167.

Da Costa, A. (2014), "Sustainable dam development in Brazil: the roles of environmentalism, participation and planning", in W. Scheumann and O. Hensengerth (eds) *Evolution of Dam Policies*, Berlin/Heidelberg: Springer-Verlag: 13–53.

Da Silva Barbosa, E.J. and Da Trindade Júnior, S.C. (2014), *ATLAS Escolar do Pará*, João Pessoa: Editora Grafset.

Da Silva Soito, J.L. and Vasconcelos Freitas, M.A. (2011), "Amazon and the expansion of hydropower in Brazil: vulnerability, impacts and possibilities for adaptation to global climate change", *Renewable and Sustainable Energy Reviews*, 15: 3165–3177.

De Castro, N.J., Da Silva Leite, A.L. and Dantas, G. de A. (2011), *Análise comparativa entre Belo Monte e empreendimentos alternativos: impactos ambientais e competitividade econômica*, GESEL-UFRJ, Texto de Discussão do Setor Elétrico no. 35. Rio de Janeiro.

De Sousa Júnior, W.C. and Reid, J. (2010), "Uncertainties in Amazon hydropower development: risk scenarios and environmental issues around the Belo Monte Dam", *Water Alternatives*, 3(2): 249–268.

EEMI (2013), *Relatório das ações socioambientais de Tucuruí*, Gerência de implementação de ações socioambientais de Tucuruí, Eletrobrás-Eletronorte.

Eletrobrás (2009), *Aproveitamento Hidrelétrico Belo Monte – Relatório de Impacto Ambiental (EIA/Rima)*. Available at: http://norteenergiasa.com.br/site/wp-content/uploads/2011/04/NE.Rima_.pdf.

Eletrobrás/Eletronorte (2011), *Relatório de sustentabilidade 2011*. Available at: www.eletronorte.gov.br/opencms/opencms/imprensa/rio20/relatorio_sustentabilidade_2011_v4_web.pdf.

Eletrobrás/Eletronorte (2013), *Relatório de sustentabilidade 2013*. Available at: http://agencia.eletronorte.gov.br/site/wp-content/uploads/2014/06/RELATORIO_SUSTEN TABILIDADE_2013-web.pdf.

Eletrobrás/Eletronorte (2016), *Plano de Cargos, Carreiras e Salários*. Available at: www.eln.gov.br/opencms/opencms/empregados/carreiras/pccs.html.

Eletronorte (2016), *Tucuruí*. Available at: www.eletronorte.gov.br/opencms/opencms/aEmpresa/regionais/tucurui/.

EPE (2011), *Plano Decenal de Expansão de Energia – PDE 2020*, Brasilia: MME/EPE.

EPE (2012), *Methodologia para Avaliação Socioambiental de Usinas Hidrelétricas*, Rio de Janeiro: EPE, 2012.

EPE (2014), *Demanda de Energia 2050*, Rio de Janeiro: EPE.

EPE (2015a), *Balanço Energético Nacional 2015 (ano base 2014)*, Rio de Janeiro: EPE.

EPE (2015b), *Plano Decenal de Expansão de Energia – PDE 2024*, Brasilia: MME/EPE.

Fearnside, P.M. (1995), "Hydroelectric dams in the Brazilian Amazon as sources of 'greenhouse' gases", *Environmental Conservation*, 22(1): 7–19.

Fearnside, P.M. (1999), "Social impacts of Brazil's Tucuruí Dam", *Environmental Management*, 24(4): 483–495.

Fearnside, P.M. (2000), "Greenhouse gas emissions from hydroelectric reservoir (Brazil's Tucuruí dam) and the energy policy implications", *Water, Air and Soil Pollution*, 133: 69–96.

Fearnside, P.M. (2001), "Environmental impacts of Brazil's Tucuruí Dam: unlearned lessons for hydroelectric development in Amazonia", *Environmental Management*, 27(3): 377–396.

Fearnside, P.M. (2006), "Dams in the Amazon: Belo Monte and Brazil's hydroelectric development of the Xingu River Basin", *Environmental Management*, 30(1): 16–27.

Fearnside, P.M. (2016), "Greenhouse gas emissions from hydroelectric dams in tropical forests", in J. Lehr and J. Keeley (eds) *Alternative Energy and Shale Gas Encyclopedia*, New York: John Wiley & Sons: 428–438.

Fearnside, P.M. and Pueyo, S. (2012), "Greenhouse-gas emissions from tropical dams", *Nature Climate Change*, 2: 382–384.

Ferreira, J.H.I., Camacho, J.R., Malagoli, J.A. and Guimarães Júnior, S.C. (2016), "Assessment of the potential of small hydropower development in Brazil", *Renewable and Sustainable Energy Reviews*, 56: 380–387.

Fundación Proteger, International Rivers and ECOA (2016), *Dams in Amazonia*. Available at: http://dams-info.org/en.

Giannini Pereira, M., Vasconcelos Freitas, M.A. and Fidelis da Silva, N. (2010), "Rural electrification and energy poverty: empirical evidences from Brazil", *Renewable and Sustainable Energy Reviews*, 14: 1229–1240.

Goldemberg, J. and Johansson, T.B. (2002), *Energy for Sustainable Development: A Policy Agenda*, New York: United Nations Development Programme.

GSE (2014), *Brasile – Le fonti rinnovabili nel contesto energetico*, Gestore Servizi Energetici. Available at: www.gse.it/it/Dati per cent20e per cent20Bilanci/GSE_ Documenti/Studi/BRASILE per cent20- per cent20Le per cent20FER per cent20nel per cent20contesto per cent20energetico.pdf.

Heinzerling, L. and Ackerman, F. (2002), "Pricing the priceless: cost–benefit analysis of environmental protection", *University of Pennsylvania Law Review*, 150(5): 1553–1584.

IBAMA (2016), *Ibama multa Norte Energia em R$ 35 milhões por mortandade de peixes em Belo Monte*. Available at: hwww.ibama.gov.br/publicadas/ibama-multa-norte-energia-em-r-35-milhoes-por-mortandade-de-peixes-em-belo-monte.

IBGE (2009), *Censo Agropecuário 2006. Agricultura Familiar Primeiros Resultados*. Available at: www.ibge.gov.br/home/estatistica/economia/agropecuaria/censoagro/agri_familiar_2006_2/.

IBGE (2011), *Gross Domestic Product of Municipalities 2011*. Available at: www.ibge. gov.br/english/estatistica/economia/pibmunicipios/2011/default.shtm.

IBGE (2015), *Sistema Nacional de Pesquisa de Custos e Índices da Construção Civil*. Available at: www.ibge.gov.br/home/estatistica/indicadores/precos/sinapi/.

INGETEC (2014), *Proyecto hidroélectrico Guaicaramo: estudio de impacto ambiental*, Capítulo 5, Cuarto Informe Parcial, Revisión 4, Documento No. EMG-EIAPHG-06.

INPE (2014), INPE-EM: Estimativa de emissões dos gases do efeito estufa (GEE) por mudanças de cobertura da terra. Available at: http://inpe-em.ccst.inpe.br/#.

INPE (2016), *Projeto PRODES: Monitoramento da Floresta Amazônica Brasileira por Satélite*. Available at: www.obt.inpe.br/prodes/index.php.

Iorio, M. and Caravaggio, N. (2016), "Management of water resources in the Amazon Region", in C. Gorse, and M. Dastbaz (eds) *Sustainable Ecological Engineering Design: Selected Proceedings from the International Conference of Sustainable Ecological Engineering Design for Society (SEEDS)*, Springer International Publishing Switzerland: 279–292.

IPCC (2014), *Climate Change 2014: Synthesis Report. Contribution of Working Groups I, II and III to the Fifth Assessment Report of the Intergovernmental Panel on Climate Change* [Core Writing Team, R.K. Pachauri and L.A. Meyer (eds)] Geneva: IPCC.

Kaul, I., Grunberg, I. and Stern, M.A. (1999), *Global Public Goods: International Cooperation in the 21st Century*, (ed.) United Nation Development Programme (UNDP), New York: Oxford University Press.

Kelman, J. (2001), *Relatório da comissão de análise do sistema hidrotérmico de energia elétrica*. Available in: www.kelman.com.br.

La Rovere, E.L. and Mendes, F.E. (2000), *Tucuruí Hydropower Complex – Brazil*, Prepared for the World Commission on Dams (WCD).

Lopez, H. (2008), "The social discount rate: estimates for nine Latin American countries", *Policy Research Working Paper*, *4639*, The World Bank, Latin America and the Caribbean Region – Office of the Chief Economist.

MAB (2004), *Dossiê – Ditaduracontra as populações atingidas por barragens aumenta a pobreza do povo brasileiro*, Movimento dos atingidos por barragems. Available at: www.riosvivos.org.br/arquivos/571179614.doc.

Magalhães, S., Marin, R.A. and Castro, E. (2009), Análise de situações e dados sociais, econômicos e culturais, In: *Painel de Especialistas (2009): Análise Crítica do Estudo de Impacto Ambiental do Aproveitamento Hidrelétrico de Belo Monte, International Rivers*: 23–35.

Manyari, W.V. and de Carvalho, O.A. (2007), "Environmental considerations in energy planning for the Amazon region: downstream effects of dams", *Energy Policy*, 35(12): 6526–6534.

Medeiros, H.F. (2009), Avaliação de Impactos do Projeto de Aproveitamento Hidrelétrico de Belo Monte Sobre a Vida Selvagem, Incluindo Implicações Socioeconômicas, In: *Painel de Especialistas (2009): Análise Crítica do Estudo de Impacto Ambiental do Aproveitamento Hidrelétrico de Belo Monte, International Rivers*: 167–184.

Merona, B.D., Juras, A.A., Dos Santos, G.M. and Cintra, I.H.A. (2010), *Os peixes e a pesca no Baixo Rio Tocantins: vinte anos depois da UHE Tucuruí*, Centrais Elétricas do Norte do Brasil S.A. – Eletrobrás Eletrónorte, Israel Hidenburgo Aniceto Cintra.

Molina, J. (2009), Questões hidrológicas no EIA Belo Monte. In: *Painel de Especialistas (2009): Análise Crítica do Estudo de Impacto Ambiental do Aproveitamento Hidrelétrico de Belo Monte, International Rivers*: 95–107.

Norte Energia (December 2014), *UHE Belo Monte*. Available at: http://norteenergiasa.com.br/site/informativo-home/.

Norte Energia (January 2015), *UHE Belo Monte*. Available at: http://norteenergiasa.com.br/site/informativo-home/.

Norte Energia (2016), *Norte Energia: Usina Hidrelétrica de Belo Monte*. Available at: http://norteenergiasa.com.br/site/ingles/belo-monte/.

OECD (2016), *OECD Factbook 2015–2016: Economic, Environmental and Social Statistics*, Paris: OECD Publications.

ONS (2016), *Mapas do SIN*, Available at: www.ons.org.br/conheca_sistema/mapas_sin.aspx.

PAC2 (2014), *Balanço 4 anos, 11 Balanço 2011 a 2014*, Brazilian Government, Retrieved from: www.brasil.gov.br/infraestrutura/pac.

Pearce, D. (1976), "The limits of cost–benefit analysis as a guide to environmental policy", *Kyklos*, 29: 97–112.

Pearce, D., Atkinson, G. and Mourato, S. (2006), *Cost–Benefit Analysis and the Environment: Recent Developments*, Paris: OECD Publications.

Pinto, L.F. (2008), *Tucuruí: A barragém da ditatura*, Belém: Edição Jornal Pessoal.

Pinto, L.F. (2012), De Tucuruí a Belo Monte: a história avança mesmo?, *Bol. Mus. Para. Emílio Goeldi. Ciênc. hum.*, 7(3): 777–782.

PNUD, Fundação João Pinheiro and IPEA (2013), *Atlas do Desenvolvimento Humano no Brasil*. Available at: www.atlasbrasil.org.br/2013/.

Portal Brasil (2015), Prorrogado até 2018, *Luz para Todos deve beneficiar mais um milhão de brasileiros*, Palácio do Planalto, Presidência da República. Available at: www2.planalto.gov.br/noticias/2015/05/prorrogado-ate-2018-luz-para-todos-deve-beneficiar-mais-um-milhao-de-brasileiros.

Posner, E. and Adler, M.D. (1999), "Rethinking cost–benefit analysis", *Yale Law Journal*, 109: 165–247.

Raadal, H.L., Gagnon, L., Modhal, I.S. and Hanssen, O.J. (2011), "Life cycle greenhouse gas (GHG) emissions from the generation of wind and hydro power", *Renewable and Sustainable Energy Reviews*, 15: 3417–3422.

Rocha, A. (2008), *Todos convergem para olago! Hydrelétrica Tucuruí. Municípiose Territórios na Amazônia*, Belém: NUMA/UFPA, 2008

Santos, T., Santos, L., Albuquerque, R. and Corrêa, E. (2012), Belo Monte: Impactos Sociais, Ambientais, Econômicos e Políticos, *Revista de la Facultad de Ciesias Económicas Y Administrativa*. Universidad de Narino, 13(2): 214–227.

Sartori, D., Catalano, G., Genco, M., Pancotti C., Sirtori, E., Vignetti, S. and Del Bo, C. (2014), *Guide to Cost–Benefit Analysis of Investment Projects – Economic Appraisal Tool for Cohesion Policy 2014–2020*, Prepared for the European Commission, Luxembourg: Publications Office of the European Union. Available at: http://ec.europa.eu/regional_policy/sources/docgener/studies/pdf/cba_guide.pdf.

Scherer, C., Cavalcante, D. and Saneh, G. (2003), *Norsk Hydro in Brazil – Adubos Trevo, Acro Alumínios and Alunorte*, Observatorio Social. Available at: www.observatoriosocial.org.br/sites/default/files/04-01-2003_01-norsk_hidro-ingles.pdf.

SIDRA (1990), *Banco de dados agregados*, Sistema IBGE de Recuperação Automática. Available at: www.sidra.ibge.gov.br/bda/.

Steinhurst, W., Knight, P. and Shultz, M. (2012), *Hydropower Greenhouse Gas Emissions: State of the Research*, Synapse Energy Economics, Inc.

Stern, N. (2006), *Stern Review: The Economics of Climate Change*, UK Government Economic Service. Available at: www.hm-treasury.gov.uk/stern_review_report.htm.

Survival International (2010), *Il ritorno delle grandi dighe: una grave minaccia al futuro dei popoli indigeni*, Milano: Survival International. Available at: http://assets.survival international.org/documents/375/Rapporto_Survival_Grandi_Dighe.pdf.

Teodoru, C., Prairie, Y. and del Giorgio, P. (2010), Spatial Heterogeneity of Surface CO_2 Fluxes in a Newly Created Eastmain-1 Reservoir in Northern Quebec, Canada, *Ecosystems*, 14: 28–46.

Tundsi, J.G., Goldemberg, J., Matsumura, T. and Saraiva, A.C.F. (2014), "How many more dams in the Amazon?", *Energy Policy*, 74: 703–708.

UN-REDD (2016), *Reducing Emissions from Deforestation and Forest Degradation Programme*, United Nations. Available at: www.un-redd.org/.

Westin, F.F., dos Santos, M.A. and Martins, I.D. (2014), "Hydropower expansion and analysis of the use of strategic and integrated environmental assessment tools in Brazil", *Renewable and Sustainable Energy Reviews*, 37: 750–761.

World Bank (2016), *World Development Indicators*. Available at: http://data.worldbank. org/data-catalog/world-development-indicators.

12 Careful with that switch!

Willingness to save energy and income distribution

Gionata Castaldi, Alessio D'Amato
and Mariangela Zoli

Introduction

Averaged worldwide, the residential sector accounts for approximately 30 per cent of the energy consumed by all sectors (Swan and Ugursal, 2009). In the 28 European Union countries, households are one of the largest users of energy, consuming almost 27 per cent of final energy consumption (excluding energy used for transport) in 2013.[1] As energy is mainly produced by exploiting fossil fuels, the housing sector consumption is responsible for a significant part of global greenhouse gas (GHG) emissions (Mattinen et al., 2014).

Nevertheless, the household sector has considerable energy conservation potential and it is a worthwhile focus of attempts aimed at decreasing overall energy consumption. A prerequisite for the development of effective conservation strategies and policies is to carefully investigate individual behaviours towards energy conservation to understand whether there exist different types of energy consumers that can be distinguished according to their energy-saving efforts.

A growing literature from various fields has examined the determinants of individual energy behaviours, focusing in particular on the role that environmental beliefs, social norms and personal values may have in affecting energy-saving behaviours, such as buying energy efficient appliances, recycling paper, glass and plastic and conserving electricity (e.g. Barr et al., 2005; Alcott, 2011). Such studies investigate the impact of behavioural interventions, which may be aimed at voluntary behavioural changes, by targeting individuals' perceptions, preferences and abilities or at changing the context in which decisions are made, for instance by providing financial rewards or energy-efficient equipment (Abrahamse et al., 2005). Among behavioural instruments to promote energy-conservation actions, for instance, the provision of information (both general about energy-related problems, and specific on various energy-saving measures households can adopt, and both private and public; see, e.g., Delmas and Lessem, 2014) can be proved to be useful to increase households' awareness of their energy usage and of their possibilities to reduce it.

Besides intrinsic motivations, other factors that may have an impact on energy behaviours are socio-demographic characteristics. The age of the households' members, for instance, has been shown to increase energy consumption, as older people can be less aware of environmental problems or their specific needs may influence their energy use (O'Neill and Chen, 2002; Lenzen et al., 2006). Nevertheless, this aspect is still debated: Wang et al. (2011), for instance, estimate that age is significantly and positively correlated with electricity-saving behaviour in urban areas, while Weber and Perrels (2000) find that the household types that consume more energy are middle-aged couples, and elderly singles/couples come next followed by young families.

Another relevant aspect is education: highly educated people tend to have a higher concern for the future and the environment, which can affect their energy consumption decisions. This is especially true for high levels of education, such as having at least a university degree (Veisten et al., 2004; Bachus and van Ootegem, 2011). Clearly also contextual factors (the dwelling type, its size and age, the geographic location and weather) are directly connected with energy-saving possibilities and may have a significant role. Usually, older houses are less energy efficient and bigger houses are more prone to energy consumption (O'Doherty et al., 2008; Bachus and van Ootegem, 2011). Households living in urban areas with high population density generally have a lower energy intensity than rural households (Herendeen, 1978; Herendeen et al., 1981), even though people living in rural areas are more prone to protect the surrounding environment.

Among the investigated determinants of energy-saving behaviours, however, a relevant driver is represented by households' disposable income. In discussing the relation between income and energy use, some studies at macro level refer to the well-known Environmental Kuznets Curve: Bachus and Van Ootegem (2011), for instance, report that energy use rises until a level of about $25.000 gross domestic product (GDP) per capita. The rise is exponential at a level of development below $15.000 per capita GDP and becomes moderate between $15.000 and $25.000. At higher levels of per capita GDP, services dominate industry and eco-efficiency becomes such a central issue that energy use declines, suggesting that an inverted U-shaped relation may exist between per capita GDP and energy consumption.

At individual/household level, however, the relation between disposable income and energy use is more complex and existing literature does not provide clear-cut evidence. According to some studies (e.g. Anker-Nilssen, 2003), energy consumption rises with income as high-income individuals tend to have lower environmental concerns. O'Doherty et al. (2008) also find that energy consumption in Ireland is potentially higher for high-income households, even though, given the widespread availability of energy-saving tools and devices in their dwellings, it is not clear whether the related environmental impact is larger or not. Scasny and Urban (2009) find that households' income is negatively related to energy-saving behaviours.

Given the complexity of the relation between energy consumption and individual disposable income, it is interesting to investigate the impact that household's income may have in affecting energy-saving decisions, by controlling for other potential drivers of these behaviours. The analysis of the relation between income and energy use is also valuable from a policy perspective, by considering the potential role that redistributive policies may have in determining environmental behaviours and the overall level of environmental quality. In other terms, depending on the shape of the relation between income and energy-saving behaviours, we could have that policies affecting the income distribution, though desirable from other social welfare perspectives, may have unintended (and unwanted) effects in terms of increasing the overall level of environmental degradation.

In this chapter, we aim at explicitly investigating the income–energy-saving relationship by considering UK households' behaviours as a case study. In the first part of the work, we identify the main drivers of energy-saving behaviours by estimating a Quadratic Almost Ideal Demand System (QUAIDS), through the inclusion of an estimated variable indicating the annual amount of energy saved on domestic lighting and heating system. Results suggest that the relation between energy saving and income is inversely U-shaped: energy saving increases marginally with income until a maximum threshold beyond which it starts decreasing. In the second part of the work, we focus on households' "willingness to save" with respect to their disposable income. By exploiting the theoretical framework proposed by Ebert (2007) and using results from the demand analysis, we aim at estimating how much households with different income levels are willing to save energy; more specifically, we assume a household production function where the commodity produced is exactly energy saving. Results reveal that the poorest households are willing to save around 30 per cent more than the richest ones, suggesting that income constraints can act as a driver for households' energy saving. Moreover, the willingness to save (WTS) is decreasing throughout the entire distribution, and varies less as income increases for the richest households, corresponding to the last three deciles. A possible explanation for this phenomenon could be linked, at least partially, to the fact that budget constraint is less binding for richer households.

This chapter is structured as follows: in the second section we briefly describe the data used in the analysis and the empirical framework concerning the QUAIDS model, while the third section presents results for the demand analysis. The fourth section estimates the households' WTS and how it changes with the income distribution, and the fifth section concludes.

Data and empirical framework

In order to evaluate the income–energy-saving relationship, we exploit data provided by the UK Budget Household Panel Survey (BHPS). The BHPS is an annual survey consisting of a nationally representative sample of UK households; we focus on the period from September 2008 to September 2009, included in the Wave 18, where we can find variables related to energy-saving behaviours, not always included in the survey.

Beside the BHPS, we also use data provided by the UK Meteorological Office for Weather and Forecasts, in order to estimate the impact of climatic conditions on energy savings during our reference period. Climatic data are collected in the following macro-areas: Wales, Scotland, Northern Ireland, East and North-East

Table 12.1 Retail domestic energy prices

Fuel	Gas	Oil	LPG	Coal	Electricity (Economy 7)	Electricity (standard rate)
Average price (pence/kWh)	4.49	5.87	8.17	3.69	8.54	14.39

England, North England, South England, South-East England, Midlands and East Anglia. Since the BHPS provides the household's county of residence, we estimate, for each macro-area, the average values for the two following monthly climatic variables: the mean temperature and the (log of the) hours of sun per month. To avoid multicollinearity problems, we have estimated two separate demand systems.

In order to evaluate energy-saving behaviours, we consider three qualitative variables obtained by the following questions in the BHPS:

- Question A: "Do you leave your TV on standby overnight?"
- Question B: "Do you switch off lights in empty rooms?"
- Question C: "Do you wear extra clothes rather than turn up heating?"

For each of these questions, respondents can choose among five possible answers: "Always", "Very often", "Quite often", "Not very often", "Never".

By using these variables, we provide a quantification of the related monetary amount of energy saving, on the basis of the annual savings' estimates provided by the Energy Saving Trust.[2]

In Table 12.1, we report the energy retail prices used for the estimates[3] of energy saving.

We then proceed to assign the monetary values. Referring to question A, we employ estimates of the average annual savings due to switching off electronic products rather than keeping them in standby.[4]

For question B, we use, as a proxy, estimates of the annual savings obtained when the light bulbs in the household are entirely substituted with energy-saving bulbs.[5]

Finally, for question C, we use estimates related to putting more clothes on instead of increasing the thermostat temperature of 1 degree, with a gas heating system.[6]

After considering the average annual savings for each of these variables, we assign the value depending on each behavioural typology through a uniform distribution. In other terms, we assign the initial average value to the most "virtuous" individual and a zero value to the less energy efficient ones. The values deriving from our three variables are then summed up, estimating the total amount of energy saved by each household as resulting from his/her overall behaviour.[7] Then, the share of energy savings for household *i* is calculated as the sum of the resources saved from electricity and heating on the total family expenditure:

$$w_i = \frac{A_i + B_i + C_i}{M_i}$$

where M_i is the total expenditure of the ith household.

In this way, we can use this measure of the monetary value of energy saved per unit of total annual expenditure as the dependent variable in the empirical model.

Taking stock of the literature mentioned in the introduction, we assume that the ratio w_i is affected by the household's socio-demographic characteristics, the consumer's preferences and a set of exogenous environmental goods that may influence energy saving, such as climatic conditions.

In order to evaluate the drivers of the "demand" for energy saving, we estimate a modified version of the Almost Ideal Demand System (Deaton and Muellbauer, 1980), the Quadratic Almost Ideal Demand System (QUAIDS) (Banks et al., 1997), which has the advantage of permitting goods to be luxuries at some income levels and necessities at others. Further, although the linear formulation appears to provide a reasonable approximation for the food-share curve, for other kinds of goods, in particular alcohol and clothing, distinct non-linear behaviour is generally evident. In our case, as it is possible to see in Figure 12.1, the raw data emphasize a non-linear relation between the energy-saving share and the total log-expenditure, suggesting the need to include a quadratic term.

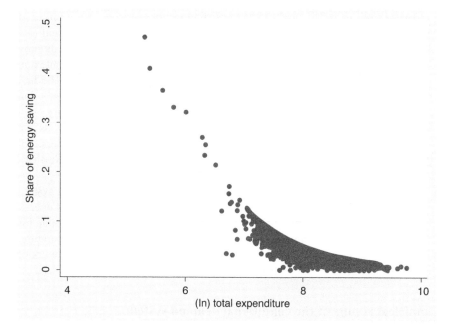

Figure 12.1 Relation between energy-saving share and total expenditure (in log)

We then adopt a class of demand analysis that has log income[8] as the leading term in a saving share model and additional higher-order income terms.

The QUAIDS model we estimate is specified as follows:

$$w_i = \alpha_i + \beta_i log(M_i) + \delta_i log(M_i)^2 + \varphi t + \eta_i T_i^p + \varepsilon_i$$

where M_i is the log annual income of each household, t is a measure of the monthly regional surface temperature or the (log) hours of sun per month, T_i^p is a vector of dummy variables which describe the main characteristics of the ith household.

In particular, we consider the following groups of explanatory variables as potentially affecting households' energy-saving decisions:

- *Economic conditions*: given the non-linear relation between the share of energy saving and total annual income, we include this variable using both a linear and a quadratic term. As further controls of the households' financial situation we consider whether the household owns the house or rents it as well as a dummy for tenures having more than four rooms. Finally, as a proxy of the household's socio-economic position, we refer to the level of education of the reference person (RP), identified according to the CASMIN classification method,[9] and the possibility of having access to internet.
- *Socio-demographic characteristics*: to account for the household composition, we consider nine different types: couple with no children, couple with no dependent children, couple with dependent children, single parents with no dependent children and with dependent children, non-elderly single, elderly single, two or more unrelated parents. Further, we consider the number of members currently working and the number of children per household (i.e. family members whose age is equal or less than 16). We also include a dummy variable for gender of the RP. To take into account the demographic context in which household members live, we include two dummy variables. The first refers to the population density, divided into areas with high population density (more than 1,000 inhabitants/km²) and low population density, with the aim of understanding whether living in metropolitan areas affects the household's energy behaviour and in which direction. The second series of dummy variables divides the sample geographically, in England, Northern Ireland, Wales and Scotland.
- *Climatic variables*: as mentioned above, we include in the demand system two climatic variables, as climate conditions affect the possibilities of energy saving. To construct this variable, we assign the mean temperature value for each region in the sample, based on the regional monthly surface temperature. We follow the same method to construct the variable related to the hours of sun per month.

Empirical results of the conditional demand system

The QUAIDS model is estimated through OLS regressions. After a test for heteroskedasticity, we adopt the White (1980) correction. We provide results for two different models, according to the climatic variables included. In Model I, we use the monthly regional mean temperature in the UK, while, in Model II, we use the monthly regional hours of sun per month. Empirical results are shown in Table 12.2.

An inverted U-shaped relation between income and energy saving is suggested by the positive sign of the linear income term and by the negative sign of the quadratic income term. This implies that the share of energy saving increases as income rises for relatively low levels of income, and then decreases. To identify

Table 12.2 Empirical results

Independent variables	Model I	Model II
(log) income	0.003252***	0.003267***
((log) income)^2	−0.000279***	−0.000280***
Owned or rented house	−0.000098	0.000080
Gender of the RP	0.000263	0.000254
(log) age of the RP	−0.020535**	−0.020592**
((log) age of the RP)^2	0.002413**	0.002415**
Elementary level of RP	−0.000078	0.000749
Middle level of RP	0.000907**	0.000892**
Middle/high level of RP	0.000663	0.000599
Tertiary level of RP	0.001481***	0.001451***
1 child per HH	−0.000531	0.000519
2 children per HH	−0.0001440*	−0.001448*
3 children per HH	−0.002751***	−0.002762***
4 or more children per HH	−0.004985***	−0.005002***
England	0.000531	0.000435
Population density	−0.001234***	−0.001296***
1 member employed	−0.000456	−0.000461
2 members employed	−0.000131	−0.000141
3 members employed	−0.001259**	−0.001278*
4 members employed	−0.001821	−0.001826
Couple with no children	0.002528**	0.002506**
Couple with no dependent children	−0.000252	−0.000271
Couple with dependent children under 18	−0.001307	−0.001323
Single parents with dependent children	0.000976	0.000961
Single parents with no dependent children	0.002169*	0.002162
Single under 60 for women, under 65 for men	0.010720***	0.010696***
Single under 60 for women, under 65 for men	0.010720***	0.010696***
2 or more unrelated adults	0.001784	0.001791
More than 4 rooms	−0.001301***	−0.001273***
Mean temperature	0.000439**	−
(log) hours of sun per month	−	0.003701*
Constant	0.052344***	0.035376*
R-squared	0.290	0.290
Adj. R-squared	0.284	0.284
Prob > F	0.0000	0.0000
Number of observations	5029	5029

Note: * $p < 0.10$, ** $p < 0.05$, *** $p < 0.01$

Table 12.3 Income thresholds on energy saving

Independent variables	Income ≤ £1250/month	Income > £1250/month
(log) income	0.007316*	–0.041709*
((log) income)^2	–0.000702*	0.001661*
Constant	0.027886*	0.274940*
R-squared	0.017	0.096
Adj. R-squared	0.015	0.096
Prob > F	0.0001	0.0000

Note: * $p < 0.01$

an income threshold corresponding to the peak of energy saved, we run two separate regressions on two sub-samples for income levels respectively lower and higher than £1,250 per month. As it is possible to see in Table 12.3, the sign of the two income terms changes significantly. Thus, the threshold seems to be reached at a medium-low income level, i.e. households' energy-saving share tends to increase for annual income lower or equal to £15,000 and decrease for higher income levels. This suggests that, in our sample, low-middle classes are more prone to energy saving compared with both very low and high-income groups.

If we consider the socio-demographic controls, we find that the gender of the RP does not affect energy-saving decisions. Age instead plays a relevant role. To account for potential non-linearity in the relation between energy saving and age, we include a quadratic term. Also in this case, a non-linear effect can be found (even though in this case the relationship is U-shaped), suggesting that households with middle-aged RP tend to conserve less energy compared with households with younger and older RP.

Concerning the education level, we find a positive correlation between higher education levels (university degree) and energy saving, confirming the evidence provided in the literature (Gatersleben et al., 2002; Bachus and van Ootegem, 2011). Further, energy saving is negatively related with the number of households' members, especially for those in which there are three or more children. Here the interpretation is straightforward: the energy consumption requirements in large households are higher, leaving little space to energy-saving opportunities. The number of employed members per household does not provide clear evidence on energy saving. Also the household typology does not seem to be relevant to explain energy-saving decisions, probably because the number of members plays a more significant role. The number of rooms negatively affects energy saving, confirming that bigger and older houses consume more energy (O'Doherty et al., 2008; Bachus and van Ootegem, 2011).

The area of residence (i.e. living in England, compared with living in Northern Ireland, Scotland or Wales) is not significant, whilst population density is negatively related to energy saving. This contrasts with other contributions, according to which energy intensity is lower in urban areas than in rural areas (Herendeen, 1978; Herendeen et al., 1981), even though the lack of recent evidences on energy consumption, and particularly on energy saving, does not provide a clear reference

Table 12.4 Income elasticity of demand for different income deciles

Reference sample and income decile	Number of observations	(Mean) income elasticity of demand
Entire sample	5036	0.83
1st decile	421	0.95
3rd decile	423	0.89
5th decile	499	0.84
7th decile	545	0.81
8th decile	528	0.78
9th decile	550	0.77
10th decile	537	0.72

benchmark. The ownership of the house does not significantly impact energy-saving behaviours.

Finally, the average temperature and the number of hours of sun per month are both positively related to energy saving. The significance of the relation thus confirms that climatic conditions play a central role in determining household energy-saving attitude.

The analysis of the income elasticity of demand (shown in Table 12.4), both for the entire sample and for the sub-sampling in different income groups, is also interesting. It is straightforward to notice that the higher the income level, the lower the income elasticity of demand for energy saving, suggesting that, as the disposable income increases, energy saving becomes a less "necessary" commodity. Thus, energy saving behaves like an inferior good: the demand decreases as the annual disposable income per household increases.

The willingness to save (WTS) analysis

In this section, we provide an estimation of the households' willingness to save on energy uses. To this end, we refer to the revealed preference approach and exploit the theoretical framework developed by Ebert (2007). This approach deals with the possibility of recovering the consumer's underlying preference ordering from the observed behaviour, when non-market goods are employed in the household production function. In this framework, the consumer uses different (both private and environmental) goods to produce a commodity that yields utility. The challenge here consists in specifying the functional form of a production function that takes into account the observable behaviour of the household and where the environmental good is used as an input, instead of being consumed directly. In our case, the observed behaviour is represented by the selected energy-saving decisions.

Following Ebert (2007), we assume that the WTS of each household is affected by a composite good related to electricity and gas consumption (which are directly related to energy saving) and environmental quality, which, in our setting, is measured by the climatic variables defined in the previous section. As we did

Table 12.5 Willingness to save

Reference sample	Model I	Model II
	(Mean) WTS for mean temperature	(Mean) WTS for hours of sun
Entire sample	15.14	25.1223
	(0.1018)	(0.1634)
1st decile	17.5278	29.0659
	(0.3760)	(0.6148)
3rd decile	16.3681	27.0210
	(0.3301)	(0.5610)
5th decile	15.2158	25.2453
	(0.3169)	(0.5138)
7th decile	14.3133	23.7568
	(0.2998)	(0.4385)
8th decile	13.7089	22.6834
	(0.2930)	(0.4761)
9th decile	13.7232	22.8384
	(0.2691)	(0.4781)
10th decile	13.4691	22.4696
	(0.2856)	(0.4334)

Notes: Standard errors in parenthesis. Coefficients estimated at a 95% confidence level.

for the demand system, we run two models, where the environmental good corresponds to the monthly mean temperature (Model I) and the hours of sun per month (Model II), respectively. Results are reported in Table 12.5 for different income levels. Estimates are obtained by a bootstrap of 500 replications (Martini and Tiezzi, 2014).

In both cases, the WTS decreases over the entire income distribution; specifically, in Model I, the poorest decile that is willing to save £17.50/month, while the richest saves £13.50/month. From the bottom to the top of the income distribution, the WTS decreases by roughly 23 per cent, a consistent variation if considered on an annual basis and by considering the household's overall budget. In particular, if we consider the annual value of the WTS and compare it with the annual average disposal income for each decile, we find that for the poorest households (first income decile) the WTS corresponds to 2.3 per cent of income, whilst for the last decile it corresponds to 0.26 per cent.

When considering Model II, the impact is roughly the same (22.7 per cent), suggesting that the poorest households need to save more energy and are willing to do so enhancing a daily pro-environmental domestic behaviour.

Clearly, this result suggests that poorer households are bounded to save energy, since a marginal improvement in domestic monetary savings is more valuable for those households. Consequently, the importance of saving energy becomes an everyday issue for poor families.

The lower willingness to save of richer families may be, on the other side, linked to weaker budget constraints considerations, as well as to the access to more efficient appliances (recall that our energy-saving actions are rather specific). This seems to suggest the possibility of a rebound effect as income increases, albeit, at this stage of the analysis such a conclusion can only be seen as a conjecture.

Discussion and concluding remarks

Energy saving is a complex issue in modern societies. Our results provide some insights on the relationship between energy saving and income distribution. Specifically, we show that energy saving is crucially linked to income distribution: both the income elasticity of demand and WTS show that low-income households need to save energy, and to do so they are more prone to act environmentally. Income distribution must therefore be accounted for when designing energy efficiency policies. Our chapter provides food for thought in this respect, as it highlights how energy behaviours change along the income distribution (focusing on the UK as a case study).

We also show that other drivers play a role in pro-energy-saving households' behaviour. Highly educated people save energy, confirming that information and awareness are extremely important. Our results are subject to important caveats. First of all, the outcome of our analysis is expected to be affected both by the specific data used and by the chosen WTS calculation procedure (borrowed by Ebert, 2007). The robustness of our results is therefore a straightforward path for future research. More broadly, extending this application to a macro level can result in interesting variabilities from country to country, depending on climate and cultural differences. A different household production function may be specified in order to address different energy problems and other environmental goods should be taken into account together with other energy-saving typologies.

Notes

1 Eurostat data, available at www.eea.europa.eu/data-and-maps/indicators/final-energy-consumption-by-sector-9/assessment (last accessed 04/10/2016).
2 www.energysavingtrust.org.uk/Info/Our-calculations.
3 In determining the response variable, we deflate the estimated energy saving with the retail price provided by Eurostat for our reference period (2008–2009).
4 For these estimates, see www.energysavingtrust.org.uk/Take-action/Money-saving-tips/Energy-saving-tips/Stop-wasting-energy-in-your-living-room.
5 For more details, see www.energysavingtrust.org.uk/In-your-home/Lighting/Saving-energy-from-lighting.
6 See www.energysavingtrust.org.uk/In-your-home/Heating-and-hot-water/Thermostats-and-controls.
7 To calculate this variable, we consider the first respondent of each household, for which we have information about specific characteristics (gender, level of education, etc.). Thus, the monetary value depends exclusively on the reference person. In order to avoid a possible bias due to the reference person's behaviour, we check the robustness of our results by computing the average monetary value per household, given the behaviour of all the members living in it. Since the distribution of these two variables are very similar, we conclude that the potential bias is minimum. We then use the variable constructed on the reference person in our analysis.

8 We consider income in place of expenditure to mitigate a potential endogeneity bias.
9 For more details, see www.nuffield.ox.ac.uk/Users/Yaish/NPSM/Casmin%20Education. htm.

References

Abrahamse, W., Steg, L., Vlek, C. and Rothengatter, T. (2005). "A review of intervention studies aimed at household energy conservation". *Journal of Environmental Psychology*, 25(3): 273–291.

Allcott, H. (2011). "Social norms and energy conservation". *Journal of Public Economics*, 95: 1082–1095.

Anker-Nilssen, P. (2003). "Household energy use and the environment: a conflicting issue". *Applied Energy*, 76: 189–196.

Bachus, K. and Van Ootegem, L. (2011). *Determinant of Energy Saving Behaviour by Households*. K.U. Leuven, INESPO.

Banks, J., Blundell, R. and Lewbel, A. (1997). "Quadratic Engel curves and consumer demand". *Review of Economics and Statistics*, 79(4): 527–539.

Barr, S., Gilg, A. W. and Ford, N. (2005). "The household energy gap: examining the divide between habitual-and purchase-related conservation behaviours". *Energy Policy*, 33(11): 1425–1444.

Deaton, A. and Muellbauer, J. (1980). *Economics and Consumer Behavior*. Cambridge: Cambridge University Press.

Delmas, M. A. and Lessem, N. (2014). "Saving power to conserve your reputation? The effectiveness of private versus public information". *Journal of Environmental Economics and Management*, 67(3): 353–370.

Ebert, U. (2007). "Revealed preferences and household production". *Journal of Environmental Economics and Management*, 53: 276–289.

Gatersleben, B., Steg, L. and Vlek, C. (2002). "Measurements and determinants of environmentally significant consumer behavior". *Environment and Behaviour*, 34: 335–362.

Herendeen, R. (1978). "Total energy cost of household consumption in Norway". *Energy*, 3: 615–630.

Herendeen, R., Ford, C. and Hannon, B. (1981). "Energy cost of living, 1972–1973". *Energy*, 6: 1433–1450.

Lenzen, L., Wier, M., Cohen, C., Hayami, H., Pachauri, S. and Schaeffer, R. (2006). "A comparative multivariate analysis of household energy requirements in Australia, Brazil, Denmark, India and Japan". *Energy*, 31: 181–207.

Martini, C. and Tiezzi, S. (2014). "Is the environment a luxury? An empirical investigation using revealed preferences and household production". *Resource and Energy Economics*, 37: 147–167.

Mattinen, M. K., Heljo, J., Vihola, J., Kurvinen, A., Lehtoranta, S. and Nissinen, A. (2014). "Modeling and visualization of residential sector energy consumption and greenhouse gas emissions". *Journal of Cleaner Production*, 81: 70–80.

O'Doherty, J., Lyons, S. and Tol, R. S. (2008). "Energy-using appliances and energy-saving features: Determinants of ownership in Ireland". *Applied Energy*, 85(7): 650–662.

O'Neill, B. C. and Chen, B. S. (2002). "Demographic determinants of household energy use in the United States". *Population and Development Review*, 28: 53–88.

Scasny, M. and Urban, J. (2009). *Residential Energy Efficiency*. OECD.

Schläpfer, F. (2006). "Survey protocol and income effects in the contingent valuation of public goods: a meta-analysis". *Ecological Economics*, 57: 415–429.

Swan, L. G. and Ugursal, V. I. (2009). "Modeling of end-use energy consumption in the residential sector: a review of modeling techniques". *Renewable and Sustainable Energy Reviews*, 13(8): 1819–1835.

Veisten, K., Hoen, H.F., Navrud, S. and Strand, J. (2004). "Scope insensitivity in contingent valuation of complex environmental amenities". *Journal of Environmental Management*, 73: 317–331.

Wang, Z., Zhang, B., Yin, J. and Zhang, Y. (2011). "Determinants and policy implications for household electricity-saving behavior: evidence from Beijing, China". *Energy Policy*, 39: 3550–3557.

Weber, C. and Perrels, A. (2000). "Modelling lifestyle effects on energy demand and related emissions". *Energy Policy*, 28: 549–566.

White, H. (1980). "A heteroskedasticity-consistent covariance matrix estimator and a direct test for heteroskedasticity". *Econometrica*, 48(4): 817–838.

Index

For Product Safety Concerns and Information please contact our EU
representative GPSR@taylorandfrancis.com Taylor & Francis Verlag GmbH,
Kaufingerstraße 24, 80331 München, Germany

Printed and bound by CPI Group (UK) Ltd, Croydon, CR0 4YY
01/05/2025
01858432-0004